Catering and Hospitality
NVQ/SVQ 2

Reception

Student Guide

SECOND EDITION

Ann Bulleid, Pam Rabone,
Caroline Ritchie, Jacqui Whibberley

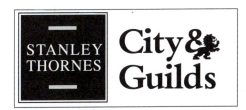
STANLEY THORNES   City & Guilds

First published in 1993 by:
Stanley Thornes (Publishers) Ltd
Ellenborough House
Wellington Street
CHELTENHAM GL50 1YW
England

Second edition published 1996

00 / 10 9 8 7 6 5 4 3 2

A catalogue record for this book
is available from the British Library.

ISBN 0 7487 2593 8

Acknowledgements

The authors and publishers would like to thank Mike Hatcher and Ron Evans for their help and advice. They would also like to thank the following for permission to use photographs and realia: Queen's Moat Houses Plc for photographs on pages 130 and 131; the Forum Hotel, London for the cover photograph and the photograph on page 145; Forte Hotels for the photographs on page 118; The Automobile Association for the illustrations on page 52; The Forum Hotel for the illustrations on pages 117, 153, 167 and 172; Hilton Hotels for the illustrations on pages 134, 146, 154 and 179.

Typeset by Columns Design Ltd, Reading.
Printed and bound in Great Britain by Redwood Books, Trowbridge, Wiltshire

Contents

Maintain a safe and secure working environment

This chapter covers:

ELEMENT 1:   **Maintain personal health and hygiene**
ELEMENT 2:   **Carry out procedures in the event of a fire**
ELEMENT 3:   **Maintain a safe environment for customers, staff and visitors**
ELEMENT 4:   **Maintain a secure environment for customers, staff and visitors**

What you need to do

- Carry out your work in line with hygiene practices.
- Take account of customers', staff and visitors' reactions when involved with emergencies and deal with them accordingly.
- Identify hazards or potential hazards and take appropriate action to deal with the situation.
- Take cautionary measures to warn customers, staff and visitors of hazards or potential hazards.
- Identify all company procedures for dealing with emergency situations.
- Comply with all relevant health and safety legislation.
- Ensure that safety and security procedures and practices are followed at all times in a calm, orderly manner.
- Work in an organised and efficient manner in line with appropriate organisational procedures and legal requirements.

What you need to know

- Why it is important to comply with health and safety legislation.
- Where and from whom information on health and safety legislation can be obtained.
- Why and what preventative actions are needed to maintain a safe environment.
- What action to take when dealing with an emergency situation such as fire, accident or the discovery of a suspicious item or package.
- Why preventative action must always be taken quickly when a potential hazard is spotted.
- How to identify and deal with safety hazards or potential safety hazards for customers, staff and visitors.
- Whom to contact in the event of an emergency and the information they will need.
- Why suspicious items or packages should never be approached or tampered with.
- Why suspicious items or packages must always be reported immediately.
- The procedures for ensuring the security of the establishment and property within it.
- Why keys, property and storage areas should be secured from unauthorised access at all times.
- What action to take when challenging suspicious individuals.
- What action to take when establishment, customer or staff property is reported missing.
- Why it is important to use correct lifting techniques.

I

ELEMENT 1:   Maintain personal health and hygiene

INTRODUCTION

When dealing with guests, the image we project can say a lot about the way the company operates. People are more likely to use an establishment, and feel more confident about the service they will receive if the staff are smart and seem to take pride in their appearance.

You are probably the first person a guest will see when they enter the establishment, and it is extremely important that you give a professional and efficient impression.

How the receptionist should and should not look

As a receptionist, working closely with other people and sometimes under pressure, you will be aware of the need to keep yourself clean and fresh. It can, for example, be very easy to get hot behind the reception desk and begin to perspire causing discomfort to yourself and people around you. Following some basic principles of personal hygiene can help you present a professional and hygienic image.

PRINCIPLES OF PERSONAL HYGIENE

Most of these principles are common sense and have a place in our daily life, but they need to be emphasised to ensure we maintain a professional and hygienic appearance throughout our working day. The principles are in no particular order of importance as each one is essential when demonstrating good hygiene practice.

- Avoid wearing too much (or too little) make-up as it can be distracting to guests and colleagues. Strong perfume or aftershave can be offensive.
- Keep hair neat and tidy. No matter how clean you are, if your hair is a mess the rest of you will tend to look untidy as well. This can give a general impression of inefficiency.
- Keep hair clean by washing regularly (at least twice a week). Washing reduces the risk of bacteria accumulating on hair and will improve your overall appearance.
- Keep hair, moustaches and beards neat and tidy. Some establishments give clear guidance about the amount of facial hair allowed. You should follow your company's guidelines.

MEMORY JOGGER

What are the principles of effective and good personal hygiene?

- Do not comb hair in sight of guests.
- Wash hands as often as necessary, but particularly:
  - before starting work
  - after visiting the toilet
  - after touching your nose, hair and ears
  - after smoking.

Dirty hands can be very off putting to guests, especially as you may need to shake hands or hand over keys to them. Your hands need to be kept clean and dry.

- Keep finger nails short, and clean. Dirt and bacteria can gather under nails and be unsightly to guests. Avoid wearing nail polish, even clear polish, as it can easily chip and become untidy.
- Wear only plain rings and other jewellery. Ornate jewellery can be very distracting to the eye, and does not represent a calm, professional appearance. It can also be dangerous as dangling necklaces and bracelets can become trapped in equipment.
- Wash and shower daily to reduce body odour and risks from bacteria. It is advisable to wear deodorant after your daily shower to help minimise offensive odours.
- Do not work if you have any symptoms of an illness likely to be transmitted to colleagues or guests. Report your symptoms to your supervisor.
- Use disposable tissues. Germs are present in our ears, nose and throat. It is very easy to infect other people by sneezing without using a tissue or by spitting or picking ears or nose. DON'T DO IT. If you need to use a tissue, use disposable ones and wash hands immediately afterwards.
- Cover cuts, bruises with clean waterproof dressing. As you are in the public eye so much it is important not to have unsightly wounds exposed for everyone to see.
- Avoid bad habits such as:
  - licking fingers when picking up paper
  - picking, scratching or touching your nose
  - scratching your head or spots
  - coughing or sneezing over other people
  - smoking or chewing
  - playing with your hair

These habits can be extremely unpleasant to watch and may be off putting to your guests and colleagues.

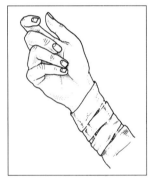

Use waterproof dressings or a clean bandage for injuries at work

Looking smart

A uniform helps to project your company's image and can greatly enhance your own appearance. Uniforms are also very helpful to our guests, as they can recognise you as a member of the team which may encourage them to approach you if they need help.

If your company does not supply a specific uniform it may well have guidelines about the type, style and colour of clothes to be worn at work. Whatever clothing you wear, whether company uniform or your own, you should comply with the guidelines.

- Keep your uniform clean, well pressed and in good repair.
- Do not carry too much in your pockets, for example, pens, tissues or money as this can look untidy and unprofessional.
- Always ensure, as far as you can, that your uniform fits you properly. It can be very uncomfortable working in a uniform which is badly fitting, and can make you feel self conscious. A uniform in the wrong size is also more likely to be torn easily or become damaged at the seams.

It is a good idea to wear different shoes for indoors and outdoors. Alternate the shoes you wear to ensure foot odour is kept to a minimum and to help reduce the strain on your feet and protect them.

MEMORY JOGGER

Why is it important to appear clean and tidy and wear the correct uniform when on duty?

3

Do not wear worn or open shoes in case of spillages or in case items, such as trays or files are dropped on to your feet. Open shoes would offer little support if you were to trip or slip on a wet floor. Low heeled, closed shoes give you most protection and help you move quickly and efficiently about your place of work. Ensure your shoes are always clean and comfortable.

Essential knowledge	Correct clothing, footwear and headgear should be worn at all times in order to: ● maintain a clean and professional appearance ● avoid the risk of contamination of food from hair and bacteria ● ensure personal freshness and eliminate the risk of body odour ● prevent accidents, i.e. through clothes or jewellery coming into contact with machinery ● ensure staff comfort during work periods

Hygiene checklist
Follow these guidelines for good personal hygiene practice:
- wash hair and body regularly
- wear a clean, well pressed uniform
- keep hair clean and tidy
- keep hands clean and dry
- keep nails clean and free of nail polish
- report any illness or contact with people with illness to your supervisor immediately
- keep all cuts and wounds covered with appropriate, clean waterproof dressings.

Do this 	● Examine your uniform. Check that it is clean, well pressed and in good repair. ● Check yourself against the listed guidelines to see how well you comply with personal hygiene principles.

MORE ABOUT HYGIENE

As a receptionist your work, probably, does not directly involve you in the handling of food. You may, however, be called upon to help with some aspects of food service, if there is a room service operation or if you are involved in serving teas and coffees in the lounge area. It is important for everyone working in an establishment where food is prepared to be aware of the dangers from food and the most common sources of food poisoning. This will mean you can take practical measures to ensure you do not put yourself or your guests and colleagues at risk.

There is some general, background information you should be aware of should you be asked to be involved in food preparation or service.

Sources of infection

There are three main sources of food poisoning, although the source which relates most to our personal hygiene practice is bacteria: germs, such as salmonella, staphylococcus or clostridium perfringens. These are naturally present all around us and can easily contaminate food if we do not practice good personal hygiene. Bacteria are microscopic and invisible to the naked eye, so it is difficult to know when you may be carrying bacteria which could cause food poisoning.

Bacteria, such as staphylococci are found naturally on the human body, particularly in the ears, nose, throat and on the hands. Other bacteria can be carried in the intestines and can contaminate food through poor personal hygiene, for example not washing the hands on leaving the toilet. Some bacteria, such as salmonella can be transferred from one source to another.

Other sources of food poisoning:

1   Natural sources, for example poisonous plants such as certain toad stools, and deadly nightshade. People who eat these plants are likely to develop food poisoning because of the natural poison they contain.
2   Chemical or metal contamination, such as pesticides, cleaning fluids, mercury, lead and copper. Food poisoning from this source can be caused through the chemical being inadvertently spilt onto food.

How germs can spread at work

FOOD HYGIENE LEGISLATION

Everyone involved in the preparation and handling of food is required to comply with food hygiene regulations. These are regulations which spell out basic hygiene guidelines aimed at reducing the risks of food poisoning.

The main hygiene risk areas have been identified and included in the legislation known as the *Food Hygiene (General) Regulations* 1970.

This legislation has been amended and updated by the *Food Safety Act* 1990 which is now the main 'enabling act' under which any future regulations will be passed. The features contained within the 1970 regulations are retained within this new Act and have been amended, where necessary, to reflect the tighter regulations contained within the new act.

The new *Food Safety Act* came about as a response to genuine public concern about the risks associated with food preparation and production and the increase in the numbers of incidents of food-related illnesses.

The *Food Safety Act* has been developed to take account and to impact on every stage of the food chain from its source to its presentation and consumption by the customer. This means that even more care and attention is needed when dealing with the service of food and drink. The Act has increased the scope and impact of penalties and includes, in brief, the following main provisions:
● includes an offence of supplying food that fails to comply with food safety requirements
● strengthens powers of enforcement, including detention and seizure of food
● requires training in basic food hygiene for all food handlers
● requires registration of all food premises
● enables Environmental Health Officers to issue emergency *Prohibition Notices* to force caterers to stop using the food premises or equipment immediately.

Complying with legislation

The impact on an establishment if they contravene hygiene regulations can be significant and could lead to a loss or even closure of the business. As an employee working within an establishment, you have a responsibility to comply with the regulations, to carry out your work to the standards expected and to ensure you attend any training in basic food handling you are required to.

The Environmental Health Officers (EHOs) are responsible for enforcing the regulations and have a number of powers which include:
● being able to enter food premises to investigate possible offences
● inspecting food and, where necessary, detaining suspect food or seizing it to be condemned
● asking for information and gaining assistance.

An EHO also has the power to issue *improvement notices* if they feel there is a potential risk to the public. They may also, where it is felt there has been a breach of the legislation, impose a *prohibition order* which closes all or part of the premises.

The *Food Safety Act* has increased the maximum penalties available to the courts and these include:
- up to two years imprisonment for offenders or the imposition of unlimited fines (in Crown Courts)
- up to £2,000 per offence and a prison sentence of up to six months (through Magistrates Courts) – up to a maximum of £20,000.

There are also penalties for obstructing an Enforcement Officer.

Complying with the legislation is important. The fines may not just relate to an employer, but can also effect an employee who contravenes and fails to demonstrate hygienic working practices.

Finding out about current legislation

When you are working in an establishment you should be able to find out about the food hygiene legislation through your manager or supervisor.

There should be information and copies of the legislation available on the premises in which you work, so it is important you find out where this is kept and make use of it. You will also find out further information through the training sessions your manager or supervisor will organise for you. The Library is also a good source of information on this subject, as well as keeping up to date through trade magazines, newspapers, etc. You will also find the local EHO Office will be able to supply information should you need it.

Do this
- Find out where the establishment displays food hygiene information.
- Look out for new hygiene information related to your work in magazines and newspapers.

Your responsibilities under the hygiene regulations

In these regulations the food handler's responsibilities are clearly detailed and form the basis of the guidelines you will need to follow if you are involved in the preparation or service of food.

In the regulations it is stated that food handlers must observe certain rules.
1 Protect food from risk of infection.
2 Wear suitable protective clothing.
3 Wash hands after visiting the toilet.
4 Not smoke, spit or take snuff in food rooms.
5 Cover cuts, lesions with clean washable dressing.
6 Report illness or contact with illness.

These regulations are enforceable by law and can result in fines if they are not complied with. The Environmental Health Officer is charged with overseeing the implementation of these regulations, as well as to give help and advice to businesses involved in preparing and selling food. You may hear of an EHO visiting your workplace or be involved in one of the visits yourself.

You will see that much of the personal hygiene requirements are very similar to those which apply to your job as a receptionist. There are additional points for you to be aware of should you be asked to prepare or serve any food.

Clean and tidy hair

When preparing food, long hair should be tied back and a head covering worn. Food can become very unappetising and off putting to the guest if a stray hair has been allowed to fall into it. Apart from being unsightly, hairs also carry germs and can infect food. You may be required to wear head covering to reduce the risk of loose hair falling into food.

When serving food you will be required to comply with the *Food Hygiene Regulations*. Long hair must be tied back, or put up and always kept away from your eyes. This style can help prevent you from touching or playing with your hair when serving customers.

If you are involved in preparing or serving food, the basic principles of good personal hygiene we have already mentioned apply.

Clean hands

Bacteria (germs) on our hands can be one of the main methods of spreading infection. Germs are easily transmitted by touching dirty cutlery, then picking up food by hand to put on a plate for a customer. This moves the bacteria from one place to the other and could result in cross contamination.

Washing your hands regularly prevents germs from contaminating food

It could also be that you have visited the toilet, returned to work without washing and now have bacteria on your hands. If you then go to make sandwiches, bacteria present on your hands can be easily transmitted to the food while you are preparing it. By washing your hands in hot soapy water after visiting the toilet you will greatly reduce the risk of infection.

When, therefore, you are involved in preparing and serving food it is even more important you:

Wash your hands as often as necessary, but particularly:
- before handling food
- when moving between jobs
- after visiting the toilet
- after touching your hair and ears
- after coughing and sneezing
- after smoking.

You will probably be aware that you are not allowed to smoke in food preparation areas, in storage areas or when serving food. Some companies have gone as far as to ban smoking in their restaurants altogether. This rule about smoking is to not only improve the atmosphere of the eating area for the guests, but it is also to reduce the risk of contamination. When smoking you can easily transmit germs from your mouth on to your hands and then on to items of food or equipment you may be handling. Smoking can also lead to ash being dropped into food and drink making it unpleasant for the guests.

Avoid using aprons and glass cloths or serving cloths for hand drying as this can lead to cross contamination. Food areas are required to have hot air dryers or paper towel dispensers.

Clean nails

Keep finger nails short and use a nail brush to clean them.

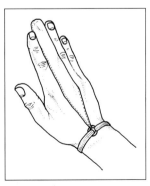

Injuries must be kept covered at work

Dirt and bacteria can gather under nails, look unsightly and spread infection to food. This is why it is a legal requirement that all wash hand basins in food areas are equipped with nailbrushes as well as soap and that disposable paper towels or hot air dryers are also supplied.

Cuts and sores

If you are required to help with food preparation you will find that waterproof plasters in the first aid kit in a food preparation area are coloured blue, so that they can be seen should they fall into the food.

The Food Hygiene Act requires you to report any sickness

Staff Sickness Notice

If you develop any illness involving vomiting or diarrhoea, or have come into contact with anyone with these symptoms, you must report it to your Department Manager before commencing work.

Other illnesses you must report to your Manager include: abdominal pain, skin rashes, fever, septic skin, lesions or discharges from your ear, nose or throat.

Reporting illness
Reporting illness is especially important if you have any symptoms linked to food poisoning, or have been in contact with someone who has, for example: vomiting, diarrhoea, stomach pains and infections. Even if you are only asked to help out with food on rare occasions it is important you report your illness, just in case.

Avoid bad habits
● Tasting food or picking at food returned to the preparation area.
● Eating food such as crisps, behind reception.
● Coughing or sneezing over food.
● Smoking in food areas.
● Using wash hand basins for washing cutlery or service utensils.

All of these habits can cause bacteria to spread and must be avoided at all times. They are also unpleasant for your guests and colleagues to see.

Wear protective clothing

If you are asked to help in a food preparation area you will, probably, be asked to wear an overall or an apron. This can prevent the risk of transmitting bacteria which have been carried in on outdoor clothing to food. Everyday clothing can easily be contaminated by contact with pets and general dirt.

Essential knowledge

Illness and infections should always be reported immediately, in order to:
● avoid contagion of disease with other staff members
● avoid contamination of food
● allow action to be taken in alerting appropriate people.

Do this

- Find out what you would need to wear if you are required to prepare or serve food.
- Check yourself against the hygiene guidelines to see if you comply with the personal hygiene requirements.

Case study

One day when you are on duty you notice a colleague has been quieter than usual and seems a little under the weather. As part of her duties she has been involved in serving afternoon teas as the food service team needed some help. She has mentioned to you that she has been feeling sick and has had a bout of diarrhoea.

- *What is the potential risk to your customers in this situation?*
- *What would you advise your colleague to do?*
- *What action would you take in this situation?*

What have you learned

1 Why is it important you maintain a professional and hygienic appearance?
2 Why is it important to wear a clean, well-pressed uniform?
3 Why should you report illness and sickness?
4 When should you wash your hands?
5 Give five examples of good personal hygiene practice.

ELEMENT 2:   Carry out procedures in the event of a fire

INTRODUCTION

Fires occur each week on premises where staff are working and customers or visitors are present. Many, fortunately, are quite small and can be dealt with quickly. Others lead to tragic loss of life, personal injury and destruction of property.

Some of these fires could have been prevented with a little forethought, care and organisation. The most common causes are misuse of electrical or heating equipment and carelessly discarded cigarette-ends. People are often the link needed to start a fire: by acting negligently, perhaps by leaving rubbish in a dark corner; or by being lazy and taking shortcuts in work methods.

Fire legislation

The Fire Precautions Act 1971 requires companies to comply with certain legal conditions, such as:

- providing a suitable means of escape, which is unlocked, unobstructed, working and available whenever people are in the building
- ensuring suitable fire-fighting equipment is properly maintained and readily available
- meeting the necessary requirements for a fire certificate. On larger premises, the owners are required to have a fire certificate which regulates the means of escape and markings of fire exits. These premises must also have properly maintained fire alarms and employees must be made aware of the means of escape and the routine to follow in the event of a fire

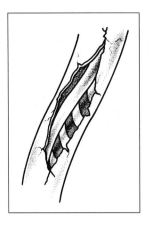

Damaged wiring

● posting relevant emergency signs around the area giving people guidance on what to do in the event of a fire and where to go.

Causes of fire

Fire can break out wherever there is a combination of fuel, heat and oxygen. As part of your responsibility in ensuring the safety of yourself, colleagues and customers you need to be aware of some of the most common causes of fire. These are:

● *rubbish*. Fires love rubbish. Accumulations of cartons, packing materials and other combustible waste products are all potential flashpoints

● *electricity*. Although you cannot see it, the current running through your electric wiring is a source of heat and, if a fault develops in the wiring, that heat can easily become excessive and start a fire. Neglect and misuse of wiring and electrical appliances are the leading causes of fires in business premises

● *smoking*. The discarded cigarette end is still one of the most frequent fire starters. Disposing of waste correctly will help reduce fires from this source, but even so, remember that wherever cigarettes and matches are used there is a chance of a fire starting

● *flammable goods*. If items such as paint, adhesives, oil or chemicals are stored or used on your premises they should be kept in a separate store room and well away from any source of heat. Aerosols, gas cartridges and cylinders, if exposed to heat, can explode and start fires

● *heaters*. Portable heaters, such as the sort used in offices to supplement the general heating, can be the cause of a fire if goods come into close contact with them or if they are accidentally knocked over. Never place books, papers or clothes over convector or storage heaters, as this can cause them to overheat and can result in a fire.

Preventing fires

Being alert to the potential hazard of fire can help prevent emergencies. Potential fire hazards exist in every area of the workplace, so regular preventative checks are essential as part of your everyday working practice.

● As far as possible, switch off and unplug all electrical equipment when it is not being used. Some equipment may be designed to be permanently connected to the mains (e.g. fax machines or telephone switchboards); always check the manufacturer's instructions.

● If new equipment is being installed, ensure this is carried out properly and arrange a system of regular maintenance.

● Electrical equipment is covered by British Safety Standards, so look for plugs that conform to BS1363 and fuses that conform to BS1362.

● Ensure there are sufficient ash trays available for smokers to use.

● Inspect all public areas, staff rooms and store rooms to ensure all discarded smoking material is collected in lidded metal bins and not mixed with other waste. Smoking should be forbidden in storage rooms and in front of guests.

● As often as possible, look behind cushions and down the side of seats to check a cigarette end has not been dropped by mistake or forgotten on a windowsill or ledge. You could check for this whenever you are tidying cushions, or after guests have left an area.

● Ensure rooms and corridors are free of waste and rubbish, especially in areas where litter tends to collect, such as in corners and underneath stairwells.

● Place all accumulated waste in appropriate receptacles, away from the main building.

● Check that all external stairways and means of escape are kept clear.

● Make sure that fire doors and smoke stop doors on escape routes are regularly maintained. These doors are designed to withstand heat and to reduce the risks from smoke. They must not be wedged open or prevented from working properly in the event of a fire. Fire exits must never be locked.

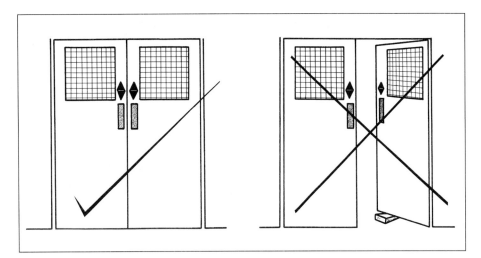

*Fire doors used correctly
(left) and incorrectly (right)*

IN RECEPTION

Fire hazards

In reception there are two main fire hazards. The electrical equipment and paper used on a busy reception desk and the seating or waiting area for the general public.

Much of the electrical equipment used on a reception desk remains in use twenty-four hours a day. Care must be taken to ensure that the wiring and connections are in good condition and maintained according to the manufacturer's instructions. If the reception area, desk or station, closes for a period of time, make sure that any equipment, which is not left permanently switched on, is turned off and unplugged.

Waste paper must not be allowed to collect unchecked. It should be placed in the appropriate bins, which should be safely emptied whenever they get full.

When tidying up the reception area never clean ashtrays by emptying them into the normal reception rubbish bins. If necessary, collect all the smoking debris in one ashtray and keep it separate until it can be safely disposed of. A cigarette end that is out but still warm can ignite paper.

The seating or waiting area of reception needs to be checked regularly to make sure that no smoking materials have been left unattended or forgotten. Areas where there is upholstery or wood, like chairs and curtains, need to be checked especially carefully.

Regular checks should also be made of any electrical equipment in the area, table lamps for instance, to ensure that the plugs are properly connected and the wiring safe.

If there is an open fire in the reception area, make sure that it is safe by placing a guard around it.

Do this

- Make a list of all the electrical equipment in your reception area.
- Note which equipment should be turned off and unplugged when not in use, and which has to remain connected all the time.

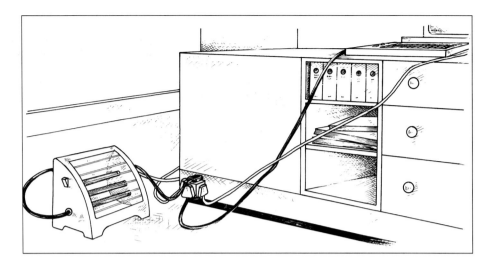

Dangerous wiring behind the reception desk

Fire safety conditions

The following conditions must always be met within a working area.
- Fire doors should not be hooked or wedged open (see illustration on page 11). Check that they close automatically when released. Fire stop doors held by magnets need to be closed from 11 p.m.-7 a.m.
- Fire extinguishers should be available, full and not damaged.
- Fire exit doors should be easy to use and accessible.
- Emergency lighting should be maintained and visible at all times. Make sure that the lights are not obscured by screens, drapes, clothing, etc.
- Signs and fire notices giving details of exit routes must be available in all areas and kept in good condition.
- Alarm points should be readily accessible and free from obstruction.
- Fire sprinklers and smoke detectors must be kept clear of obstruction for at least 24 inches in all directions.
- Fire exit doors and routes must be kept clear at all times and in a good state of repair.

Do this

- Carry out a full survey of your own work area and identify any potential fire hazards. List the hazards under the following categories: combustible material, flammable liquids, flammable gases, electrical hazards.
- Discuss the potential dangers with your colleagues and agree ways of minimising the risk.
- Revise your own working methods to minimise fire risks.

Discovering a fire

If you discover a fire, follow the sequence of events given below:
1   sound the alarm immediately
2   call the fire brigade
3   secure the guest list
4   evacuate the area
5   assemble in the designated safe area for roll call.

Sounding the alarm
The function of the alarm is to warn every person in the building that an emergency has arisen and that fire evacuation procedures may need to be put into action. Most alarms are known as *break glass* alarms, and, as the name suggests, you have to break the glass to make the alarm sound.

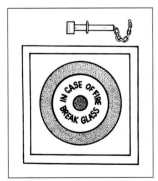

A break glass alarm

Calling the fire brigade

The responsibility for calling the fire brigade falls to different people in different establishments. Often it is a receptionist or telephonist who will be expected to deal with the call. Make sure that you know who is responsible for this in your establishment. Many establishments are connected directly to the fire station which will be alerted as soon as the alarm rings.

When calling the fire brigade, be ready with the following information:
- your establishment's address
- your establishment's telephone number
- the precise location of the fire.

You may like to write down the necessary information about the establishment and keep it near the telephone in case of an emergency. If you do have to make an emergency phone call, make sure that you listen for the address to be repeated back to you before replacing the telephone receiver.

Securing the guest list

You may be the only receptionist on duty at the time of the fire. It may therefore be your responsibility to secure and remove from the danger area a list of all the guests who are registered as staying in the establishment at the time of the fire. The fire brigade needs this list to check that no one is left behind in the building. Follow your company's policy.

Evacuating the area and assembling outside

It is essential for everyone to be able to escape from danger. If you do not have specific duties to carry out in the evacuation procedures you should leave the premises immediately on hearing the alarm.

When evacuating the premises:
- switch off equipment and machinery
- close windows and doors behind you
- follow marked escape routes
- remain calm, do not run
- assist others in their escape
- go immediately to an allocated assembly point
- do not return for belongings, no matter how valuable.

You and all of your colleagues should be instructed on what to do if fire breaks out. Customers and visitors should also be made aware of what to do in the event of a fire and made familiar with the means of escape provided. This is usually done by means of notices in all public areas and rooms. Where accommodation is provided for foreign guests, notices should be printed in the most appropriate languages.

Do this

- Write down the procedure in your establishment for securing the guest list.
- Find out if you might ever be responsible for this activity.

Fighting fires

Fighting fires can be a dangerous activity, and is generally to be discouraged. Personal safety and safe evacuation must always be your primary concern. If a fire does break out, it should *only* be tackled in its very early stages and before it has started to spread.

Before you tackle a fire:
- evacuate everyone and follow the emergency procedure to alert the fire brigade. Tell someone if you are attempting to tackle the fire

- always put your own and other people's safety first; never risk injury to fight fires. Always make sure you can escape if you need to and remember that smoke can kill. Remember the rule: *if in doubt, get out*
- never let a fire get between you and the way out. If you have any doubt about whether the extinguisher is suitable for the fire do not use it; leave immediately
- remember that fire extinguishers are only for 'first aid' fire fighting. Never attempt to tackle the fire if it is beginning to spread or if the room is filling with smoke
- if you cannot put out the fire, or your extinguisher runs out, leave immediately, closing doors and windows as you go.

Fire-fighting equipment

Types of equipment
On-premise fire-fighting equipment is designed to be used for small fires only and is very specific to the type of fire. Hand extinguishers are designed to be easy to use, but can require practice and training in how to use them.

All fire-fighting equipment is designed to remove one of the three factors needed for a fire: heat, oxygen or flammable material. Fire extinguishers are filled with one of the following:
- *water*. This type of extinguisher provides a powerful and efficient means of putting out fires involving wood, paper and fabric
- *dry powder*. These extinguishers can be used to put out wood, paper, fabric and flammable liquid fires, but are more generally used for fires involving electrical equipment
- *foam*. The pre-mix foam extinguishers use a combination of water and aqueous film, and are effective for extinguishing paper, wood, fabric and flammable liquid fires
- *carbon dioxide*. These extinguishers are not commonly in use, but can be used in situations where there are flammable oils and spirits, and in offices where there is electronic equipment.

Fire blankets are also used to extinguish fires. These are made from a variety of materials: some are made of woven fibreglass while others have a fibreglass base and are coated with silicone rubber on both sides. Fire blankets are generally housed in a wall-mounted plastic pack with a quick-pull front opening.

A fire blanket can be used to put a barrier between the user and the fire. Fire blankets remove the oxygen a fire needs to burn.

An establishment may also have fire hoses which are linked to the water supply. These can be used in the same situations as the red water-based extinguishers and are usually activated by the action of removing the hose from its mounting.

Maintaining equipment
Fire-fighting equipment is essential in areas where there is a potential risk from fires. It is essential that equipment is:
- *maintained regularly and kept in good condition*. The fire brigade or your supplier will carry out annual checks and note on the extinguisher when the check was carried out
- *kept clear from obstruction at all times*. The equipment must be visible and readily available. Obstructions can prevent easy access and may result in unnecessary damage to the equipment
- *available in all areas of work*. Different types of extinguishers are needed for different fires, so the most suitable extinguisher should be available in the area. Guidance can be sought from the fire brigade or equipment suppliers
- *used by trained operators*. Fire extinguishers can be quite noisy and powerful and can startle you if you have not used one before. It is important that the user

---

MEMORY JOGGER

What are the different types of on-site fire-fighting equipment and what are the types of fires each can help to control?

---

knows the best way of utilising the extinguisher to tackle a fire in the most effective way.

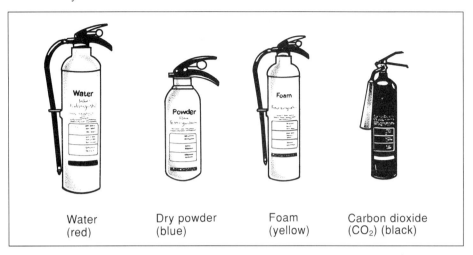

| Water (red) | Dry powder (blue) | Foam (yellow) | Carbon dioxide (CO_2) (black) |

Fire extinguishers

1 Fire extinguishers must be wall mounted on wall brackets (unless designed specifically to be floor standing) and should not be used as door stops.
2 When a fire extinguisher is discharged it must be replenished as soon as possible, and at least within twenty-four hours.
3 Every establishment should have a scale drawing indicating the location of fire-fighting equipment.

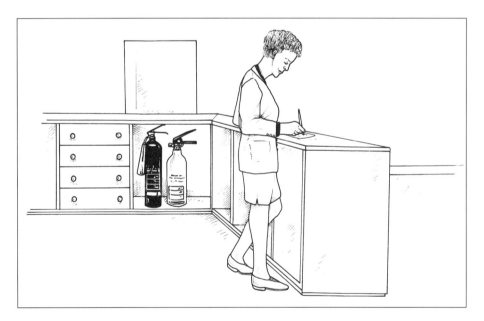

Fire extinguishers next to the reception desk

Complying with fire legislation

The fire legislation has been developed to ensure premises and working practices are safe for employees, customers and visitors. As mentioned in the introduction, failure to observe the regulations can lead to damage to property and, in more serious situations, loss of life. The legislation has been developed for everyone's safety and everyone has a role in ensuring they do not ignore fire notices and information provided about fire exits, and in ensuring they take part in fire evacuations and fire drills when necessary.

Finding out about the fire legislation

In your work area there will be notices and information posted around the building.

Details about the fire regulations will also be kept on site for you, your manager or your supervisor to refer to.

The local fire station will have a nominated Fire Officer who gives advice and guidance to establishments on how well they are complying with the regulations and who will identify any improvements in the evacuation drill that may be needed. The local Fire Officer will also be keen to give advice and support and, where appropriate, assist in the training of staff within the business.

Do this

- Find out where your nearest fire exits are located and the route you need to follow to reach your nominated assembly point.
- Identify the fire extinguishers available in your area and learn how to use them. If there is a training session under the guidance of the fire brigade, they will usually agree, or even suggest it.
- Look out for potential fire hazards in your area and remove or report them immediately.
- Take part in practice fire drills in your establishment and learn to recognise the type of sound made by the alarm in your building.

Case study

You are carrying out a security check of your establishment and you notice that two of the fire extinguishers have been removed from their wall brackets and the fire exit near the delivery area is blocked with old cardboard boxes
- *What would be your main concern if you found these problems?*
- *What immediate action would you take?*
- *What longer-term action could be taken to prevent this happening again?*

What have you learned

1 What are the possible causes of fire in the working environment?
2 What is the first thing you should do on discovering a fire?
3 What type of extinguisher would you use for putting out:
   - an electrical fire
   - a fire in an upholstered chair
   - a fire in a store room where chemicals are stored?
4 List four points you need to remember when evacuating your department if the fire alarm sounds.
5 Why is it important to comply with your responsibilities under the fire regulations?
6 How does a fire blanket work in preventing a fire from spreading?
7 Why should fire escapes and exits be kept free from rubbish and doors unlocked when people are on the premises?
8 Why must the guest list be secured?

ELEMENT 3: Maintain a safe environment for customers, staff and visitors

INTRODUCTION

The safety of everyone who works or visits an establishment should be foremost in the minds of everyone. As a main part of any employee's work they have to carry out procedures and comply with regulations which have been designed to encourage good working practices and to reduce the risks of injury to themselves and others. These regulations are also designed to make the working environment more comfortable and safer to work in.

The *Health and Safety at Work Act* 1974 (HASWA) set out to detail the responsibilities of employees and employers to take a 'general duty of care' and to place an emphasis on the need for preventative measures to be enacted and managed. The act encouraged the constant re-evaluation of systems and processes which prevent accidents and reduce risk to everyone in the establishment.

The *Health and Safety at Work Act* 1974 is an 'enabling' Act in that it imposes a general duty of care, but has the flexibility to be adapted to suit future needs. Regulations passed under the 1974 Act include, so far:
– *Health and Safety (First Aid) Regulations* 1981
– *Reporting of Injuries, Diseases and Dangerous Occurrences* 1985 (RIDDOR)
– *Control of Substances Hazardous to Health Regulations* 1988 (COSHH)

Under the *Health and Safety at Work Act* 1974 there are certain responsibilities with which both employers and employees must comply. Those given below are ones you should be particularly aware of.

Employers' responsibilities

Employers must, as far as is reasonably practicable:
● provide and maintain plants and systems of work that are safe and without risks to health
● make arrangements to ensure safety and the absence of risks to health in connection with the use, handling, storage and transport of articles and substances
● provide such information, instruction, training and supervision as will ensure the health and safety of employees
● maintain any place of work under their control in a safe condition without risks to health and provide at least statutory welfare facilities and arrangements.

These duties also extend to include customers and others visiting the premises.

Employees' responsibilities

As an employee you also have responsibilities and must:
● take reasonable care of your own health and safety
● take reasonable care for the health and safety of other people who may be affected by what you do or neglect to do at work
● cooperate with the establishment in the steps it takes to meet its legal duties
● report any physical conditions or systems which you consider unsafe or potentially unsafe to a supervisor (otherwise you may be held responsible should an accident occur).

These responsibilities have been drawn up for the benefit of everyone in the workplace, to ensure that the risk of accident or injury to anyone is minimised through promotion of a thoughtful and considerate approach to work practices.

MEMORY JOGGER

What are the employees' responsibilities under the *Health and Safety at Work Act* 1974?

Many working days can be lost through accidents, which more often than not are caused through carelessness and thoughtlessness. As a result, the business suffers reduced productivity and, in serious cases, loses considerable trading time if forced to close while the premises are made safe.

Under the HASAWA, Health and Safety Inspectors (often under the umbrella of the Environmental Health Office) have the authority to place prohibition notices on premises if they persistently fail to meet the standards set by law. This might occur if there were a physical problem in the building or in equipment such as loose or unsafe wiring.

Whatever the cause, it is important that you and your colleagues have a positive and active approach to maintaining the safety of the environment in which you operate.

Health and Safety inspectors

These appointed representatives have a number of powers under the Act which include being able to:
- enter premises at reasonable times
- test, measure, photograph and examine as they see fit
- take samples or dismantle equipment
- view Health and Safety records, accident books, etc.
- serve *improvement notices* requiring action within a period of not less than 21 days
- prosecute *any* person contravening a statutory provision (penalty is a maximum fine of £5,000 and/or term of imprisonment up to two years)

Cautionary measures

1   When you spot a hazard, if practicable, remove it immediately and report the situation to your supervisor. Most establishments have a standard Health and Safety Report Form stating action to be taken and follow up procedures.
    - If you are unable to remove the hazard, as in the case of a doorway blocked by the luggage belonging to a large party of guests, monitor the situation and if it appears the goods are not to be moved quickly, report the problem to your supervisor.
    - By taking immediate action over a potential hazard you will be contributing to your own wellbeing and that of your colleagues.
    - Some hazards, however, may be due to poor working practices or faulty building design and they will need a different approach and more time to solve.
2   You may also need to place signs, such as 'Caution Wet Floor' to warn others of the potential hazard they are approaching. In some cases you may even need to cordon off an area whilst you deal with, or make arrangements to deal with, the hazard.
3   Other cautionary measures will include ensuring you keep potentially dangerous items such as chemicals under lock and key, or out of reach of others.
4   Take note of all signs warning of dangers or potential hazards, especially those associated with:
    - use of machinery
    - hazardous chemicals
    - cleaning fluids.

    In some instances you may need to draw the attention of others to the signs.

Essential knowledge	Preventative action should always be taken quickly when a hazard is spotted, in order to ● prevent injury to staff and customers ● prevent damage to buildings and staff ● comply with the law.

HAZARDS IN THE RECEPTION AREA

Many of the accidents which are caused in reception can be avoided if staff work tidily and have thought for their colleagues who work with them. Many hazards are caused by trailing wires not properly secured and, as it is a very busy and congested area, by things being left around, blocking passage ways and causing falls.

Luggage blocking the way and presenting a hazard

Much of the health and safety legislation focuses on people having a thoughtful and commonsense approach to their work and the safety of others. Many of the accidents which happen on premises, whether it be to staff, customers or visitors, occur as a direct result of someone not doing the right thing at the right time.

HAZARD SPOTTING

Health and safety legislation is aimed at preventing accidents from happening and ensuring the environment is safe for everyone within it. Some of the most common causes of accidents in the workplace are caused through basic mistakes.

A hazard is defined as something with the potential to cause harm.

A risk can be expressed as the likelihood of that harm actually arising.

By being aware of the potential danger of hazards you will be able to contribute effectively to the safety of the area in which you work. The guidelines given below show areas in which you can start contributing towards maintaining a safe environment.

Safety points to remember

- Be constantly aware of obstacles on the floor or in corridors and remove them, returning them to their rightful place.
- Watch out for damaged floor coverings or torn carpets: it is very easy to catch your heel and trip over a carpet edge.
- Make sure electrical cables or wires never run across walkways. Always keep them behind you when you are working to reduce the risk of damage to them.
- Clean up spillages as soon as they occur.
- If cleaning up spillages use wet floor signs to warn people of the danger.
- Never handle electrical plugs with wet hands. Water conducts electricity: this can cause death.

● Never use equipment that appears faulty or damaged. You are increasing the risk to yourself by doing so. Report the problem immediately and ensure the equipment is repaired.
● Use a step ladder to reach to the top of shelves. Never stand on piles of cases or boxes.

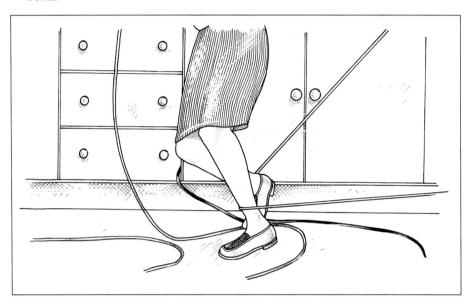

Loose and tangled wiring

HAZARDOUS SUBSTANCES

The *Control of Substances Hazardous to Health Regulations* 1988 (COSHH) form part of the Health and Safety Regulations and lay down the essential requirements and a step-by-step approach to protecting people exposed to them. In the bar the most likely exposure to chemicals is through the use of cleaning and associated chemicals.

The COSHH regulations set out the measures employers and employees have to take. Failure to comply with COSHH constitutes an offence and is subject to penalties under the *Health and Safety at Work Act* 1974.

Substances hazardous to health include:
● those labelled as dangerous (e.g. toxic, corrosive)
● those where exposure over a long time is thought dangerous (e.g. pesticides)
● harmful microorganisms
● substantial concentration of dust of any kind
● any material, mixture or compound used at work, or arising from work activities, which can harm people's health. In the bar hazardous substances may include bleach, ammonia, chlorine, detergents, methylated spirits, solvents, pipe cleaning fluid.

COSHH requires an employer to:
– assess the risk to health arising and state the precautions needed to reduce the risk
– introduce appropriate measures to prevent or control the risk
– ensure the control measures are used
– where necessary, monitor the exposure of employees
– inform and instruct employees on a regular basis.
COSHH requires an employee to:
– know what risks there are in using certain substances
– understand how these risks are controlled
– take the necessary precautions.

When storing hazardous substances it is important:
● they are stored in a locked area
● they are clearly labelled in a securely capped container
● to have first aid instructions and method of summoning assistance
● to have a system of work related to their use

The Health and Safety Executive has the responsibility of advising on safety matters and of enforcing the HASAWA if the obligations of this Act are not met. This is one reason why serious accidents must always be reported to the Executive.

In the case of hotel and catering establishments, local authorities appoint their own inspectors; Environmental Health Officers who work with companies and colleges on matters associated with health and safety.

REPORTING HAZARDS

Under the HASAWA, every company must have a procedure in place for employees to report potential hazards they have identified. In some companies there may be *safety representatives* whose role is to bring the hazard to the supervisor's attention. The safety representative may be part of a *Health and Safety Committee* which will meet regularly to deal with matters of safety and to ensure appropriate action is taken.

Your department may have a standard Hazard Report Form which you would complete to help you and your supervisor deal with the hazard through a formalised procedure. You may also be involved in carrying out regular safety audits in your department aimed at ensuring that planned preventative work is implemented.

Under the HASAWA it is your responsibility to be aware of potential hazards and to take the necessary action to prevent them from becoming actual hazards.

Do this

● Carry out a hazard-spotting tour of your area noting any actions needed and highlighting potential dangers.
● Find out how you are required to report health and safety hazards in your place of work.
● Examine the equipment you use in your department. Is the wiring in good condition? When was the equipment last serviced? Discuss any problems found with your supervisor.
● List all the safety notices you can see in your area.

DEALING WITH SUSPICIOUS ITEMS AND PACKAGES

In any area of work there may be times when an unattended item, package or bag raises suspicion. This could lead to an emergency, and, if not handled correctly, may result in danger or injury to people in the area.

It is important to treat any suspicious item seriously. Be aware of the dangers it potentially contains and be prepared to inform people of your suspicions quickly and calmly.

A suspicious package which is not dealt with immediately may result in serious injury to people in the area or serious damage to the building. It is an essential part of your daily work to keep alert to dangers from suspect packages and follow laid-down procedures when dealing with the problem.

Recognising a suspicious item or package

It is difficult to give precise guidance about where you may discover a suspicious package, or what size or shape it might be. It may be one of the following:
- Something that has been left unattended for some time, such as a briefcase next to a chair, or a suitcase left in a reception area.
- Something that looks out of place, like a man's holdall in the ladies' cloakroom, or a full carrier bag near a rubbish bin.

In fact, anything that sticks out in your mind as somewhat unusual could count as a suspicious item.

A full carrier bag left next to an empty rubbish bin might be enough to arouse suspicions

On discovering a suspicious item

- Do not attempt to move or touch the item. The action of moving or disturbing the item may be enough to start off a reaction leading to an explosion or fire.
- Remain calm and composed. Try not to cause panic by shouting an alarm or running from the item. People and property can be injured through a disorderly or panicked evacuation.
- Report the matter to your supervisor or the police immediately. Check your establishment's procedures to find out who you should inform.
- If possible, cordon off the area and move people away. It may be difficult to do this without causing people in the area to panic, but it is essential that no one attempts to move or touch the item, so you will need to warn people to keep clear.
- At some point it may be necessary to evacuate the building, or the part of the building nearest to the suspect package. This may be a decision taken by your supervisor, or the police if they are involved. If it is thought necessary to clear the area, follow your company procedures for the evacuation of the building.

MEMORY JOGGER

What are the actions to take if you discover a suspicious item in or around your area of work?

Essential knowledge

- Suspicious items or packages must never be approached or tampered with in case they contain explosive materials which may be set off.
- Suspicious items or packages must always be reported immediately, to prevent serious accidents occurring involving bombs and explosives.

Reporting a suspicious item

If you are reporting a suspicious item make sure you are able to tell your contact:

1 what the suspicious package looks like:

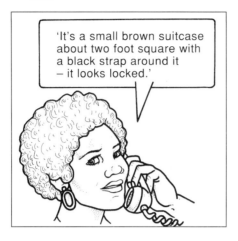

2 the exact location of the suspect item:

3 the precautions you have taken so far:

4 the existence of any known hazards in the surrounding area, e.g. gas points:

5 the reason for your suspicion:

6 any witnesses to the placing of the package or item:

Do this

- Carry out a survey of your work area to identify places where suspicious items or packages could be left.
- Find out what procedures your establishment follows for dealing with suspect packages.
- Carry out regular checks in your area.

DEALING WITH AN ACCIDENT

Within the normal course of your work you may be required to deal with an accident or an emergency resulting in someone sustaining an injury. Often these injuries are not life-threatening, but occasionally they may be serious enough to warrant the person involved being taken to hospital, or being unable to carry on their work for that day.

Most organisations have several people trained in dealing with emergencies and administering first aid. These *first aiders* are often spread around the different departments to ensure that someone is available at all times. Organisations are legally required to have trained first aiders on the premises and to display a list detailing their place of work and contact telephone number on notice boards.

First aiders are usually the people who deal with an emergency before a doctor or an ambulance arrives (if necessary). They have a responsibility to respond to emergencies as they arise, and are trained to diagnose the course of action needed to deal with the injured person. You would immediately call a first aider when an accident occurs.

Recording an accident

All accidents need to be reported as soon after the event as is practicable. Any accident is required by law to be reported and recorded in an accident book located on the premises. Any accident resulting in serious injury must be reported to the Health and Safety Executive within three working days. Your establishment should have procedures for dealing with this.

In the case of an accident to a member of staff, ideally the person who received the injury would complete the accident book. However, it may be necessary for an appointed person to report the accident on their behalf.

The following information is essential:
1   the date and time of the accident
2   the particulars of the person affected:
- full name
- occupation
- nature of injury or condition
3   where the accident happened
4   a brief description of the circumstances.

If an accident happens to a customer or visitor there will probably be different records available. Check on the type of records kept by your own establishment. If there are any witnesses, their details and description of events should also be recorded together with a note of what action was taken and by whom.

Accident record keeping is important, not only to comply with the legal requirements under health and safety legislation, but also to ensure details are available for possible insurance claims. Accident reporting can also be a great help when analysing trends and identifying where there may be a need for preventative training.

Complying with the regulations related to accidents

The current regulations governing the notification and recording of accidents are contained in the *Reporting of Injuries, Diseases and Dangerous Occurrences Regulations 1985* (RIDDOR). These regulations are about ensuring that a company has procedures in place to manage the reporting of accidents. They are separated into five main areas:

1 fatal or specified major accidents or conditions
2 notifiable 'over three days' injuries
3 reportable diseases
4 dangerous occurrences (whether there is an injury or not)
5 other accidents.

Each establishment is responsible for ensuring there are procedures in place which enable employees to comply with the regulations. Failure to follow the RIDDOR requirements can lead to prosecution under the Act.

Do this

- Establish where the Accident Recording Book is located.
- Find out whether there are different procedures and records for accidents involving customers and visitors to those involving staff for your establishment.
- Find out the procedure for reporting accidents to the emergency services.

Who is a *first aider*?

The term *first aider* describes any person who has received a certificate from an authorised training body indicating that they are qualified to render first aid.

The term was first used in 1894 by the voluntary first aid organisations and certificates are now offered by St John Ambulance, St Andrew's Ambulance Association and the British Red Cross. The certificate is only valid for three years, to ensure that first aiders are highly trained, regularly examined and kept up to date in their knowledge and skills.

First aid organisations (left to right): St John Ambulance, St Andrew's Ambulance Association, British Red Cross

Once the first aider is dealing with the casualty their main aims are to:
- preserve life
- prevent the condition worsening
- promote recovery.

Their responsibility is to:
- assess the situation
- carry out diagnosis of the casualty
- give immediate, appropriate and adequate treatment
- arrange, without delay, for the casualty to be taken to a hospital or to see a doctor if appropriate.

Giving information to the first aider
Once the first aider arrives at the accident they will need certain information from you before they begin their treatment.

Be prepared to tell the first aider as much as you know about:
- *the history of the accident*. How the accident happened, whether the person has been moved, what caused the injury
- *the symptoms*. Where the casualty is feeling pain, what other signs you have observed, whether the symptoms have changed
- *the treatment given*. What has already been done to the casualty and, to the best of your knowledge, whether the casualty has any other illness or is receiving treatment or medication.

Initial response to an accident

Whether you are a first aider or not, in the event of an accident it is the initial response to the situation and the way laid-down procedures are followed that can make the difference to the treatment received by the injured person.

You need to know what immediate response you should give if a person near you sustains an injury. Many of the points are common sense, and will depend upon the extent of the accident and the speed with which you can contact the relevant people.

When dealing with accidents the following points are important.
- *Remain calm when approaching the injured person*. The injured person will probably be frightened by the situation they are in, or may be in pain, and they will benefit from someone taking control of the situation. This may help reduce the feeling of panic, helplessness or embarrassment they may be experiencing.
- *Offer reassurance and comfort*. Keep the casualty (if conscious) informed of the actions you are taking by talking in a quiet, confident manner. Do not move the person but keep them warm, covering them with a blanket, or a coat if necessary. By keeping them warm you are minimising the risk of shock which can often cause the condition of the injured person to deteriorate. By preventing them from moving you are allowing time for them to recover and reducing the possibility of further injury.
- *Do not give them anything to drink*. If the casualty is given something to drink they may not be able to have an anaesthetic if necessary. A drink may also make them feel worse and may cause nausea.
- *Contact, or instruct someone else to contact, a first aider*.
- *Stay by the casualty* if you can, to reassure them and ensure they do not cause further injury to themselves.
- *Minimise the risk of danger* to yourself, the injured person and any other people in the area.

In the case of:
1 *gas or poisonous fumes*: if possible, cut off the source.
2 *electrical contact*: break the contact either by removing the injured person from the source, or removing the source. Do this by using something that does not conduct electricity, such as a wooden broom handle. Make sure that you do not come into contact with the electrical source yourself. Take precautions against further contact.
3 *fire, or collapsing buildings*: move the casualty to a safe area after temporarily immobilising the injured part of the person.

MEMORY JOGGER

What would you do if you were not a first aider and you were in the vicinity when someone had an accident?

Do this

- Find out the name and work location of your nearest first aider (a list should be displayed in your work area).
- Find out how you can acquire training in first aid.

Contacting the emergency services

If you or your supervisor decide that assistance is required from the emergency services, or you have been asked to call them by the first aider you will need to pass on certain information:

1 *your telephone number*, so that if for any reason you are cut off, the officer will then be able to contact you
2 *the exact location of the incident*. This will help the ambulance or doctor to get to the scene of the accident more quickly
3 *an indication of the type and seriousness of the accident*. This will allow the team to bring the most appropriate equipment and call for back-up if necessary
4 *the number, sex and approximate age of the casualties involved*. If possible, you should also explain the nature of their injuries
5 *any special help you feel is needed*. For example, in cases where you suspect a heart attack.

It might be a good idea to write down the information you need to pass on before calling the emergency services.

If you do call 999, you will be asked to state the service required: in the case of accidents you would normally state 'ambulance'. The officer responding to your call will be able to pass on messages to any other emergency services necessary, such as gas or fire.

Establishment procedures

Procedures vary from company to company as to who has authority to call the emergency services so it is important that you find out how you are expected to deal with the situation in your own place of work.

CORRECT LIFTING TECHNIQUES

One of the most common sickness problems related to work is back injury. It affects not only those in manual jobs, but also sedentary workers. Under the Health and Safety Regulations, the Manual Handling Operations Regulations are intended to reduce the risk of injury and set out simple steps to take to reduce injury. Back injury can put people out of work for a while as well as have a long-term debilitating effect on a person's health. Prevention of back injury is a must.

When lifting at work where there is a risk of injury, there are a number of questions to consider. For example, in the longer term:
● is the lifting operation necessary – could it be eliminated?
● could the lifting operation be mechanised/automated?

As well as these longer-term issues it is also important that an employee gives thought to how they are going to move an object before they do it. They could:
– 'walk the route' to check how to lift and move the object without causing injury
– get someone else to help if the load is heavy
– get someone else to help if the load is bulky or an awkward shape
– use lifting techniques which do not put strain on the back (see diagram)

If lifting a load, make sure it is not too heavy or awkward for you to move on your own. If you need help, ask. Back injuries are one of the most common reasons for people having to take time out from work. The picture overleaf illustrates the correct way of lifting heavy objects.

The correct way to lift a heavy object

FINDING OUT ABOUT AND COMPLYING WITH THE REGULATIONS

Health and safety is the responsibility of us all. Failure to comply with the requirements laid down in the Acts may lead to an occurrence which could lead to prosecution. An injured person may be able to sue their employer, or a fellow employee, for breach of their statutory duty. This could lead to damages being awarded through the Civil Courts, or being prosecuted in the Criminal Court.

Information about the health and safety aspects of your work should be made available by your manager or supervisor. There may be a *Health and Safety at Work* handbook available when your join an establishment detailing your responsibilities and those of your colleagues. There will also be information available in the form of posters and statutory notices posted around the building and on staff notice boards.

During training sessions you will be given information about the regulations and how they affect your work. You should also be given guidance on working practices (such as lifting techniques) which will ensure you do not put yourself or others at risk from injury.

Case study	*The area in which you are working is very busy and is used as an interim storage area for work which needs to be stored away or archived (finance information mainly). You often have to work round these boxes. Recently you have been asked, as part of your job, to help move the boxes on a daily basis to their correct storage area. You are happy to help as it means the working area will be kept much clearer and will be easier to work in.*
	● *Before you get involved in this work what are the main health and safety points to remember?*
	● *What should you find out from your supervisor?*
	● *What steps should you take to ensure you are complying with the HASAWA?*

ELEMENT 4:   Maintain a secure environment for customers, staff and visitors

INTRODUCTION

Maintaining effective security should be the concern of everyone working within an establishment and is an essential part of good business practice. There may be staff within your own organisation employed as *Security Officers* whose role will include all aspects of protecting people on the premises, looking after the security of the building and the property contained within it.

Effective security practices can help protect the profit of the business by reducing the likelihood of losses through, for example:
● *theft*, whether through break-ins causing damage to the building or through walk-outs where customers leave without paying for their service
● *fraud*, by customers or staff
● *missing stock*.

Profitability can be affected both by the immediate loss of property or damage to the building and by bad publicity, which can damage the business through loss of custom.

Your role

Whether or not there are security staff employed within your organisation, you will find there are many situations within your working day where you need to be security conscious. It is easy to become complacent or lazy in your working habits, which can lead to an opportunity being seen and seized by a thief. A common example of this is a member of staff leaving a cash drawer open after transactions for speed or ease of use, allowing a customer to remove cash from the till when the cashier turns away.

Daily work patterns may also present an opportunity to be exploited by a thief. When we work in an area we become familiar with our surroundings, used to seeing things in a certain place and following procedures in a certain way. It is often these patterns that are observed by potential thieves and which can lead to break-ins, thefts and fraud.

Being aware of potential breaches of security and knowing how to report them or the action to take is an essential starting point. Think about the way you work and how security conscious you are. Make sure that you always follow the basic security practices listed below.

● Handle all cash transactions away from the customer and other unauthorised persons, preferably out of their sight, especially when counting your float.
● Never handle cash without some sort of receipt or authorisation to justify the transaction and remember you must always follow your company's policy concerning the handling of cash.
● Keep security issues and procedures confidential: you can never be sure who might overhear you discussing a sensitive issue.
● Never accept or return guests' property, unless it has been properly recorded. You should always follow your company's procedure.
● Keep your own belongings, such as handbags or wallets, secure and out of sight in a locked compartment or drawer.
● Keep alert to anything or anyone which looks suspicious, for example: an occupied car parked outside the building for a long period of time, boxes or ladders placed near to windows, fire exits left open.
● Keep keys, especially master keys, under close supervision. You will probably find that your establishment has a log book for recording the issue of keys.
● When visitors arrive for staff or guests, check that they are expected before giving them directions on how to move around the establishment. Never allow visitors to enter a dangerous or restricted part of the establishment unescorted. Whenever practical ask visitors for identification.

MEMORY JOGGER
What are the guidelines to follow to help ensure there are no breaches of security in your working area?

It is important for you to follow any particular security procedures that are in place in your establishment. These procedures are often there both for your benefit and to minimise any loss to the business.

Do this

● Think about your working day. List the things you do where attention to security is essential.
● Now write down your ideas for improving security within your job. Discuss your ideas with your supervisor.
● Find out what security procedures you are required to follow within your work area.

DEALING WITH LOST OR MISSING PROPERTY

From time to time company, customer or staff property may go missing. This can be due to a variety of reasons, such as:
● customer property may have been left behind in a guest room or public area
● company property may have been moved without people knowing and may, in fact, be misplaced rather than lost
● a member of staff may have been careless about returning property, such as dirty linen to the linen room, or crockery to the crockery store
● items may have been stolen from the property. You may hear this type of loss called *shrinkage* or *pilfering*, especially when referring to food or liquor missing from refrigerators or cellars.

In most establishments there will be procedures for dealing with any missing property. If you discover that property has gone missing it is important you follow the correct procedure. The type of information you should report will probably include:
● a description of the missing item/s
● the date and time you discovered the item/s were missing
● who reported the item/s missing
● where the item/s were last seen
● the name and address of the owner if the item/s belonged to a guest
● the location where the item/s are normally kept
● details of any searches or actions taken to locate the item/s.

In some cases your establishment may decide to report the loss to the police. This is common where the item missing is of value or where a substantial amount of goods has gone missing. In some establishments all losses are reported to the police whether theft is thought probable or not. If the police are involved, you may be required to give them information, so it is essential for you to be clear on the circumstances of the losses.

Essential knowledge

Keys, property and areas should be secured from unauthorised access at all times in order to:
- prevent theft
- prevent damage to property
- prevent damage to the business from customer loss of confidence.

RECORDING LOST PROPERTY

In most establishments there are procedures for recording lost property. This usually covers personal property lost by customers, visitors or staff rather than property which may have been deliberately removed from the premises.

If someone reports they have lost an item it is usual for this to be recorded in a Lost Property Book. A page from one of these is shown overleaf.
- The information required should be recorded clearly and accurately. This information can then be used as a reference point for any property found on the premises.
- When recording lost property it is particularly important to take a contact address or telephone number so that the person can be contacted should the item/s be found.
- If you should find property it is your responsibility to report the find so that it can be returned to the appropriate person.
- In some organisations, found property is retained for a period of, for example, three months and then either returned to the person who reported it or sent to a charity shop.

SECURING STORAGE AREAS

Throughout the building there will be areas designated as storage, whether for customers or staff. These areas can often be used by a variety of people in the course of a day, so security of the area and the contents are essential.

Storage areas, particularly those allocated for use by customers (such as secure lockers in hotels) are especially sensitive and can lead to a great deal of damage to the business if items from such areas are lost or go missing.

Some items can be easily removed from the premises and are therefore of particular concern.
- *Small items* such as linen, cutlery, crockery, food, wine, toiletries, etc. can be easily concealed in a carrier bag or suitcase and removed without too much difficulty.
- *Larger items* such as televisions, irons, hairdryers and computers can also be removed, but will generally need more thought and planning beforehand.
- *Valuables* such as jewellery, watches and money can be easily concealed and removed from the premises and are often more difficult to trace.

It is sometimes extremely difficult to make an area completely secure, especially as the premises are often host to a large variety of people. It is therefore important to minimise the risk as much as possible by following some fundamental guidelines.

LOST PROPERTY RECORD					
Date/time loss reported	Description of item lost	Where item lost	Lost by (name, address, tel. no.)	Item found (where, when, by whom)	Action taken

A page from a Lost Property Book

Before we explore those guidelines, complete the 'Do this' exercise below. This will help you to identify areas which are not as secure as they could be. This may be due to a lost key, poor working practice or laziness on the part of the staff concerned.

Securing access

By carrying out regular checks like those given in the 'Do this' exercise below, you could highlight the need for improvement and increase the security of your area.

The following points show how you might prevent unauthorised access to certain areas.
- Ensure access to storage areas is restricted to specific individuals. This will make it easier to trace any missing items and is likely to reduce the risks.
- Ensure that property taken out or put into the store is correctly recorded according to company procedure.

Do this

- Draw up a list of all of the designated storage areas within your department and indicate whether they are secured storage areas (i.e. lockable) or unsecured storage areas. Make sure you include every area in your list, including those made available for customers, staff and the storage of company property.
- Once you have drawn up the list, tick those areas which are kept secure at all times. Identify the gaps, then discuss with your colleagues ways of improving the security of these areas.

● Limit the number of duplicate and master keys and keep a record of all key holders. Limiting access to keys makes it easier to control the movement of items around the building.
● Never leave keys lying around or in locks: this is an open invitation to an opportunist thief.
● Never lend keys to other staff, contractors or visitors; especially master keys. If you have been issued with a master key, you have responsibility for the access to that particular storage area.
● Follow any organisational procedures regarding the reporting of lost keys. It may be necessary to trace the lost key or have a new lock fitted to ensure the security of the area.
● If you are working in a hotel, keep guest keys out of sight and reach. If they are visible, it is possible for someone to work out which guests are in or out; if they are within reach, an unauthorised person may take them.
● If you are working in a secure area, e.g. a guest room or liquor store room, always lock the room when you are leaving, even if only for a few moments.

These guidelines are by no means exhaustive, but should help you maintain the security within your area of work and raise your awareness of the potential risks.

MEMORY JOGGER

How could you ensure that you secure the areas within your establishment where access is restricted?

Do this

● Add your own ideas to the guidelines listed above, taking into account the list of storage areas you drew up earlier.
● Keep the list in a prominent position, such as your notice board or locker to remind you about the 'do's and don'ts' of effective security practice.

DEALING WITH SUSPICIOUS INDIVIDUALS

Since you are working in the business of hospitality, there will inevitably and frequently be strangers within the building.

As part of your job you should keep yourself alert to the presence of strangers in areas reserved for staff, i.e. in the staff areas, offices and corridors. Non-staff may have a legitimate reason for being there: they may be visiting or delivering some material. On the other hand, they may have found their way in and be looking for opportunities to steal.

An individual may seem suspicious to you for a number of reasons. The following list will give you some pointers to potential problems, but remember that behaviour and situations may or may not indicate that an offence is taking place. An individual fitting any of these descriptions might be said to be acting suspiciously:
● someone wearing an incorrect uniform, or a uniform that is ill-fitting or worn incorrectly
● someone asking for directions to certain areas where you would not expect them to work; for example someone wearing kitchen whites and asking directions to a bedroom
● someone carrying company property in an area not open to them
● someone who appears lost or disorientated (remember that they *may* be innocent new employees)
● someone who just *looks* suspicious: perhaps they are wearing heavy clothing in summer, or carrying a large bag into the restaurant. Large bags or coats can be used to remove items from your premises
● someone who seems nervous, startled or worried, or is perspiring heavily
● someone booking into a hotel for a stay without luggage
● a guest asking for details of someone else staying in the establishment. (In this case, it is better to pass on the enquiry rather than give out information to a stranger.)

Responding to a suspicious individual

If you see someone on the premises you do not recognise, or who looks out of place it is important that you:

1 challenge them politely: ask if you can help them, or direct them to the way out
2 if it is possible, ask a colleague to keep an eye on them and report the presence of a stranger to your supervisor immediately.

Procedures for dealing with strangers will vary depending upon the establishment in which you work.

In all cases, *do not put yourself at risk*. Do not approach the person if you feel uncomfortable or potentially threatened by them. Merely reporting any suspicions you have, whether it be about customers, staff or visitors can often be of great help to the security and long-term health of the business.

> **MEMORY JOGGER**
>
> What would you need to do if you noticed someone acting suspiciously?

Do this

- Find out what procedures are laid down by your organisation for dealing with people acting in a suspicious manner.
- Discuss with your supervisor how you think you might challenge someone should you need to.

DISCLOSABLE INFORMATION

During the time you are at work there may be people who ask you questions. These may be general questions about the operation of the bar, or may be specific about one aspect of the business. It is important that when this happens you are discreet and careful about what you say. It may be that by answering these questions there could be a breach of security, or have a more indirect effect on the business (e.g. an idea being used by a competitor).

If you are unsure what you can or cannot say to someone about the business or how it operates, it is best to say nothing and to check with your manager or supervisor.

It is also a useful idea to mention to your manager or supervisor the questions you have been asked to avoid a problem in the future.

REPORTING UNUSUAL/NON-ROUTINE INCIDENTS

Much of the work we do involves patterns and routines. If something disturbs that routine or seems out of the ordinary it is important these incidents are reported to the appropriate person (usually your manager or supervisor). It may be the incident does need further action to be taken, but it also may result in a bigger problem being avoided. In cases where you see something which is a little bit out of the ordinary it is important it is reported.

Case study

The hotel is busy and has been used for a conference event over the last two days. You are on an early shift and a non-resident has been to you to report that she thinks someone has stolen her handbag from the table in the lounge at which she has been sitting having coffee with a friend.
- *What would you do if faced with this situation?*
- *How would you record the incident?*
- *What would you report to your manager?*

What have you learned		

<table>
</table>

What have you learned

1 Why is it essential to maintain secure storage areas within your establishment?
2 List five potential security risks within your own area.
3 Why is it important you are aware of security risks?
4 How can you prevent keys from being misused?
5 What should you ensure you do when leaving a secure area?
6 What should you do if you see someone acting in a suspicious manner?
7 How can you reduce the risk of items being taken from your own work area
   a belonging to the guests
   b belonging to the staff?
8 Why is it important you only give disclosable information to others?
9 Why is it important to report all unusual/non-routine incidents to the appropriate person?

Get ahead

1 Find out more about how the *Food Hygiene Regulations* relate specifically to food handlers.
2 Identify situations you face in your daily work where the *Food Hygiene Regulations* apply to you.
3 Carry out some research and find out how bacteria can be transmitted through poor personal hygiene practices.
4 Find out about the *recovery position* in first aid. When would you need to use this? Why is it effective?
5 Find out what immediate response you could give in the case of: burns and scalds, fainting, strokes and heart attacks.
6 Talk to your first aiders. Find out what kind of events they commonly deal with in your establishment.
7 Invite a fire prevention officer to your establishment to talk about fire prevention and fire fighting in more detail.

Maintain and deal with payments

This chapter covers:
ELEMENT 1:   **Maintain the payment point**
ELEMENT 2:   **Deal with payments**

What you need to do

- Be correctly prepared at the beginning of your shift with all the opening and hand-over procedures completed.
- Follow company procedures at all times, especially when actually handling cash, handing over change or handing over cash to authorised persons.
- Never hand over cash to unauthorised persons.
- Look after and change, as appropriate, receipt and audit rolls.
- Create and maintain customer bills accurately and securely.
- Complete all the closing-down or hand-over procedures at the end of your shift.
- Correctly carry out your establishment's procedures for handling and recording cash and non-cash payments.
- Enter the correct price or code and inform the customer of the amount due.
- Acknowledge the receipt of non-cash payments.
- Issue receipts.
- Produce the accompanying documentation efficiently, accurately and neatly.

- Store the payment and accompanying documentation securely.
- Give receipts and vouchers where appropriate.
- Ensure that the payment point is secured from unauthorised access.
- Work swiftly, efficiently and calmly under pressure.
- Understand the security requirements for handling cash, tokens and vouchers.
- Understand the importance of audit rolls and receipt rolls, etc. to the accurate handling of cash, tokens and vouchers.
- Learn why opening, closing and hand-over procedures are so important.
- Become aware of the importance of security in the handling of cash.
- Become aware of, and deal with, any unusual or unexplained behaviour or situations.
- Work within a specified time frame.
- Deal with customers in a polite and helpful manner.
- Comply with all health and safety regulations and all relevant legislation at all times.

What you need to know

- Why you should always have a sufficient amount of change and how to anticipate and deal with any shortages of change before they arise.
- The prices in your establishment, and the codes for them on the cashiering machines, if applicable.
- How to issue a receipt.
- How to calculate and issue change.

- When change is applicable.
- Why security both of the cash and of access to the payment point are so important.
- How to work swiftly and efficiently, so that the work can be accurately completed in a reasonable time.
- How to deal with vouchers and tokens.

- What the establishment's procedures are for processing non-cash payments.
- How to authenticate all forms of non-cash payments.
- How to prepare the appropriate documentation to accompany non-cash payments.
- How to deal with any problems or discrepancies that occur.
- Why all forms of payment should be stored securely.
- How to ensure the security of the payment point.
- How to deal with unexpected situations.
- The procedures of your establishment for dealing with cash, token and voucher payments.
- How to deal with customers in a polite and helpful manner at all times.

INTRODUCTION

MEMORY JOGGER

Who do company procedures protect?

Cash handling is an important part of a receptionist's job. It is also a very vulnerable area in that it is a temptation to theft, fraud and violent behaviour. For these reasons security is of vital importance when handling cash: security not only of the cash, but also of customer accounts and the back-up paperwork. Anyone who handles large amounts of cash is a target for thieves and conmen. The cash-handling procedures within your establishment will have been designed to reduce the risk of theft and fraud, and your own vulnerability. Non-cash payments are not as vulnerable to simple theft as cash payments, but they are more vulnerable to fraud. With non-cash payment it is also possible for the company who underwrites the credit payment, i.e. a bank, to refuse to honour the payment, i.e. a cheque. The bank has the right to do this if the credit payment is not accepted correctly. You must never lose sight of the fact that any form of payment is always potentially fraudulent, as are any refund claims. You must therefore familiarise yourself thoroughly with the procedures necessary to deal with payments and follow them carefully. If you do not understand why something is done in a specific way, ask your supervisor, but never deviate from the procedure without authorisation, because the system may have been designed specifically to protect you and other members of staff.

ELEMENT 1:   Maintain the payment point

OPENING, CLOSING AND HAND-OVER PROCEDURES AT A PAYMENT POINT

In most residential catering establishments the facility to pay bills is available to customers twenty-four hours a day, seven days a week. This is because there is no set time at which a customer may choose to check in, or out, or pay for some service. However, there are fairly regular high- and low-activity periods, although the actual routine will vary from establishment to establishment. For instance, in an hotel which caters mainly to business people you would expect most customers to book in after the end of a normal working day, that is after 5.30 p.m., and you would expect most to check out between 8.30 and 9.00 a.m. so that they can get in a full day's work. Tourists or holiday makers often check in and out at times which coincide with trains, boats and planes arriving and departing. The quietest time is usually during the afternoon. Thus there are fairly standard shifts for most receptionists. Examples are as follows:

- An early shift will start sometime between 7.00 a.m. and 8.00 a.m. and go on until mid-afternoon, around 3.00 p.m.

- A late shift will start around 3.00 p.m. and continue until around 11.00 p.m.
- There may also be a day shift, 9.00 a.m.–5.00 p.m. Those who do this shift often tend to do a lot of administration work.
- Between 11.00 p.m. and 7.00-8.00 a.m. there may be a night shift in a busy hotel, but it is more common in most establishments for the reception desk to be partially closed down and for there to be one person to simply take registration details and cash as applicable. These staff would have their own floats and tills.

In other places such as clubs and restaurants, those handling cash may work straight shifts with no hand-over being necessary, the shifts coinciding with the opening hours.

The payment point is open for most of the time that an establishment is open, and a receptionist starting or finishing a shift will have to go through various different procedures depending upon what time of day or night they are starting or finishing.

Opening a payment point

When a start is made early in the morning, or as an establishment opens, you would be considered to be opening a shift. You would perform the following tasks:

- You will have to fetch, or receive, the float and any other monies from where they had been stored overnight. This would normally be some sort of safe and would be authorised by the duty manager.
- When you have received the float you should count it, in the presence of the manager who is giving it to you. Both of you would then agree on the amount that had been handed over. In most establishments there will be a book which you will sign to this effect.
- The receptionist would also have to set up the payment point ready for the customers who will depart that day.

<table>
<tr><td colspan="1">**FLOAT RECEIVED BOOK**</td></tr>
<tr><td>Date</td></tr>
<tr><td>Time</td></tr>
<tr><td>Amount</td></tr>
<tr><td>Till</td></tr>
<tr><td>Number/Department</td></tr>
<tr><td>Issued by/Handed over by</td></tr>
<tr><td>Received by</td></tr>
</table>

- Next you would ensure that the till or other billing machine is ready for use, and would put the float securely in the cash drawer. Ensuring that the till or other billing machine is ready for use will vary from establishment to establishment. In essence it means that the receptionist will ensure that the till rolls are in and working, and that, in an hotel, the customers' bills are up to date, giving priority to those customers who are due to check out that day. In other establishments the receptionist should ensure that the paperwork necessary to create bills is available.

MEMORY JOGGER

So that you can operate the payment point efficiently, what materials should you always have available?

- You should then check to see if any transactions took place after the payment point had closed down at the end of the previous shift. This will mean that you will have to check with any night staff to see what transactions took place, e.g. extra bar bills, etc., and make sure that they are entered onto the customers' bills.
- You should also check to see if there are any special charges, discounts or promotions which must be applied to the bills.
- There may well be a hand-over book in which any such details have been noted which you should consult. In an hotel it is common for the receptionist who opens the shift to also have been the receptionist who was on duty during the late shift the night before. This allows for continuity, and means that it will be the same receptionist who checked the customer in, and opened up their bill, who is there the next day to have it ready for presentation.

The exact procedure for opening a payment point will depend upon the policy of each establishment. You will have to learn the procedure used in your establishment.

Handing over a payment point

In an establishment which is open for more than eight hours it is normal for there to be a hand-over of the cashiers role. Normally hand-over takes place during the after-noon in an hotel, because it is usually the quietest time of the day. The hand-over takes place when the late shift takes over from the early shift. The following points and tasks should be noted, but the exact order and precedence of each task will depend upon the individual establishment.

Two receptionists looking at the hand-over book

1 The payment point does not close during this procedure, which is why it is referred to as a hand-over period.
2 During this time the till rolls will be read, or some other computerised reading will be taken to show how much business has been done to this point.
3 The cash, and other forms of payment, will be totalled up against the readings, and the float removed.
4 The float should be the same amount as it was when the cash point was opened in the morning.
5 The cash, or other forms of payment should total the reading from the cash machines.
6 The float will be formally handed over and recorded as it was in the morning, and the till roll and takings removed by an authorised person to a secure place for banking.

7   The receptionists will also discuss any relevant points which have arisen during the shift – perhaps not all the restaurant bills from lunch time are in, or the float is running short of change and action should be taken now, etc.

Closing a payment point

At the end of the working day, the payment point will be closed down, or another hand-over will take place if the establishment has a full night reception shift. This hand-over would follow the same procedure as the afternoon one. If the cash point closes, procedures will be different:

● A reading of all the business done to date will be taken, and the till roll removed.
● The takings will be counted against the cash point reading, and the float will be counted out again, but this time it will be handed back to management for safe storage over night.
● All the customers' bills will need to be completely up to date, and, if applicable, made available to the authorised night staff.
● The hand-over/shift comment book will also need to be completed.

Exactly how these activities will be completed will vary from establishment to establishment and be based upon its size and the number of payment points that it has. Remember that you must *never* deviate from your establishment's procedure because it is designed to safeguard you as much as anyone else.

Remember these points:
● If you do not open, close and hand over at a payment point correctly, the cash takings for the entire establishment may be recorded incorrectly and mistakes will be very hard to trace.
● In some establishments cash handlers are required to make up any cash discrepancies at the end of their shift from their own pocket.
● If you do not open, close and hand over at a payment point correctly all mistakes may be attributed to your shift and you may have to make up any cash discrepancies, whether or not the error occurred during your shift.
● Even when you are very rushed never accept or hand over cash unless it has been signed for, or authorised in some way.

Do this ✔

● Find out what type of cash machines your establishment has and where they are.
● Write down for yourself what you are supposed to do when opening, closing or handing over at any of these cash points.
● Find out who is authorised to hand over the float to you and to whom you should give it back.
● Ask your supervisor what the establishment's policy is about cash shortages, or overages.
● Find out how people who want to pay their bills during the night would do so (if this is applicable to your establishment).
● Discuss with your supervisor, and then make a list of, all the types of things which should be written in the hand-over book, or discussed during a shift hand-over.
● Find out where the customers' bills are kept whilst the cash points are closed.
● Find out how you would get access to the bills if you were opening up a cash point by yourself.

HOW TO MANAGE A FLOAT

The float which you receive at the beginning of your shift is to enable you to give change to your customers. It is not possible for you or the management to know exactly how all of the customers will pay, whether they will use cash, vouchers or some form of credit, or whether, if they give you cash, they will give you the exact amount or require change. This means keeping an eye upon the cash in your drawer, so that you never run out of change. If a customer is in a hurry to pay and leave they do not want to hang around whilst you try to find change for their bill, they will simply become angry at your inefficiency. To prevent this happening you should always follow the procedure described below.

1 When the change starts to run low you should notify an authorised person about the situation. They will probably ask you what kind of change you are running low on and how much more you think you need. This is something that you will learn to judge accurately as you become more experienced.

2 The change will then be brought to you by an authorised person, and they will usually ask you to give them the same amount of money back in large-denomination notes. You may or may not be asked to sign for this transaction, it will depend upon company procedure. The total amount of money in your till should not be affected by this activity.

3 In some establishments, when you receive the float the exact breakdown of the float will be recorded, in others just the total amount will be recorded.

4 Periodically during the day authorised persons will remove the cash from all of the cash drawers. This is to prevent the build up of cash, which would make the payment points a tempting target for thieves. When this happens, and when you are extracting the float from the takings at the end of the day, you should try to make sure that the money remaining in the cash drawer, or making up the float, is in small change so that change is always available for the customers' benefit.

5 On some shifts everyone may pay by non-cash methods, so that you never run out of change. On other days everyone may pay by large-denomination notes and you may run low frequently. This is a fact of business life, and you should not worry if you have to request more change frequently. You will not be able to provide an efficient service to the customers if you do not have the right equipment – in this case enough change.

6 *Never* allow yourself to run out of change. Do not, in a panic, take change from other members of staff and then have to try to extract it from the cash point at a later date.

Essential knowledge	● The float consists of an amount of change which will enable you to give back some money to a customer if they hand over too much in payment of a bill.
	● Because customers tend to hand over large denominations of money, such as £20.00 notes, at some stage you will find that you have used up all your change.
	● Change for the floats either comes from takings within the establishment, or from the bank.
	● Management will normally hold some extra change back, in a safe, so that when a cash point gets low on change it can be replenished.
	● As it may take a while to contact a busy manager, never let the change in the float run completely out before asking for it to be replenished, otherwise you may have to keep a customer waiting.

Do this	● Find out what the float size for each cash point is in your establishment, and if possible why it is set at that level.
	● Write down the procedure within your establishment for requesting extra change. Make a special note of who is authorised to provide it.
	● Find out whether or not you have to list the exact breakdown of the float when you receive it and when you hand it back.
	● Ask your supervisor to explain to you how they become aware of the fact that they are running short of change.
	● Ask your supervisor if, because of the type of customer within your establishment, you require more change at certain times than others.

DEALING WITH AUDIT ROLLS, RECEIPT ROLLS AND CUSTOMER BILLS

Whenever you handle cash, tokens or vouchers there should be some paperwork to back up your action. This is for your own protection as well as to enable the establishment to judge how efficiently its business is running. It also enables any queries in the future to be traced back to the source and understood. Perhaps a customer may have paid twice, both the husband and wife accidentally paying. The establishment will want to confirm that this is what happened before they give a refund, and also why it happened so that they can prevent such an error occurring again.

There are three main ways of compiling and recording this information, and complying with legal requirements. One is using a manual system, one is using a computerised system, and the third a combination of the two.

On a conventional mechanised, electronic till there will be two rolls of paper. One is a till roll, or receipt roll, and one is the audit roll. When a payment takes place the details of the payment will automatically be printed onto both rolls. The receipt roll will be pushed out of the machine so that it can be given to the customer as proof of purchase, and the audit roll will remain within the machine and have printed on it an exact replica of the information on the receipt roll.

A till showing the receipt roll and the audit roll

At the end of the day, when the payment point is closed down, and perhaps during the day, during hand-over periods, an authorised person will cause a total of the business to date to be recorded on the audit roll (and it may also appear automatically upon the receipt roll as well). They will then take away the relevant part of the audit roll and compare it with the actual takings to date, to make sure that there are no discrepancies. You, the receptionist, will not have access to the audit roll, but will be able to see it. You will have access to the receipt roll. At the beginning of each shift you should check to ensure that there is enough of each roll to last throughout the shift, plus spares. If customers are held up whilst the till rolls are being replenished it will make them impatient, and make the establishment look inefficient.

In a computerised payment point it is unlikely that there will be an audit roll. Instead there will be a program to which only authorised persons have access, and this program will automatically record each use of the payment point.

In both types of machine the receipt roll may be replaced by the customer's bill. This would be quite legal as long as the items on the bill are printed out by the machine and not recorded by hand. The customer's bill then acts as their receipt.

Obviously, therefore, you must make sure that there is a plentiful supply of bills available for use during the shift, whether they be individual bills or an automatic feed supply to the cash point.

The exact procedure will vary from establishment to establishment, and from machine type to machine type.

Remember:
● Whenever a cash transaction takes place there should be some paperwork to justify the transaction.
● It is a legal requirement that whenever a good or service is purchased a receipt must be given as proof of the transaction.
● In order to prevent members of staff behaving in an illegal way some paperwork can only be accessed by authorised senior members of staff.
● Accurate knowledge about the income of an establishment is essential if it is to stay in business. Thus accurate recording of income, by receptionists, is also essential.

Case study

There was an accident on the way to work which blocked the traffic, and so you were late arriving for your shift. You had a very busy session and now you are cashing up at the end of your shift. The payments in your till do not match with the till readings.
- *How do you know that there is a discrepancy?*
- *What action must you take?*
- *What action can you take in the future to prevent this from happening again?*

Do this

- Find out what kind of audit rolls, receipt rolls, and customer bills are used in your establishment. Are they the same for each payment point?
- Find out where the replacements are kept and if access to them is restricted.
- Make a list of who is authorised to read the audit rolls or programs. Make a note of their job titles as well.
- During a quiet period ask your supervisor to show you how to change the receipt roll of any machine that you are likely to have to use.
- If all the customer bills are numbered, ask your supervisor what to do if you make a mistake and a bill cannot be used. (Do not worry if you damage one or two bills at the beginning, your establishment will have a procedure for dealing with this event.)

SECURITY OF THE PAYMENT POINT

Given that cash is such a temptation for thieves, it is obvious that all receptionists have to be very careful about security. You also have a duty to ensure that the customer is only asked to pay for those goods or services which they have used, and that they are charged for every good and service used.

In some establishments payment points may be physically separate from other parts of the reception area, and even be within a secure cubicle.

In other establishments the payment point is incorporated within the main reception desk.

If you are the receptionist authorised to deal with payments during a shift then you are responsible for the security and safety of all the money in your cash drawer and for the safety and confidentiality of the customers' bills.

A reception desk with a glassed-in area for the cashiers

43

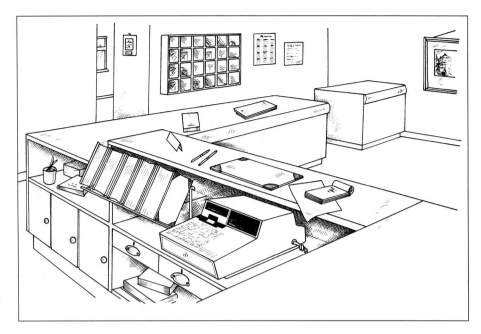

A payment point within the main reception desk

There are several golden rules which you should observe at all times:

● Never leave the cash point unattended for any period of time.
● Never hand over cash, tokens or vouchers to, or receive cash from, anyone, even an authorised person, without the correct explanatory paperwork.
● Never allow anyone except the customer, or a properly authorised person, to look at the customers' bills.
● Never allow anyone without proper authorisation into the area of the payment point.
● If you have to make an adjustment to a customer's bill, get the proper authorisation and signature before you do so.
● Whenever you have the smallest doubt about the honesty of anyone's actions, immediately contact your supervisor.

In addition to these points, each establishment will have a security procedure which has been set up to deal with each payment point's specific security needs. You must always follow this procedure.

Essential knowledge	● Any amount of cash is always a temptation to a thief.
	● Members of staff are just as likely to steal from an establishment as a stranger.
	● Whilst you are the receptionist at a payment point you are responsible for all the cash moving through that area. You are therefore responsible for any discrepancies between what should be there and what actually is.
	● If unauthorised persons gain access to customer bills, they may alter the totals for their own illegal reasons. The customer will therefore not be charged correctly, with serious consequences for the business. An unauthorised person may also damage the payment point.

Do this

- From time to time when you are in charge of a payment point you may need to leave it – you may need to go to the toilet for instance. Find out what the procedure is within your establishment if this type of situation should arise.
- Make a list of all those people who are authorised to have access to the customers' bills, and why they have that authorisation.
- Discuss with your supervisor and then make a list of when you should hand over monies, to whom, why, and what is the required authorisation.
- Do the same activity with monies received.

DEALING WITH CUSTOMERS AND UNEXPECTED SITUATIONS

Anticipating customer needs will enable you to prevent most problems. If most people check out between 8 and 9 a.m. make sure all the bills are ready by 7.30 a.m. This is called being aware of a potential problem and diffusing it before it occurs. The ability to do this comes through observation and experience.

When you are responsible for a vulnerable area, like a payment point, you must learn to become aware of all unexpected behaviour, because of the potential trouble it could indicate. However, you must not overreact, and possibly embarrass a genuine customer who may appear to be behaving oddly.

You cannot anticipate all potential problems. If a customer walks towards a payment point with a heavy coat on on a summer's day, it may be that they have a gun or other weapon under the coat, as they intend to try to rob the establishment. It may also be a customer who has just come to this country from a much hotter one, and is finding the English summer a little cold. If someone comes into the reception area and just sits and watches what is going on, it may be a person with dishonest intentions; it may also be a friend of a guest who has arrived early and is merely killing time.

Bearing in mind that you must *never* leave an open payment point unattended, the following points are useful guidelines as to what you can do and what you should not do.

- If you have any reason to believe that there is something unusual going on you must immediately do something and not let it pass hoping that nothing will happen.
- You should always follow the establishment's policy in dealing with the situation. This would normally be to contact your supervisor, or the security department if your establishment has one, and report your suspicions.
- Approaching a potentially suspect person by yourself may not be a wise thing to do, nor possible if you are alone at the payment point. It could be dangerous.
- Being aware of behaviour also means keeping an eye out for packages, etc. left lying unattended. These may have simply been forgotten, or they may be much more dangerous.

MEMORY JOGGER

Why must customers always be dealt with in a calm and polite way?

Do this

- Find out what your establishment's policy is for reporting unusual or suspicious behaviour.
- Consciously try to become aware of anyone who is behaving in an unusual fashion when they enter a vulnerable area, like a payment point.
- Ask your supervisor and other receptionists about problems which arise frequently. Find out how they deal with them.
- Make a note of when you have a problem at a payment point. After a week or so, look at your notes and see if some problems are occurring regularly. If they are, discuss with your supervisor how you could anticipate them, and so prevent them from happening.

1 Why must you follow your establishment's procedures strictly with regard to the operating of a payment point?
2 What problems may you cause yourself if you do not open, close and hand over a payment point correctly?
3 What is a 'float'?
4 Why should you always have a sufficient amount of change available in the cash drawer?
5 What is the difference between an audit roll and a receipt roll?
6 Why shouldn't the receptionist on duty have access to the audit roll or program?
7 Why must the customer have a receipt?
8 Why must a receipt be printed?
9 What should you do if an unauthorised person wants access to a payment point?
10 Why should you never hand over any monies without the proper authorisation documents?
11 What should you do if you think that someone is behaving in an unusual fashion? Why shouldn't you approach them directly?

ELEMENT 2: Deal with payments

COMPILING A CUSTOMER'S BILL

In places like supermarkets the customer's bill is often created by swiping the bar code on an item over a computer reader. This reader then tells the cash register how much to charge for the item, and then when all the items have been 'read' it totals up the amount automatically. The cashier does not need to know the price of any item individually, and so they have quite an easy task when compiling a bill. This procedure cannot be followed in the service industries: you cannot put a bar code on a bedroom, for instance, or a glass of wine.

This means that you must be very skilful and accurate when compiling a bill, and know exactly what price to charge for each good or service that the customer has purchased. Obviously you will not be able to remember all of the prices of everything which the customer can buy, especially in a very large establishment, therefore the establishment will have a set of procedures for keeping the receptionists up to date.

The basic components of a bill in an establishment which provides accommodation are:
● accommodation
● food
● drink
● telephone.

Some other common items may be:
● special video or television channels
● laundry or valet services
● newspapers
● mini bars in the rooms
● charges for the use of some leisure facilities.

On top of this, each establishment may have their own specialised services to sell. In a club, for instance, there will be a membership fee, or perhaps an extra charge if a guest of a member uses particular facilities, etc. The basic components on the bills of an establishment serving meals will be food and drink.

Two bills showing charges for various items

When the bill is not going to be presented to the customer straight away – they may be staying for several days – then this is called posting the charges to the bill. It is simply a method of keeping the bill up to date. The basic principles behind compiling a bill do not vary, however, whatever is on the bill. They are as follows:

● You must know what types of charge should be on the bill, e.g. if a customer stayed over night they probably slept, ate and drank.

● Quite commonly all charges of one type are posted at the same time. For instance, if the system is not fully computerised, all telephone charges may be read at a quiet period of the day and then put onto all of the customers' bills (as well as just as they leave). If you notice that one room which is occupied has no charges you should check to make sure that this is correct.

● If when you come to compile the bills you notice that one type of charge is missing you should check. This can be done by contacting the appropriate department and asking if this service was used, and if so where is the charge for it.

● Once you are sure that you have collected all the charges you must ensure that you enter the correct figure on the bill; if the customer is a single person they must be charged at the single rate, if they are entitled to any discounts they must receive them, and so on.

● When all the charges are entered onto the appropriate cash register, they can be totalled ready for presentation to the customer, or sub-totalled if the customer is not yet leaving and may use some other services. Common sense should tell you what is the most suitable action to take.

When compiling a bill the most difficult part may be ensuring that the customer is charged the correct amount for any good or service they have used. This can be a problem because the receptionists cannot remember all the possible prices within the establishment, or else because the establishment may offer special discounts or packages to certain people at certain times so that the normal prices do not apply.

So that you can post the correct charges, there should be appropriate price lists at the payment point and if any of the customers are receiving special rates you should be given details of this before the customer arrives at the establishment, or starts to use the appropriate service.

In establishments where a manual system operates (a manual system is one where there is no computer to automatically post charges to a customer's bill), you may be given checks or dockets from various departments, i.e. you may be given checks from the restaurant at the end of lunch service for those residents who ate lunch. The dockets should be signed by the guest, showing that they have received this service, then you can enter this charge onto the customer's main account. These dockets must be kept in case of any queries when the main bill is actually paid. When you enter a charge such as a room charge, there may not be any supporting documentation, just a description of a room type or a room number. In this case you would enter this information which would enable the correct charge to be posted to that customer automatically by the machine.

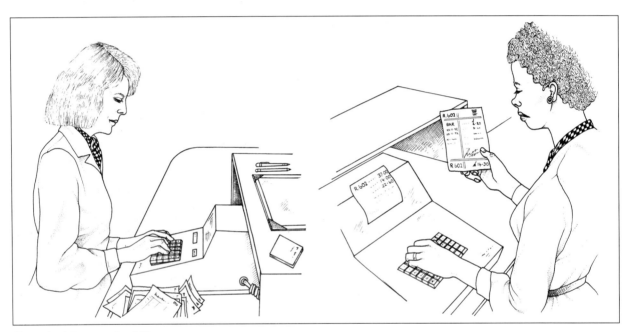

Receptionists preparing bills

In some establishments which are highly computerised, it may not be part of the duties of the person operating the payment point to compile the bill because the charges are entered at source. This means that when the customer has a drink in the bar, for instance, it is recorded on the computerised bar till. The computer will automatically post the charge to the main account in reception. In this case you may merely be required to total and print bills as and when required.

Whatever system is used in any part of your establishment, there will be a set of guide lines for you to follow so that you will know, once you have collected all the necessary charges, how to record them and create a bill. Whatever system is used you must take great care to make sure that the correct figure or code is entered onto the right bill and that the bill is ready for presentation at the appropriate time.

The bill should be totalled and made ready for presentation to the customer when the customer requires it. For certain bills it may be possible to anticipate when the customer is most likely to call for their bill. In these cases the receptionist can have the bill prepared in advance, so as to prevent possible delays if many bills are likely to be required at once. Likely busy periods are morning departures from the reception payment point, or meal payments after the meal is finished.

A well-run payment point and a badly-run payment point

Remember the following points:
● It is illegal to charge a price other than the one advertised for any good or service.
● All basic prices must be displayed for the customer to see easily, whether for food, drink, accommodation or other services.
● It is very bad for the reputation of any establishment to accidentally over or under charge the customers.
● A messy bill, with lots of corrections, would indicate that the establishment, and its staff, are very inefficient.
● Before a customer pays a bill they have the right to check its accuracy.
● If a bill is not accurate, or has many corrections, it makes the establishment look inefficient.
● Once a bill has been checked and agreed then the customer and the establishment have made a legal contract about the amount which is to be paid. If the receptionist made a mistake in calculating the bill it cannot be added at a later stage. The money is lost.
● Once a transaction has been made, a printed receipt must be provided as proof of that transaction.
● Any deviation from the correct procedures may result in a non-cash payment not being accepted and honoured by the issuing company.
● In some establishments it is policy that any shortages due to staff error be made up by the member of staff concerned.

Do this

● Find out if your establishment uses a manual, computerised or semi-computerised system for compiling bills.
● Practise compiling bills according to your establishment's procedures for any payment point which you are likely to have to work in.
● Make a list of those bills which are compiled for immediate presentation and those which are updated regularly for future presentation. On the list, write down why the bill is produced in this format.
● If your establishment uses codes to compile bills, make a list of all the codes and what charges, and how much, they represent.
● Make a list of all the different price lists within your establishment. Check to see that they are available at the appropriate payment point.

PRESENTING AND ACKNOWLEDGING CUSTOMERS' BILLS

There is always an appropriate time to present a bill to a customer, and this is normally upon request. The bill may be presented either by the person working at the payment point – if the customer collects the bill – or by a member of staff who takes the bill to the customer. The procedure depends both upon within which department the bill is required and upon the individual establishment.

When a customer asks for their bill it should be presented in a written format. Normally it is printed by a cashiering machine, but in some establishments it is hand written. If it is hand written great care should be taken to ensure that the writing is clear and legible. The customer should be presented with the bill in a written format so that they can see what charges are on the bill and therefore how the total amount was arrived at. The customer should be allowed time to study the bill, if they choose to do so, before the actual payment is collected.

When the bill is presented it should be done so discreetly – that is to say so that only the customer receiving the bill can see what charges are on it. There are several reasons for this:

● The customer may be entertaining someone else, perhaps for business or as a treat, and they prefer that the other person not know the amount.
● There may be certain items on the bill which they may want to keep confidential.
● The customer may simply not want anyone else to know how much they did or did not spend, or what discounts they received, etc.

When creating or totalling a bill it is essential that the correct prices or codes are used, otherwise the bill will not be correct and unnecessary delays and embarrassment will be caused whilst the errors are corrected. It is also essential to use the correct price and code when accepting payment in any form. The correct price must be entered so that:

● you can give the correct change, if applicable
● the reading on the receipt roll and audit roll match that of the amount of payment received
● you charge the customer the correct amount of money.

The correct code or ledger information (if a bill is not paid immediately and is sent, for example, to a company for payment, it is called a ledger payment) must be entered when receiving payment so that the accounts department will know how much money to expect in cash and how much in other forms of payment. This information will either be indicated on the keys of the billing machine or there will be a list of codes available at the payment point. You must make yourself familiar with the establishment procedure and codes.

Once payment has been made, even if it is a non-cash payment, the customer must receive a machine-printed receipt showing the amount that they have paid. If the bill was created by machine rather than by hand then it can be used for this purpose. However, if the bill was hand written the customer must be given a receipt from the billing machine's receipt roll as proof of the transaction.

The exact procedure will vary from establishment to establishment and from machine to machine.

A till receipt stapled to a hand-written bill

Essential knowledge	One customer may be paying for others, and so may want the total of the bill to remain anonymous to all except themselves and the establishment.

Do this

- Find out how your establishment presents bills to different types of customer and in different departments.
- Make a list of why some bills are presented in one fashion and some in another.
- Find out what types of receipt are issued at each payment point that you are likely to work at, and learn to create them yourself.
- Ask your supervisor if there are specific times of the day when certain customer bills are most likely to be required. If there are, ask why these busy times occur and what action you can take to anticipate them so that you will be able to react swiftly and efficiently to them. (What work should you have done in advance? What should you have checked?)
- Ask your supervisor what you should do if some one other than the customer, another guest perhaps, says that they have come to collect the bill on the customer's behalf.

CASH, VOUCHER AND TOKEN PAYMENTS

Once a customer is satisfied that their bill is accurate, they will pay. You may not always be able to give change to a customer – this depends upon the method they choose to pay by – but you are always able to, and by law must, give a printed receipt for each transaction which takes place.

Cash payment means payment using the coinage and/or printed money of the country which you are in. If a customer pays by this method they are entitled to the appropriate amount of change, again in the coinage or printed money of that country.

When voucher or token payments are made no cash changes hands. This is a method of payment where the actual exchange of cash took place before the customer visited your establishment. For instance, a customer may buy a book of tokens from a national chain of hotels. Each token represents one night's accommodation and breakfast in any of the company's hotels. The customer then decides which hotel they are going to stay in, and for how many nights. They may choose to stay one night in an hotel in York, one night in Bath, two nights in London and so on. When they check out of the hotel they hand over the token for their accommodation instead of a cash payment. They may have used other facilities as well, such as the restaurant, and they would pay cash for these transactions. If the customers did not have breakfast one morning they would not be entitled to any change because the token, or package, which they are using is an inclusive one.

When customers pay with special tokens or vouchers, the basic procedure for accepting such payments is as follows:
- When you are offered payment in any form other than cash, check that your establishment accepts the type of payment.
- Accept the token or voucher and cancel it using the method required by your establishment.
- Place the token or voucher securely in your cash drawer.
- If the voucher is for less than the total of the bill, the difference, in cash, should be requested from the customer.
- If the face value of the token or voucher is for more than the total amount of the customer's bill you will not under normal circumstances be able to give them back any change. You must follow your establishment's policy on this very closely.
- Give the customer a receipt.

Essential knowledge	All tokens and vouchers must be cancelled in the approved fashion to prevent them being reused and the establishment being defrauded.

Some tokens or vouchers may be a form of part payment. Sometimes organisations promote themselves by having special offers. They may say, for instance, that at the weekend a child can stay for free if they stay in the same room as their parents. When this type of token or voucher is presented at the payment point, a certain portion of the bill is not charged to the customers, i.e. the child's accommodation, but the rest is, i.e. the parents' accommodation plus any bar and restaurant bills.

Although a customer is not entitled to change if they do not use up all the facilities available on a voucher or token, if there was an emergency and they had to cut short their visit, the management might allow the customer to use up the unused facilities on their voucher at another time. For instance, if some customers had bought a voucher entitling them to three nights' accommodation but someone became very sick and they had to return home early, the management might say that they could come and stay for one night, to use up their voucher, upon another occasion. However this would be a decision which the managers would make and not you.

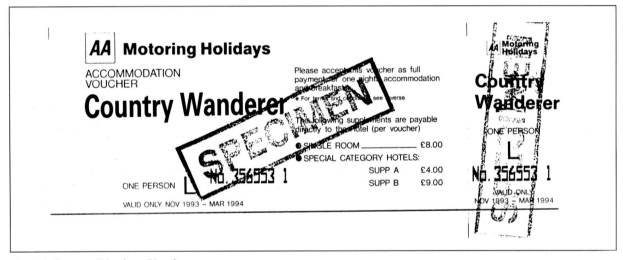

An AA Country Wanderer Voucher

An AA Driveaway Voucher

Whatever type of token or voucher payment is used, you must make sure that it is one which is accepted by your establishment. There should be a list of those which are acceptable at the payment point. Normally if a customer is going to settle their account using a voucher or token, they tell the reception desk when they arrive, or check before they use the appropriate facility. However, there may be customers who present the voucher when they ask for their bill. If the voucher or token is one which is accepted by the establishment it would simply be accepted and the appropriate information recorded on the bill. If it is not a token or voucher which is acceptable to the establishment, then you would have to inform the customer that you cannot accept it and ask for some other form of payment. If the customer insists that the voucher should be accepted, then you should be courteous and polite, explain that you are not able to help them, and ask your supervisor to deal with the problem. Problems often arise if people do not read the expiry dates, or exact terms on free and special offers.

When a voucher or token is accepted in lieu of a cash payment it must be cancelled immediately so that it cannot be used again. There are various methods for doing this:
● There may be a section on the token or voucher which should be filled in by you.
● It may be company policy to write 'cancelled' across the voucher or token.
● The establishment may have special date stamps which can be used to show when the voucher was accepted and by what department.

Storing the payment

Assuming that everything is alright, the payment in cash, token or voucher form should be accepted, cancelled where appropriate, and stored in the correct compartment of the cash drawer.

As soon as the payment has been placed in the cash drawer it must be closed for security reasons to make it less vulnerable to theft. On some machines it is not possible to start a second action unless the cash drawer has been fully closed from the first one.

If cash, tokens or vouchers are not placed neatly in the cash drawer then it will be much harder, and much slower, finding change when it is necessary, and if the notes are muddled up into different denominations it is quite easy to give out the wrong change anyway.

An untidy till drawer

RECEIPTS

Once payment in any form has been accepted the customer is entitled to a printed receipt. The receipt does not necessarily have to show the exact breakdown of the bill, but should show where and when the transaction took place, how much it was for and what type of service it covered, i.e. accommodation, food, the use of leisure facilities, etc. If the customer's bill is printed by the billing machine it can act as the customer's receipt. This saves the customer from having to have an extra piece of paper to carry around with them, and saves you time in having to produce the receipt.

If the customer's bill is also their receipt, it is customary for the bill to be in triplicate. This means that it will have three, self-duplicating, copies. The top copy of the bill is given to the customer, with their change if they are due any, and acts as their receipt. The bottom two copies are kept by the hotel and used by the accounts department to make sure that all actions have been correctly charged for, and all monies taken correctly recorded. If the customer's bill was hand written they would have to be given a printed receipt from the till roll. (See page 50.)

Exactly what you will have to do to accept payment and issue receipts will depend upon the type of billing machines your establishment uses, the vouchers and tokens it accepts and the establishment's procedures for accepting payment. You must find out all this information as quickly as possible.

A bill in triplicate

Remember that:

- Once you have received and accepted payment, even if you have charged the wrong amount, you will find it very difficult, if not impossible, to ask for the difference later when the error is found out.
- Each customer is entitled to a printed receipt for every transaction that takes place.
- Some customers may ask for special receipts for business purposes, for example VAT receipts.
- If the payments which you receive are stored in a muddle then you will find it hard to get change when you need it.
- When people pay with tokens and vouchers they may not be entitled to be given any change, even when the face value of the voucher comes to more than the total bill.
- Your establishment is unlikely to accept all of the token and voucher payments which are available, it will only accept some of them.

Do this

- Make a list of all of the vouchers and tokens your establishment accepts.
- Make a list of how to cancel vouchers and tokens once they have been accepted.
- Find out what your establishment's policy is if a customer wants to pay with a voucher or token which the establishment does not normally accept.
- Find out if the billing machines tell you how much change you should give a customer when they pay by cash, or if you have to work it out.
- Find out what type of receipts your establishment issues. Are they the same for all payment points?

NON-CASH PAYMENTS

There are various types of non-cash payment. Each must be treated slightly differently, but no matter which establishment you work in the basic acceptance and validation procedures for each type of payment remain the same. The main types of payment are as follows:

- *cheques* – bank, giro or building society cheques; sterling traveller's cheques; Eurocheques
- *credit cards* – Access/Mastercard; Visa/Barclaycard
- *charge cards* – American Express; Diners Club
- *direct debit cards* – Switch cards; Visa.

Cheques

Cheques are issued by banks, the post office (giro cheques) and building societies. If you are presented with a normal cheque then it means that the customer has an account with the issuing establishment into which they pay money with which their cheques will be paid. A normal cheque can only be used in the country and currency in which it was issued. This means that a cheque from a Barclays bank anywhere in the UK can be accepted anywhere within the UK and the amount written on it will be in pounds sterling.

A Eurocheque is similar to a normal cheque but it can be accepted anywhere within the European Union and written in any currency. This means that a customer from France can bring a Eurocheque issued by a bank in France to the UK and pay for goods and services in sterling.

A Eurocheque

A sterling traveller's cheque is slightly different. In this case the customer may not have an account with the issuing establishment, and the issuing company may not be a bank as such, but part of a financial institution, for instance Thomas Cook or American Express traveller's cheques. In this instance the customer will have bought – paid cash for – the traveller's cheques and when your establishment accepts them they will get their money from the issuing company, which already has the money.

People tend to carry cheques with them rather than cash if they are not sure how much their bill will come to and because it is a more secure form of payment than cash. If cheques are stolen then the customer can report this to the issuing company and they can cancel them, and no money is lost. This is not possible with cash. This means however, that when accepting a cheque payment you must always consult the establishment's cancelled/invalid lists. These lists will also record the number of any bank cards which are no longer valid.

ACCESS INVALID CREDIT CARD LIST 25.2.97

CARD NUMBER	EXPIRY DATE
5534 9948 7535 9630	10/97
7984 5555 2341 9804	9/97

An invalid/cancelled cheque and bank card list

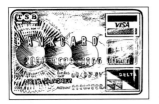

Bank card

A bank card is a small plastic card issued by a bank or building society which contains information to enable a receptionist to verify the ownership of a cheque.

Bank, giro, building society and Eurocheques should all be supported by the relevant bank card. The bank card has a cash figure on it, usually a multiple of £50, and the signature of the customer. This is to enable the person accepting the cheque to check that the bill total is not for more than the issuing establishment will accept, (the cash amount on the bank card) and by checking the signature on the card against the signature on the cheque that the cheque has been written by the correct person. Traveller's cheques are usually supported by a passport or official ID card. Here the receptionist is able to look at the photograph and signature and establish the identity of the customer. If there is no supporting card or passport the cheque should not be accepted.

Basic procedure for accepting bank, giro, building society and Eurocheques

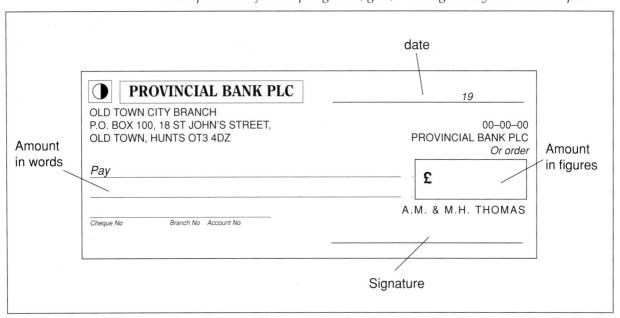

1 Show the customer the bill, so that they can write out the amount owing on the cheque.
2 Take the filled out cheque from the customer and check the following points:
   ● that the date is written in correctly
   ● that the amount, both in writing and figures, is written correctly
   ● that the signature on the cheque is the same as that on the bank card
   ● that the signature is written on the original paper strip (if a new one has been

pasted to the bank card, then when you run your thumb over the back of the card it catches on the different surface)
- if your establishment has a validation machine, hold the card under the ultra violet light to check that the hologram is a true one and not a two-dimensional fake.
- that the bank card is valid, e.g. not out of date
- that it is the correct bank card – this can be verified by making sure that the sort code on the cheque is the same as the sort code on the bank card (except with a Barclays Bank bank card because the bank card is also able to be used as a credit card under certain circumstances)
- that the total of the bill does not exceed the guarantee figure on the bank card (if it does, you must follow your establishment's procedure for dealing with the cheque).

3   Compare the bank card and cheque with the cancelled/invalid list; make sure that it does not appear on it.
4   Write the card number on the back of the cheque (you may also be asked to write down other information but that will depend upon your establishment's procedures).
5   Place the cheque in the cash drawer.
6   Give the customer back their bank card, plus a copy of the bill, and a printed receipt if applicable.

If the bill total is for more than the amount guaranteed on the bank card, your establishment will have a set of procedures for you to follow. This usually means that other information is entered on the back of the cheque, so that if the cheque should not be honoured by the issuing company the customer can be traced and asked to pay by another method.

Your establishment will also have a set procedure to follow if the cheque or bank card number show up on the cancelled/invalid list. Make sure that you are familiar with the procedure and follow it, because if you accept payment from a cheque or bank card which has been withdrawn, the issuing company will not honour the cheque and your establishment, and perhaps you, will lose money. If, on the other hand, you retain an invalid card correctly you may be financially rewarded.

In some establishments cheques are not hand written, they are printed out by the billing machine. In this case the above procedures remain the same except for point 1, which will now become
1   Show the customer the totalled bill, take a cheque from them to print on the billing machine and return it to the customer for checking and signing.

Then continue as before with points 2 to 6.

Basic procedure for accepting sterling traveller's cheques
Before accepting a sterling traveller's cheque you should note the following:
- An unauthorised traveller's cheque means that the second signature is not yet filled in. The first one was filled in when the customer bought the traveller's cheques.
- Traveller's cheques are issued for standard amounts, i.e. £5. £20, £50, etc. This means that when a customer uses this method to pay, the amount on the traveller's cheque is unlikely to be the same as the amount on the bill.
- If the value of the traveller's cheque is greater than the value of the bill then the customer should be given change for the difference. For example if the bill is for £79.50 and the customer gives traveller's cheques worth £80.00, they would be entitled to 50p change. If on the other hand a customer's bill came to £55 and they gave the receptionist £50 worth of traveller's cheques, then the difference would have to be made up, usually by the customer paying £5 in cash.
- Often a customer may use more than one traveller's cheque to pay for one bill. For example they may use two £50 cheques to pay for a £100 bill. This is an acceptable, standard practice.

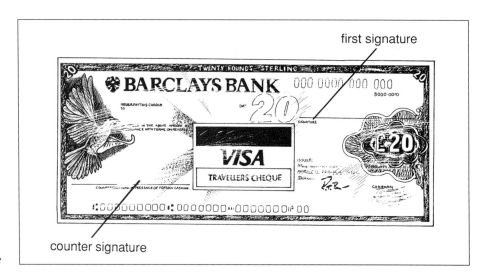

first signature

counter signature

A sterling traveller's cheque

● Customers who are entitled to change may only be given change in sterling. Only banks and other licensed premises are legally allowed to issue foreign cash.

When accepting a sterling traveller's cheque:

1 Show the customer the totalled bill.
2 Accept from the customer unauthorised traveller's cheque(s), usually for more than the total of the bill.
3 Accept from the customer an authorised form of identification, usually a passport or an official ID card.
4 Ask the customer to date the traveller's cheque and countersign it (that is to enter the second signature). This second signature should only be entered in front of the person receiving the payment so that they can authenticate the signature.
5 Check the signature and the photograph in the passport or on the ID card against the signature and person in front of you.
6 If it is your establishment's procedure, write down the passport or ID card number on the back of the traveller's cheque.
7 Receive the difference between the total of the traveller's cheques being offered and the total of the bill, if applicable.
8 Give the correct change, the identification documents and a printed receipt to the customer.
9 Place the traveller's cheque(s) safely and correctly in the cash drawer.

Credit cards and charge cards

Some cards are issued by banks, e.g. Barclays Bank, and others are issued by large financial institutions, e.g. American Express. Some are only acceptable within the UK and some are acceptable internationally. Not all establishments accept all credit and charge cards. This is because they have to pay commission to the issuing company. Your establishment will have a list of those charge and credit cards which it accepts, and you should familiarise yourself with it so that you only accept the listed cards.

As far as accepting payment by credit or charge card is concerned, the receptionist will follow the same basic procedures. This is because the main difference in the type of card is how the establishment receives its final cash payment from the issuing company. Another difference which the receptionist will see is that the internationally accepted cards, which tend to be charge cards, normally have a higher guarantee limit, and the establishment will have a higher floor limit for this type of card.

A cheque is guaranteed by a bank card, and checking against the cancelled/invalid list. A charge card or credit card payment is guaranteed by the card's printed limit,

Credit cards

by the floor limit of the establishment, by an authorisation code and by checking the cancelled/invalid list.

Floor limits
- The 'floor limit' is the establishment's credit limit without authorisation for a non-cash payment. Its purpose is to try to reduce fraud.
- Each establishment will probably have different floor limits for each type of non-cash payment.
- If the total of a bill exceeds the floor limit, an authorisation code must be sought from the issuing company otherwise they have no legal obligation to accept the charge.
- Once an authorisation code has been obtained no adjustments may be made to the customer's bill. If an adjustment has to be made, a new floor limit for the new amount must be sought.

Authorisation codes
An authorisation code is needed whenever the bill total is for more than either the card's stated limit, the establishment's floor limit, or both. In this case you must contact the issuing company by following the establishment's procedure. This will normally be to telephone a special number. You will give the issuing company the following information:
- the name of the establishment
- the reference number of the establishment
- the name, number and expiry date on the card
- the total of the bill.

The issuing company, if everything is fine, will then give you a number. This is the authorisation code. It guarantees that the issuing company will reimburse the establishment for the total of that bill even if the customer should run out of money.

If there is a problem then you will be asked to retain the card and inform the customer why you are doing so. If this happens your establishment will have a standard procedure to follow to help you do this.

Always remember that when a card is cancelled, whilst it may be that the customer is trying to defraud your establishment, it could also be that they are a genuine customer whose last payment simply got held up by, say, a postal strike. If they are a genuine customer they will be deeply embarrassed, and would not want anyone else to know what has happened. Therefore you must be discreet. In all circumstances you *must* follow your establishment's procedures, as well as asking for another form of payment.

Basic procedure for accepting credit and charge cards
In some establishments the method of accepting credit and charge cards is manual and in others it is incorporated into a computerised system. The procedures vary slightly from one another so both are described below. It may also be useful for your future career to learn both systems.

A manual acceptance system
1 Give the customer the totalled bill.
2 Accept from the customer the credit or charge card.
3 Check that this is a card which is accepted by your establishment, and check the floor limits for this type of card.
4 Check the following details on the card:
   - that it is still valid, i.e. the expiry date has not yet been reached
   - the cash guarantee limit of the card
   - that the signature is the original one by running your thumb over it (if a new paper strip has been added with a new signature written on it, your thumb will catch on the edge of the new strip)

MEMORY JOGGER

What are floor limits and authorisation codes?

MEMORY JOGGER

What must you check before accepting a credit card payment?

- if your establishment has a validation machine place the credit or debit card under the ultra violet light to check that the hologram is real, not a two-dimensional fake.

5 Take a blank voucher and the credit card, and run them through the imprinting machine.

6 Write the following information onto the voucher:
   - date
   - department
   - sales number, if applicable
   - your initials
   - a brief description of what is being paid for, e.g. 'hotel accommodation'
   - the amount of the bill in the amount section and the total section
   - the authorisation code, if applicable.

7 Give the voucher back to the customer to sign.

8 Check the signature of the customer on the voucher against the signature on the card.

9 Give the customer the customer's copy of the voucher, their card and a printed receipt.

10 Place the establishment's copies of the voucher in the correct place in the cash drawer.

A mechanised acceptance method

1 Give the customer the totalled bill.

2 Accept from the customer a credit or charge card.

3 Check that it is a card which is accepted by the establishment.

4 Swipe the card through the appropriate machine (there will be a machine through which to swipe the card, or it will be incorporated as part of the billing machine). The machine will automatically check the card and provide an authorisation number. When the checks have been completed successfully the machine will print out a duplicate voucher.

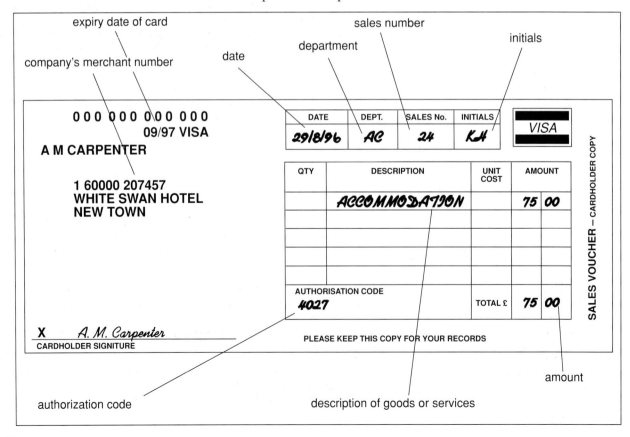

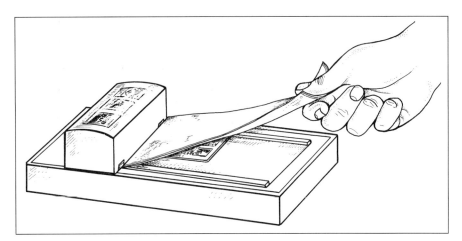

A credit card and voucher in an imprinter

5 Ask the customer to sign the voucher.
6 Check the signature on the voucher against that on the card (the card may be valid, but it may not be the owner of the card who has presented it to you).
7 Give the customer the customer's copy of the voucher, their card and their copy of the bill.
8 Place the establishment's copies of the voucher in the correct place in the cash drawer.

In some establishments there may be a combined manual and mechanised system. Here the normal procedure would be for the receptionist to validate the card by swiping it through an authorising machine and entering the total of the bill. The machine would automatically show the authorisation code on a digital display, and you would complete processing the card via the manual system. This system is more popular now than an entirely manual system, because it saves time and all cards can be validated quickly and efficiently at any time of day or night.

If at any stage you are not happy with the transaction – for example you cannot get an authorisation code, the signatures do not look the same, etc. you should not accept the payment, but, following the establishment's procedures, get assistance from another member of staff.

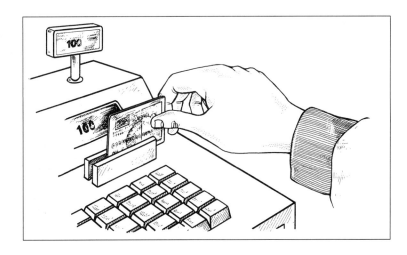

An authorisation machine

This is especially true if the payment point is very busy because, if you take a long time to deal with one customer, others will be queuing up behind and become very frustrated. It is also very difficult to be discreet when there is a problem with lots of other people around all trying to pay their bills, and therefore able to overhear any conversation which might be going on.

Direct debit cards

These are cards which directly debit the customer's bank account with the total of the bill, and place that amount into the establishment's bank account. It is therefore similar to accepting cash, in that there is no waiting period for the payment. However, the procedure for accepting payment by this method is very similar to the mechanised credit or charge card system. The most common card of this type is a Switch card.

Many people choose to carry them in preference to cash, as a security measure. Establishments are happy to accept them because as long as they are correctly accepted the establishment is guaranteed its money straight away.

Basic procedures for accepting a direct debit card
1   Give the customer the totalled bill.
2   Accept from the customer the direct debit card.
3   Check that it is a card which is accepted by the establishment.
4   Swipe the card through the appropriate machine (there will be a machine through which to swipe the card, or it will be incorporated as part of the billing machine). The machine will automatically check the card. When the checks have been completed successfully the machine will print out a duplicate voucher.
5   Ask the customer to sign the voucher.
6   Check the signature on the voucher against that on the card (the card may be valid, but it may not be the owner of the card who has presented it to you).
7   Give the customer the customer's copy of the voucher, their card and their copy of the bill.
8   Place the establishment's copies of the voucher in the correct place in the cash drawer.

As with any other form of non-cash payment, if you are not happy with any part of the acceptance or validation procedure you should follow your establishment's procedure for dealing with problems in a non-cash payment situation. This will normally involve explaining the problem to a more senior member of staff, in the first instance.

DEALING WITH ERRORS OR SPOILT CHEQUES OR VOUCHERS

From time to time, especially when you first start training, you will make errors. Your supervisors expect a *few* problems to occur, and there will be an establishment policy for dealing with them. However, when a cheque or voucher is spoilt or written incorrectly there are several basic steps to follow which will be part of your establishment's procedure. These steps are as set out below.

Cheques

● If any part of the cheque is written out incorrectly (often it is the date), the customer can cross the error through, write down the correct information and initial the error.
● As long as the cheque is still clearly legible it will not matter if there is more than one correction on it, but all the corrections must be initialled by the customer.
● If there are a lot of corrections it is better to cancel the cheque by tearing it up in

front of the customer so that they can see you doing it, and giving them the torn cheque if they require it. In this case a new cheque would be written out.

Credit or charge cards

- If there are any errors the voucher must be voided.
- The voucher should be torn up, in front of or by the customer, and they should be given the torn voucher if they require it.
- A new voucher should be written out.

Do this

- Write down the procedure for accepting a cheque if it is for more than the guaranteed cash limit on the card.
- Make a list of forms of ID other than a passport acceptable to your establishment when accepting sterling traveller's cheques.
- Make a list of all the credit cards and charge cards which your establishment accepts.
- Make a list of your establishment's floor limits for each card which is accepted.
- Find out where the cancelled/invalid lists are kept. Make sure that there is one beside the cash point.
- Write down exactly what you should do if you are at all worried about accepting a non-cash payment.
- Find out whether your establishment uses a manual or mechanised credit and charge card authorisation system, and learn how to use it.
- Write down the procedure which your establishment uses to cancel unusable cheques and vouchers.

SECURITY OF THE PAYMENT POINT

Given that any form of payment is a temptation to dishonest people, it is obvious that security of the payment point is very important. If unauthorised persons gain access to a payment point they will be able to gain access to the customers' bills, as well as cash and other forms of payment.

If a person gains access to the payment point they may be able to find out unauthorised information about various customers of the establishment. If a media VIP is staying they may not want fans, press or other interested people to know which room they are in otherwise they will get no peace from visitors and telephone calls. The information gained can also be used for more serious ends, perhaps in a divorce court.

MEMORY JOGGER

Why must you never leave the payment point unattended?

Unauthorised people may also behave in other dishonest ways, for example they may alter the totals of the customers' bills, i.e. lower their own. They may also simply steal, i.e. remove cash and other valuable items.

For these reasons payment points must be kept secure, and are sometimes physically separate from the other parts of the reception area, and can even be within a secure cubicle. In other establishments the payment point is incorporated within the main reception desk.

If you are the receptionist authorised to deal with payments during a shift then you are responsible for the security and safety of the contents of your cash drawer and for the safety and confidentiality of the customers' bills.

There are several golden rules which you should observe at all times:
- Never leave the payment point unattended for any period of time.
- Never allow anyone except the customer, or a properly authorised person, to look at the customers' bills.

● Never allow anyone without proper authorisation into the area of the payment point.
● If you have to make an adjustment to a customer's bill, get the proper authorisation and signature before you do so.
● If you have to void a voucher or cheque, actually tear it up in front of the customer so that they can be certain that it has been destroyed.
● Whenever you have the smallest doubt about the honesty of anyone's actions, immediately contact your supervisor.

Beyond this, each establishment will have a security procedure which has been set up to deal with each payment point's security needs. You must always follow this procedure.

Essential knowledge

Security of the payment point is important for the following reasons:
● The payment of any bill is potentially open to fraud.
● A common fraud would be for an unauthorised person to gain access to the payment point and alter a bill total, either manually or on a computer record.
● If unauthorised persons gain access to a payment point they may gain access to confidential information.
● Any payment point which has been opened up for service is very vulnerable to theft and fraud. They must never be left unattended or unsecured.
● An unattended payment point may be damaged.

Do this

● From time to time when you are in charge of a payment point you may need to leave it, you may need to go to the toilet for instance. Find out what is the procedure within your establishment if this type of situation should arise.
● Make a list of all those people who are authorised to have access to the customers' bills, and why they have that authorisation.
● Discuss with your supervisor and then make a list of when you should hand over any form of payment, to whom, why, and what is the required authorisation.

DEALING WITH CUSTOMERS REQUIRING REFUNDS

You may be the first person to hear about a problem for which a customer feels that they are entitled to a refund. This is because the payment point is where they settle their account. When dealing with such customers you should remember the following points:
● From time to time refunds either in cash or credit will need to be made by all establishments.
● Not all refunds are the result of errors or bad service, etc., however most are.
● A customer requiring a refund will usually be unhappy about something and therefore will require especially sympathetic handling.
● Applications for refunds are open to misuse such as fraud, just as payments are.
● Because all applications for refunds are potentially fraudulent, all refunds must be appropriately authorised.
● The issuing of a refund must be authorised and recorded; if cash is handed over without being recorded, the person who handed it over is open to accusations of cash discrepancies, i.e. theft.
● All applications for refunds must be recorded so that management can take action to prevent the problem reoccurring.

There are three basic reasons why a customer may ask for a refund, but in each case they may be, or appear to be, very angry, and so require to be treated very politely and diplomatically. The reasons are as follows:

1   If something has gone wrong, for example the customer asked for a room with a bath and was promised it, and got a room with a shower, then they are entitled to be angry. If they sent clothing to be cleaned and it has not arrived back on time, they are caused great inconvenience. This means that when you are dealing with them you will have to be especially tactful.

2   A customer may be 'trying it on'. That is to say, seeing if they can get a price reduction even if they are not really entitled to it. A senior member of staff, after investigating the incident, will have to give authorisation for the refund once they have become satisfied that the incident has occurred. The customer usually appears very angry in order to intimidate the establishment's staff. This is why a senior member of staff should investigate and deal with the problem.

3   A customer may have a problem, but they may have caused it themselves, for example when they sent off their laundry they did not say they wanted a special service, so they did not get one. Again a senior member of staff will have to investigate the incident, and make a decision about whether or not the guest is entitled to some form of compensation.

In all these cases it is you, the receptionist, who often gets the first blast of anger. Your establishment will have a procedure to deal with this. If you follow it and remain calm the incident can be defused and remedies offered, but if the receptionist takes the customer's anger personally and becomes angry in return the problem will get worse.

Validating and issuing a refund

Your establishment will have a procedure for validating and issuing refunds. You must never deviate from this procedure because it is designed to protect staff as well as the establishment.

Remember that:
● issuing a refund means giving money away from the business. It can only be done if a senior member of staff has authorised it
● giving money away means that the money in your cash drawer will be short, so you must have documentation to justify the shortage.
● as a refund claim is as potentially open to fraud as any other payment transaction, the claim must be validated before the refund is issued.

Most establishments will follow the same basic rules and only the fine detail will vary from establishment to establishment. The basic procedure is as follows:

1   The establishment becomes aware of a problem. This may happen in two ways. In the first type of incident the establishment's staff become aware of the problem, and alert the appropriate senior member of staff. For instance a customer who has paid for secretarial services may have sent a fax which becomes damaged and unusable as it goes through the machine, and may have to reproduce that work again. Here the management know that there is a genuine problem before the customer is aware of it and complains and can work out the remedial action to take, i.e. secretarial services deleted from the customer's bill and a 'free' secretary offered.
    In the second type of incident the customer becomes aware of the problem first. For instance they may have ordered early morning tea in their room, which was added to the bill overnight, but the tea never arrived.

2   The next action is for the appropriate senior member of staff to be contacted, as they already were in the first example. The senior member of staff will quickly investigate the incident.

3   Once the senior member of staff is sure that the incident happened, they will authorise you to make a refund. They will do this by writing up the incident in a refund book, which will be similar to the example given overleaf.

4   If the refund is a cash refund then cash is removed from the cash drawer and given to the customer. There will normally be a duplicate book for the customer to sign saying that they have received the cash, with the bottom copy going into the cash drawer to justify the reduction in cash. If the refund is a credit refund, that is to say that there is an adjustment made on the customer's bill, then no cash changes hands but when the customer comes to pay the bill there will be a reduction on it for the agreed amount.

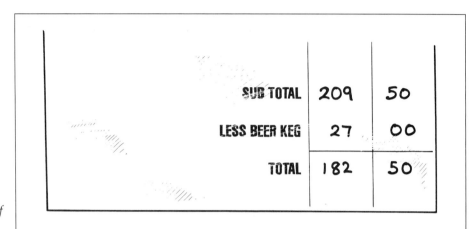

SUB TOTAL	209	50
LESS BEER KEG	27	00
TOTAL	182	50

A customer's bar bill with a reduction against the price of the beer

REFUND BOOK					
Date	Details	Cash Refund	Credit Refund	Authorised By	Cashier

A refund book

5   If the refund is a credit or charge card refund, then you will have to fill in a voucher which is very similar to a credit or charge card voucher, however it will say refund. You will take an imprint of the customer's card, or run it through an authorisation machine, according to your establishment's procedures. The customer will sign the voucher and retain their copy. However, when the customer eventually receives their statement from their credit or charge card company they will find that the refund amount has been deducted from their statement, not added on to it.

6   If the senior member of staff is not satisfied that the refund is justified then they will not authorise it, they will deal with the customer in private away from the public work areas. If there is no authorisation you must *never* give out a refund, even if it is only for a tiny sum like 50p, because you may not know the whole story.

In all establishments the basic procedures will be as described above; however there will variations in the documentation to be completed and in the members of staff who are authorised to issue refunds. You must learn the procedure for your establishment.

Do this

● Find out what is your establishment's procedure for dealing with applications for refunds.
● Find out who is authorised to give refunds in your establishment.
● Find out where the refund authorisation book is kept.
● Find out if there is a special key on your billing machine which is used to indicate that a credit refund has been given.
● Over a period of a month make a list of all the refunds which you are authorised to deal with. Analyse the list and see if any of the incidents occur regularly. Discuss them with your supervisor.
● Ask your supervisor how they deal with very angry customers, and learn some techniques from them for handling people who are upset or angry.

DEALING WITH CUSTOMERS AND UNEXPECTED SITUATIONS

Customers expect an efficient service at all times. This should be true, but sometimes it may not be. If you are unable to assist a customer straight away remember to remain polite and calm at all times, and if you are unable to deal with the customer at all, contact someone who can.

Anticipating customer needs will enable you to prevent most problems. If most people check out between 8 and 9 a.m. make sure all the bills are ready by 7.30 a.m. This is known as being aware of a potential problem and defusing it before it occurs. The ability to do this comes through observation and experience.

You cannot, however, anticipate all potential problems. If a customer walks towards a payment point with a folded paper held in both hands, it may be that they have a gun or other weapon under the paper, as they intend to try to rob the establishment. It may also be a customer who has a strange way of holding their newspaper. If someone comes into the reception area and just sits and watches what is going on, it may be a person with dishonest intentions, it may also be a friend of a guest who has arrived early and is merely killing time.

The ability to deal well with unexpected situations comes mainly through personal experience, and observing how others deal successfully with incidents. The estab-

Does this man's newspaper hide a gun?

lishment's procedure for dealing with unexpected incidents has been set up to provide a set of guidelines to work within, but common sense is also required.

When you are responsible for a vulnerable area, like a payment point, you must learn to become aware of all unexpected behaviour, because of the potential trouble it could indicate. However, you must not overreact, and possibly embarrass a genuine customer who happens to be behaving oddly. Bearing in mind that you must *never* leave an open payment point unattended, the following points are useful guidelines as to what you can do and what you should not do.

● If you have any reason to believe that there is something unusual going on you must immediately do something and not let it pass hoping that nothing will happen.

● You should always follow the establishment's policy in dealing with the situation. This would normally be to contact your supervisor, or the security department if your establishment has one, and report your suspicions.

● Approaching a potentially suspect person by yourself may not be a wise thing to do, nor possible if you are alone at the payment point. It could also be dangerous.

● Being aware of suspect behaviour also means keeping an eye out for packages, etc., left lying unattended. These may have simply been forgotten, or they may be much more dangerous.

Essential knowledge	● Realising when people are behaving in a very unusual way can help you to anticipate and therefore prevent a problem happening.
	● An open payment point is very vulnerable to potential misuse.
	● An incident in the reception area may be specifically designed to remove you from the payment point so that an unauthorised person can gain access to it and the customers' bills

Do this

- Find out what is your establishment's policy for reporting unusual or suspicious behaviour.
- Consciously try to become aware of anyone who is behaving in an unusual fashion when they enter a vulnerable area, like a payment point.
- Ask your supervisor, and other receptionists about problem areas which frequently arise. Find out how they deal with them.
- Make a note of when you have a problem at a payment point. After a week or so look at your notes and see if some problems are occurring regularly. If they are, discuss with your supervisor how you could anticipate them, and so prevent them from happening.

Case study

You are operating the payment point, which is situated in the foyer of the hotel. The foyer is quite grand and has a marble floor. A customer comes in and slips on the marble, falling heavily to the ground. They remain there looking rather dazed.
- *What should you do?*
- *What must you not do?*

What have you learned

1 If a customer gives you a form of payment which is more than the total of the bill, under what circumstances should you not give them change?
2 Why must vouchers and tokens be cancelled immediately?
3 Why must cash drawers be kept closed when not in actual use?
4 Why must the customer be charged the correct price for a good or service?
5 Why should the customer be able to look at the bill before they pay it?
6 Why must price lists be displayed?
7 Why must printed receipts be given?
8 Why must all refunds be authorised?
9 What do you need to guarantee a bank, giro or Eurocheque?
10 What do you need to guarantee a sterling traveller's cheque?
11 Which type of cheque can you give change to? In what currency?
12 If an error is made on a credit or charge card voucher what is the most secure way of voiding it?
13 What credit cards and charge cards are accepted by your establishment?
14 How should all cheques and vouchers be held securely at a payment point?
15 Who should cheques and vouchers be given to and why?
16 Why shouldn't unauthorised people have access to a payment point?
17 Who is able to authorise refunds?
18 What should you do if a refund is not authorised?
19 Where should a refund by recorded if it is:
   a   a cash refund,
   b   a credit refund?
20 Why must you remain calm and helpful all the time?
21 Why must you never leave a payment point unattended?
22 Why must you report all unusual situations?
23 Why must you follow company procedure at all times?

Get ahead

1 Find out why your establishment only accepts certain vouchers and tokens.
2 Find out why some vouchers and tokens can only be used at certain times.
3 The government says that customers must have a printed receipt for each action to protect them. From whom will it protect them and how?
4 Your establishment should have a list of procedures which you must follow when operating a payment point. Some of those procedures are to protect the establishment, some are to protect the receptionist, some cover both areas. Identify which procedures protect the establishment, which the receptionist, which both. How do they do this?
5 Find out what 'fidelity bonding' means.
6 Learn how all the payment points in your establishment work, not just the ones in your area.
7 Find out how all the charges on a customer's bill are arrived at, and how they get to the various payment points in the establishment.
8 Find out what a 'ledger' payment is, and how the account is settled with your establishment.
9 Find out why it is useful for management to have the details of all refunds recorded. What use do they make of this information?
10 Find out what are the most common reasons for your senior staff to refuse to give a refund. What do they do when this type of situation occurs?
11 Find out how much commission your establishment pays for each type of credit or charge card it accepts.
12 Find out why your establishment accepts the cards they do.
13 Find out how long it takes for the establishment to actually receive the money in the bank if they accept payment by any non-cash method.
14 Make a list of the most common ways that conmen are able to defraud establishments using non-cash payment methods.
15 Find out the legal position if very confidential information about customers is given out to unauthorised persons by your establishment.

Develop and maintain positive working relationships with customers

This chapter covers:

ELEMENT 1:   **Present positive personal image to the customer**
ELEMENT 2:   **Balance needs of customer and organisation**
ELEMENT 3:   **Respond to feelings expressed by the customer**
ELEMENT 4:   **Adapt methods of communication to the customer**

What you need to do

- Learn to deal with all customers in a polite and professional manner at all times.
- Learn to work efficiently under stress.
- Learn to identify all individual customer needs accurately and anticipate them, where possible.
- Learn to observe when a customer is feeling very strongly about something and procedures to deal with those feelings.
- Learn how to help customers without being pushy or rude and to reassure customers they are being taken seriously.
- Identify an incident from a complaint, assess its seriousness and prioritise your response to the event.
- Identify your establishment's procedures for dealing with customers' needs.
- Identify how your establishment requires you to present yourself.
- Only give that information to customers which is within your authority.
- Identify what senior management are available at what times, should any difficulties arise outside your ability to act.
- Identify the equipment and supplies which you will need to work efficiently.
- Make sure equipment is available, up to date and in good working order.
- Learn to work within current health and safety, and all other relevant, legislation.
- Learn how to communicate with and respond to people from different cultures, of different ages and with differing needs.
- Learn how to ascertain if communications have been understood correctly.
- Identify other personnel within the establishment who are able to communicate by different methods, e.g. a foreign language, sign language.

What you need to know

- What standards of behaviour and personal appearance your establishment expects you to maintain.
- Why an angry or upset customer must be dealt with straight away.
- Why you must always try to assist and be polite and courteous to customers.
- Why you should not give assistance to a customer which is beyond your authority.
- What assistance you are unable to give and why.
- When to get assistance from your supervisor.
- How to record any incidents or complaints and why you must follow company procedure.

- Why any complaint or incident must be identified, its seriousness assessed and be resolved as soon as possible.
- What equipment you will need for each job and how to maintain and replenish that equipment.
- How to constantly seek to improve your relationships with your customers, with professional limits.

- The importance of communicating accurately and establishing a good rapport with your customers.
- What facilities your establishment can offer and which are available to people with special needs.
- When and how to seek assistance when there is a problem in communicating with a customer.

INTRODUCTION

One of a receptionist's most important tasks is dealing with customers. For most customers you will be the first and last person they deal with, and for a few the only one. This means that how you behave is crucial to how the customer perceives the rest of the establishment, and whether or not they use it or any of its facilities. You will have to develop great skills of tact and diplomacy in order to be able to cope with all the situations which will arise, and learn to remain calm under all circumstances. Without customers you will have no work.

All customers are individuals and need to be treated as such. Most of the work involved in dealing with customers will be routine, and you will easily be able to help them if you have a good enough knowledge of how your establishment works and the facilities available within the local environment.

However, you must also remember that you have obligations, or limitations, upon your behaviour with regard to the establishment that you work for. Some of these are legal requirements, and so you must try to achieve a balance between the needs of the customer and the limitations of the establishment.

ELEMENT 1:   Present positive personal image to customer

When you are at work, especially in a reception area, you are acting as the public representative of your establishment, and how you behave will affect how the customers think about your establishment. Sometimes, when you are very busy, you may feel very pressured, for instance if one customer wants to go through their bill in great detail whilst others are queuing impatiently to pay and leave. If you snap at the customer querying their bill and try to rush through the explanation, they will become offended and very difficult. Remember your customers have come out to enjoy themselves or for business purposes, not to deal with your problems.

MEMORY JOGGER

Why must you always be polite to customers, even when you are very busy?

You must learn to deal efficiently with these pressures in a way that pleases the customer and enables you to use your time most effectively. For instance, you can ask another member of staff to help the customer who is querying their bill, which will leave you free to attend the other customers. If there is no one else about you can promise to send on a written explanation of the bill to the customer, and so on.

If you do agree to send written information you must remember to send it at the first possible opportunity, otherwise you risk losing the positive image which you have given to the customer about the establishment.

If the customer requires assistance which you are unable to give, perhaps they require a video recorder for their room, ask your supervisor or another member of staff for assistance. However, you should *never* be unable to serve a customer because you have forgotten to prepare some equipment correctly for your shift.

When you first start work you will not know about every product which the establishment sells, nor how to present them, but you must make it a priority to find out

MEMORY JOGGER

Why must you make sure that all the equipment and supplies you need for your shift are ready before you start?

as soon as you can, so that you are able to:
● answer customer enquiries correctly, and make positive recommendations when required
● ensure that all the equipment which you need to serve your customers is available, e.g. blank customer bills, spare till rolls
● work as efficiently as possible, because you have everything you need to hand
● give your customers the best, most efficient service possible
● reduce pressure on yourself at busy times, so that you can react more positively to your customers' requirements.

Your establishment will set certain standards of behaviour and personal appearance for all staff. For instance you may be required to wear a uniform. This is partly to help create the correct establishment image, but also for hygiene and safety reasons. For more information on health and safety at work see Unit NG1.

Your behaviour as much as your appearance will affect how the customer perceives you, and the establishment will have standards of behaviour which they will expect you to maintain. For instance, in all establishments you will be required to present a cheerful face to all of your customers, no matter how much, say, your feet hurt. In some establishments you may be required to take messages, in others this will be done by the concierge. In all cases the information must be handled efficiently by all members of the establishment.

From time to time you may notice that a customer needs something and be able to offer it to them before they request it, for instance a pen to sign a bill. When this happens you should provide what the customer needs before they have to ask for it because the customer will feel that they have been well looked after and so will feel more positive about your establishment. They may even stay longer or book again!

Essential knowledge

● A customer will always respond positively to a positive member of staff and negatively to a negative one.
● Organisational standards are designed to enable you to provide the customer with the level of service which they expect.
● If you do not prepare your equipment and supplies correctly at the start of your shift, you will not be able to work efficiently.

Do this

● Make a list of all the equipment and supplies you need to have ready at the start of each shift in order to do your job efficiently.
● Find out how to order new supplies when that is necessary.
● Find out how to have equipment repaired if it should become faulty.
● Ask your supervisor what standard of dress and behaviour is expected of you, and always stick to it.
● Ask your supervisor about legislation relating to safe working practices.
● Practise smiling even when you are under pressure.

What have you learned

1 Why must you always be courteous, even when you are very busy?
2 Why must you always maintain the standard of behaviour required by your establishment?
3 How can you find out what these standards are?
4 How can you build a positive working relationship with your customers? Why should you do so?
5 Why must you always be properly prepared at the start of your shift?
6 Where do you get more equipment and supplies from, when you need them?
7 Why must you maintain health and safety regulations?

<table>
<tr><td>

Case study

</td><td>

It will be Christmas in a couple of days. One of the other receptionists suggests that all the female members of staff buy a pair of Father Christmas earrings and wear them, as part of the seasonal festivities.
● *What would you like to do?*
● *What are you going to do?*
● *Why?*

</td></tr>
</table>

ELEMENT 2: Balance needs of customer and organisation

<table>
<tr><td>

Essential knowledge

</td><td>

● A comprehensive, accurate knowledge of the establishment's facilities, and those of the local area, will enable you to answer 90% of enquiries in a professional, efficient manner.
● Inaccurate information will result in angry and embarrassed customers.
● When you are unable to deal with an enquiry, someone else *will* be able to, and the enquiry must be passed to them as soon as possible so that the customer's needs can be attended to swiftly.
● Some information is confidential, it must never be given out. To do so may break the law and/or cause the customers, or staff, great embarrassment.
● Not all comments require action, but all should be acknowledged so that the customer does not feel ignored.
● Comments which need action, good or bad, should be passed to the appropriate person for action as soon as possible.
● You can have a direct bearing upon the success of the business if you encourage the customers to use facilities which they might not otherwise have done.
● If you over promote, 'hard sell', you may put the customers off and prevent them from using one of the establishment's facilities.

</td></tr>
</table>

<table>
<tr><td>

MEMORY JOGGER

Why should you continuously try to help the customers?

</td><td>

In order for you to be able to balance the needs of your customers against the capabilities of your establishment, you must have a detailed knowledge of your establishment's facilities. You must also be aware of what type of information is confidential, and the legal requirements in force. This will enable you to deal with most of the situations you are likely to find yourself in.

DEALING WITH CUSTOMER ENQUIRIES

Enquiries fall into two categories, those which require confidential information and which you may not answer and those which require non-confidential information which you may answer.

Non-confidential enquiries

Many customers hold the belief that receptionists will be able to answer any query that is put to them, and nine times out of ten you will be able to do so. This is because although you will be asked many questions most of them will be about the same subjects. As long as you know about these areas you will be able to help. Most questions fall into the four categories listed below.

</td></tr>
</table>

1 One type of question will be about the establishment and its facilities. This means that you are as likely to be asked if you can book an early morning call, as you are about the opening times of the restaurant and what type of food it serves. You must therefore make sure that you know what facilities your establishment has, when customers can use them, and if there are any extra charges, perhaps for leisure facilities. You must also be able to direct the customers accurately to any part of the establishment that they wish to get to. When customers ask about facilities and services which the establishment sells you must take care to give accurate answers. For instance if you work in an historical building, a customer might ask if you have four poster beds. If you said yes when in fact they were half tester beds, then you would have broken the Trades Description Act, by selling something you don't have. What you should have done is given the customer an accurate description of any old-fashioned beds that your establishment has and then the customer could make up their own mind as to what they wanted to do, or which type of bed they wanted to sleep in.

2 Another common query will be about local facilities; how to get to the local station, what time main-line trains run, numbers of local taxi companies, and so on. If you have a good working knowledge of the facilities or have easy access to guides and other sources of information again you will be able to help. You will find all the information sources that should be readily available on a reception desk listed on pages 132–3. Your establishment may have a concierge's or porter's desk, and it may be company policy that they deal with certain enquiries and bookings. In this case you should explain to the customer and direct them to the correct place.

3 Some queries may require that the customer needs to speak to another member of staff, perhaps they have special dietary needs, or want a baby's bottle warming, etc. In this case you should locate the required member of staff and enable the customer and staff member to talk to each other. In order to deal with this type of enquiry you will have to know the names and responsibilities of all the supervisory staff in the establishment and how to contact them.

4 Sometimes customers may ask you questions to which you don't know the answers. In this case you should tell them that you don't know, but that you will find out or pass them on to someone who can help them. If you give out the wrong information, because you *think* that it may be right, you may actually cause the customer a lot of inconvenience and embarrassment. For instance if you say that the establishment does have high chairs for babies in the restaurant and the customer arrives with his family to find out that they do not, the customer will feel angry and foolish, the child will be hungry and irritable and the waiters greatly inconvenienced. An even worse incident would occur if you were to say that the establishment has easy access for wheelchair users, but when the customer arrived they found out that it did not and were unable to enter the establishment without help.

It is not possible for you to be able to anticipate every single thing that all the customers could possibly ask you, but if you say that you do not know, it will give you a breathing space to find out the answer or to find out whom to pass the enquiry on to. When customers ask very unusual questions they do not normally expect you to be able to answer them immediately, but they do expect that whatever answer they get will be accurate.

Steps making entry difficult for a wheelchair customer

Confidential enquiries

From time to time you may be asked for information it would be indiscreet for you to give out, or for confirmations of details that you are not authorised to give. In these situations you must exercise great tact and diplomacy. For instance if someone came to the desk and asked the room number of another guest you have no way of knowing whether or not the guest in the room wants to see the guest at reception. Your establishment will have a code of practice relating to this. Normally you would ask the guest in reception for their name then phone the guest in their room and say that the guest in reception would like to speak to them. Providing the guest in the room wanted to talk to the guest in reception you would either connect them by internal phone or direct the guest in reception to the resident guest's room. If the resident guest did not want to communicate with the guest in reception they would say so and you would act according to their instructions, perhaps to take a message, or to say that the guest in reception had got the wrong person, etc.

Someone might also come in and ask for information about another member of staff, their address for instance. You should never give out this type of information, as you have no way of knowing who the person asking is.

Remember though, if you do take a message you must see that it reaches its destination, whether it be for a customer or a member of staff. To pass on information accurately you should always write it down at the time you take it.

Always remember to remain calm, professional and discreet in these circumstances as it is nothing to do with you why one person may or may not want to talk to another, nor why one person might enquire after another. If you do give out information which you do not have the authority to give out, you may inadvertently break the law and/or cause your company great embarrassment.

CUSTOMER COMMENTS

It is always important to treat all comments seriously. If a customer has been sufficiently motivated to bring some point to the notice of a member of staff, then staff should have the courtesy to listen politely, so that the customer feels that they are being taken seriously, and are important.

Customer comments differ from customer enquiries in that they are not asking you something, they are telling you something. This may be good or bad and may or may not require you to take some form of action.

A comment might range from someone saying that they like the floral arrangement on the reception desk, to someone saying that the tap in their bathroom seems to have developed a drip. In the first case no action other than an acknowledgement of the guest's comment is required. In the second case a message should be passed on to either the house-keeping department or the maintenance department, according to establishment policy.

From the establishment's point of view, dealing with a comment quickly and efficiently may prevent a major problem occurring. If a guest says that there appears to be a wet patch on the carpet in one of the corridors an immediate check by the appropriate person might establish whether some liquid has been spilt or a pipe has burst and is slowly flooding the floor. From the customer's point of view, it would be very inconvenient to have to change room, or move floor, merely because a comment was not taken seriously.

If the comment is favourable, for instance the customer said that the service in the restaurant had been extremely good, this should also be passed on as it encourages the staff concerned to keep up their standards of service.

PROMOTING THE ESTABLISHMENT'S FACILITIES CORRECTLY

As a receptionist you will be asked many questions about the establishment. To be an efficient and professional receptionist, as we have established, you will need to know about all of the facilities your establishment offers. Having this knowledge means that there may be times when you can encourage a customer to use more of your establishment's facilities than they had originally intended.

Most of the facilities of any establishment are promoted in brochures. These are usually available from the reception desk and constitute part of the guest packages in the bedrooms. However, simply because something is left in a room does not mean that it will be read. This is especially true if the guests are foreigners, as they may not be able to read English, or if the customer has poor or bad eyesight.

Your customers may not use your facilities either because they do not even know that they exist or because they are not aware that they can cater for their needs. When a customer asks what there is to do in the evening in the vicinity of your establishment, besides telling them about activities locally, if your establishment has a suitable facility, an excellent restaurant, a cabaret night, its own leisure facilities, etc., then you can take this opportunity to draw the customers' attention to them.

Not all of the establishment's services remain the same all of the time. It may be company policy to offer special packages or promotions at certain times of the year, such as at Christmas. You need to become aware of theses activities so that you can promote them to your customers.

The more that the facilities of your establishment are used, the more likely it is that it will remain in business.

Do this

- Make a list of all of the special features of your menu, barlist and any other special events which your customers may like, and, if applicable, when they are available.
- Make a list of all the reference books that it would be useful to have available in the reception. If they are not available ask your supervisor why this is so.
- If your establishment has a concierge or porter's desk find out what types of enquiry they deal with.
- Make a list of all of the supervisors in your establishment, what they are responsible for and how you would contact them, e.g. via a paging system, or a telephone extension or some other method.
- Write down your establishment's policy on the handling of written messages if there is no one available to deal with a specialist enquiry immediately.
- Ask your supervisor what your company's policy is about giving out any type of information about the guests in your establishment.
- Write down what you should do when someone asks you for information which it would be indiscreet and against company policy to give out.
- Write down how you feel when you are praised for doing something well.
- Discuss with your supervisor, and then make a list of, those types of comment which should be passed on and those which should just be acknowledged.
- Find out what is your establishment's method of passing on comments and make yourself familiar with it.
- From your tariff, menu or beverages lists highlight those special features that could be offered as an alternative when a customer asks about a local facility, e.g. if a foreign visitor asked about a traditional pub, is your establishment's bar a suitable alternative?
- Make a list of all of the special activities coming up in your establishment so that you can recommend them at the appropriate time.

Case study

It is quite late at night and the hotel is full. One of your late arrivals, a single person, arrives in the hotel, but has brought a partner with them. They say that both people can share the single room and no one else need know that there were two of them there.
- *What are you not allowed to do by law?*
- *Give two suggestions as to what you can do.*

ELEMENT 3:   Respond to feelings expressed by the customer

MEMORY JOGGER

Why must you respond fast and accurately to customers' feelings?

Whenever strong feelings are roused in a customer it is important that you find out why. The customer may be very happy with the service which they have received, but often these feelings are raised because they are not. Customers may also become very upset by something over which the establishment has no control, but which they must deal with as it has affected a customer, such as a customer having their pocket picked before they enter your establishment, and thus no money to pay for what they have just ordered. As mentioned before, when customers are very happy, they usually just pass comment, so when they start to express a strong feeling about something it is serious and you *must* listen. These feelings will usually be expressed either as complaints or incidents.

Essential knowledge

- A person who is angry or upset does not always act in a rational fashion. A customer who is angry or upset will be very impatient.
- If you do not start to deal with a customer who is upset immediately, they will simply become more angry and more irrational.
- As a representative of the establishment you *are* responsible for any problems which your customers come across.
- All complaints or incidents are serious, because they have caused upset to your customers who are no longer satisfied with your establishment.
- When some incidents occur, as in the case of lost property or an accident to a customer, the establishment may have a legal responsibility.
- You must never admit responsibility for an incident, because you may have committed the establishment to some legal liabilities in the future.

DEALING WITH CUSTOMER COMPLAINTS

When dealing with a customer who has a complaint you must always remember that they will be angry. Perhaps not yet angry enough to shout and threaten, but certainly unhappy enough to get extremely short with you if you do not act in a very efficient and diplomatic way. This would be true even when you, personally, are not responsible for the problem, because you as a representative of the establishment bear part of a collective responsibility for everything that happens within it. You must remember, therefore, to remain calm and polite no matter how upset the customer may get with you. Do not take the anger personally.

In order to defuse the situation as swiftly as possible you should follow the course of action recommended below, always remembering to act within your establishment's policy.

MEMORY JOGGER

What should you do if a customer decides to lodge a complaint?

● The first thing to do is to immediately acknowledge the guest and apologise to them. If they are not attended to swiftly, all it will do is make them more angry.
● Listen very carefully, without comment, unless the customer asks you to say something. Remember that when someone is angry they often tell you about lots of minor things before they get to what is really wrong. If you jump in too soon you may prevent the customer from explaining the real reason for their annoyance. Sometimes just by describing what has made them so angry will enable the customer to become more rational and calm.
● Start to deal with the complaint immediately, with the customer able to see that you are taking them seriously and actually doing something.

The situation and the customer should now become calmer. When listening to the customer's complaint you should have a calm, but interested expression on your face. This is one time when a smile could be taken as a sign of a lack of interest or seriousness, and could make the situation worse.

Some complaints are very easy to deal with. Examples of such complaints are as follows:
● If the taxi a customer has ordered has not arrived, you can phone up and find out why there is a delay.
● If the customer wanted to order tea or coffee in the lounge and the lounge waiter has gone missing, you can take the order and pass it directly on to the kitchen.

However there are other complaints which you cannot do anything about at the time. Examples of these could be as follows:
● A customer may say when checking out that they ordered foam pillows for their bed, being allergic to feathers, and as they did not arrive the customer had to sleep without pillows.
● A customer says, as they are checking out, that the newspaper which they had ordered did not arrive.

In this type of case you should write down all the details of the incident, the date, the name of the customer and what the problem is, and then you should pass on this information to your supervisor, or other appropriate person as soon as possible (according to your establishment's policy) and tell the customer that this is what you are going to do. If it is appropriate you may thank the customer for drawing the establishment's attention to the problem, for example youths gathering outside the back of the establishment late at night and making a lot of noise under the guest's bedroom windows, etc.

If you are unsure about what to do, or if the customer is being very difficult to deal with, rather than allow the situation to deteriorate, you should ask your supervisor to deal with them. If you allow the customer to get angry with you, then this will be another thing for them to complain about.

If the customer is allowed to leave the establishment still feeling that their problem has not been dealt with then that dissatisfaction is what they will remember about

Paying attention to a customer's complaint

your establishment and is what they will describe to their friends as typical of it. This will seriously damage the reputation of the establishment.

DEALING WITH CUSTOMER INCIDENTS

There are many things which can happen to customers whilst they are staying in your establishment. In most cases, no matter what the incident is, they will report it to reception. This is especially true if the customers are strangers to the area or from overseas, and so unfamiliar with the locality or the regulations of the country. As a consequence, unlike when dealing with enquiries, you will often not be able to help immediately, and will have to report the incident or redirect the customer.

A customer who has been involved in some incident, they may have lost their wallet perhaps, could be in an agitated frame of mind, or, if they have been mugged, could be feeling frightened and vulnerable. In either case they will need to be reassured that they are being taken seriously and handled in a very tactful manner.

The first thing to do is to listen, very carefully, to what the customer says has happened. You will then be able to decide what action to take. It may be helpful to jot down some notes.

When property is found in an establishment, it should be recorded in a lost property book, and stored for safekeeping (see page 31). If the customer remembered paying for something in the bar, and is now unable to find their wallet, you could check with the bar and with the lost property book to see if it can be located in either place. If the action was not successful you would have to record and report the incident according to your establishment's procedures.

Some incidents may be much more serious than a lost wallet, for example if a customer should be mugged or a child lost outside the establishment. In this type of incident where outside bodies such as the police have to be involved, senior management may also be involved and you must become familiar with company procedures for reporting such incidents to the appropriate person as soon as possible.

No matter how serious the incident is, or how agitated the customer is, you must remain calm. If you do not, then you will not be able to find out what has happened and take the appropriate action.

Do this

- Find out what is your establishment's policy for dealing with a complaint or incident.
- Find out if your establishment has a book in which complaints or other incidents are recorded, and if it has, how to fill it in.
- Find out where the lost property book is kept.
- Find out who has the authority to deal with very serious complaints.
- With a friend, pretend that one of you is a receptionist and one of you is a customer with a complaint. See if the 'receptionist' can deal with the incident to the 'customer's' satisfaction.
- Make a list of the things that make you angry at work, and another list of how you think that these problems could be sorted out. Discuss this with your supervisor.
- Ask your supervisor what was the most serious incident that they were involved in and how they dealt with it.

Case study

A customer made a reservation for a double room with a sea view by post two weeks ago. As it was for their wedding anniversary and a surprise for the spouse the customer paid in advance. They arrive today and you have noticed that all of the rooms with sea views are occupied, so they will have to have a room overlooking the high street.

- *What action should you take?*
- *What laws have you broken?*
- *How are the customers likely to react?*

What have you learned

1. In what sort of mood will a customer with strong feelings be?
2. Where can incidents involving your customers take place?
3. Why should all incidents be treated seriously, no matter how trivial?
4. What might be the consequences of delaying dealing with an incident unnecessarily?
5. What will be the consequences of dealing with an incident swiftly and efficiently?
6. Why must the problem be solved before the customer leaves the establishment?
7. Why might you find yourself doing things which are not, strictly speaking, within your job description?
8. Will your management always be unhappy to receive complaints?
9. What is the procedure for dealing with complaints that you cannot solve immediately within your establishment?

ELEMENT 4: Adapt methods of communication to the customer

Accurate communication with your customers is essential if you are to be able to provide them with whatever service they require. Not all communication is verbal, body language is also important, as can be supplementary methods of conveying information, e.g. signing, to people with special needs, e.g. the hard of hearing.

Essential knowledge

- You will probably be the first representative of the establishment that the customer meets, and you may also be the only and last person as well, so the impression you make on them will colour their views about the rest of the establishment and what they tell their friends or colleagues.
- If you do not understand a customer you will not be able to help them satisfactorily.
- If you smile most people will smile back and feel relaxed.
- Non verbal communication is as important as verbal communication.
- A person with individual, specific needs wants useful, accurate information not embarrassed sympathy.

VERBAL AND NON-VERBAL COMMUNICATION

MEMORY JOGGER

What information would a customer in a wheelchair need to have about your establishment?

Verbal communication is communication using speech. Non-verbal communication is the information which you convey by your body language. For instance if a customer comes up to the reception desk and you continue with what you are doing, without acknowledging them in any way, they will feel ignored and angry. You may be busy, perhaps answering a telephone enquiry from another customer; however, you can still smile at the new customer at the reception desk, and they will then know that you have seen them, and will be with them as soon as you can. They will feel noticed and welcome.

Verbal communication is an important skill for a receptionist to develop, and you should try to become aware of the following points.
- Customers must be able to understand what is being said to them. You should, therefore, be very careful about the words you use and their pronunciation.
- If you use a slang word the customer may never have heard of that word, or never have heard it used in that context, and so not understand you.
- If you do not enunciate your words clearly, or if you slur them, or mumble, even the most intelligent and patient customer will not be able to understand you and will become dissatisfied.
- Just because a customer does not respond to you immediately, it does not mean that they are either rude or stupid. It may mean that they are hard of hearing, or that they are having difficulties responding in a language which is not their own.

WELCOMING AND ADDRESSING CUSTOMERS

Everyone likes to be made to feel welcome when they arrive somewhere, especially if they may have had a long and difficult journey. Saying 'good morning' or 'good afternoon' with a smile on your face as soon as the customer appears is a very good start. If you know the customer – they may be a regular visitor, or have been staying for a while – use their name to personalise the conversation, for example, 'Good afternoon Mr Johnson, it's nice to have you staying with us again,' or 'Good morning Mrs Smith, how can I help you?'

It will be useful for you to learn the following points so that you become more skilled in talking to customers.
- If you do not know the name of the customer you should use the more impersonal forms, such as, 'Good afternoon, sir/madam, how can I help you?'
- When you do find out the customer's surname you can start to use it, but you should never use their first name, as this would be considered over familiar.
- If the customer is a small child you should use their first name. This is because most children would be very puzzled to be addressed by their surname and to do so would not put them at their ease.
- It requires great tact and experience to know when a child is old enough to be addressed as an adult. Addressing a young person as a child when they consider that they are an adult may be seen by them as patronising and insulting.
- If the customer you are talking to is hard of hearing, or their English is not very good, speak slowly and clearly whilst looking directly at the customer.
- Check to see if any other receptionist or member of staff speaks the appropriate language if you can identify the language a foreign guest with poor English is using.
- If a customer does not understand what you say, repeat yourself using other words and appropriate gestures. For instance if the customer does not understand when you ask them to register, show them the registration form.
- Listen very carefully when the customer says something to you, and don't be afraid to ask them to repeat themselves if you do not understand the first time; accuracy in helping people is more important than short conversations.

MEMORY JOGGER

Two children have been staying in your establishment for a week with their parents. How would you greet them?

How to deal with customers without upsetting them

As noted before, if a second customer should come to the desk whilst you are still dealing with the first, you should greet the second customer immediately and explain that you will attend to them as soon as you have finished with the first one. As long as the second customer knows that they have been seen, most people are happy to wait a few minutes. They will not be happy if you ignore them.

Bidding the customers farewell is as important as greeting them correctly, because this is often the last impression of the establishment which they will take away with them. It is also a good opportunity to try to encourage the customer to return in the future.

A simple farewell such as, 'Goodbye, Mr Johnson, I hope you enjoyed your stay with us and that we will see you again in the future,' or to a regular guest, 'Goodbye Miss Easton, it was nice to see you again and I look forward to seeing you again next month,' is sufficient. (Notice the use of the guest's name to make them feel an individual and not just part of the daily business.) This should encourage the guests to pass any comments that they might have been wondering whether or not to make and it may also stimulate the customer to make their next booking there and then if they already know the date.

Specific individual needs

All the time that you are communicating with a customer you will need to consider them as a unique individual with their own special requirements. This is especially true if your customer has any impairments or disabilities. As mentioned previously if the customer is hard of hearing or does not speak English well, you will need to be very precise and clear in what you say. You might also use other methods to communicate. For instance you could show a customer who was deaf where the restaurant was within the establishment from a plan in the brochure, or direct them to signs. You could do the same with a customer who spoke little English, or find another member of staff who spoke that language. You may also find that there can be difficulties understanding very broad dialects. For instance a person with a strong Newcastle accent may find it difficult to communicate with locals when on holiday in Cornwall, and the same care will need to be taken in communicating with them as with someone who is not English.

A customer seeking information

If your customer has a speech impediment, perhaps a slight stammer, you must listen carefully to their request, and repeat it back to them to be sure that you have understood what they wanted. If they are unable to speak you can ask them to write down their requirements.

Those with physical disabilities will also need special attention. As already noted people in wheelchairs will need to know about access, lifts and toilet facilities. But even people less disabled, such as a person who has a broken leg and is on crutches, will need extra information, again often relating to access, where the lifts are, the shortest way to walk from one point to another, how to avoid stairs, etc.

People with learning difficulties, that is to say those who have great trouble in absorbing and retaining information, or a very short attention span, can present other problems. If a customer who has learning difficulties approaches you to ask the way somewhere perhaps, it may be more sensible to take them there especially if the route is quite complicated. If they ask you to explain an item on the menu you must be careful not to appear patronising, but choose the simplest words that you can think of to explain, and speak slowly and clearly.

Do this

- Try to put yourself in the position of a customer. Next time you are in a shop observe and remember how quickly you are served and whether you are happy with the service or not.
- Find out if your establishment has a particular way in which they would like you to address the customers.
- Practise becoming aware of people entering the reception area, and smiling a greeting to them as soon as they appear.
- Get one of your friends to put on a pair of ear muffs and try to explain something to them.
- Make a list of all the people who work in your area who speak a foreign language and list what languages they speak.
- Find out what your establishment feels is a suitable phrase for bidding a customer farewell.
- If applicable, make a list of the names of all the people who have reservations for tomorrow, then, after identifying them upon arrival you will be suitably prepared to say goodbye to them all on their departure.

Case study

A young person of about 14 comes to the reception desk looking agitated because they say that they were supposed to meet their parents here but they can't remember which room they are in or at exactly what time. They give you the name of a couple who are resident in the hotel and ask if you can let them into their room to wait.

- *What should you not do?*
- *What information should you ask for?*
- *What should you do with this information?*

What have you learned

1 How will your customers feel if you ignore them?
2 Why do your customers like to be remembered and recognised?
3 Why should you address children by their first names?
4 Why must you find out exactly what the customers want?
5 What should you do if you are unable to communicate accurately with one of your customers?
6 What alternative methods could you use to communicate with people who have difficulty in understanding you?
7 Why is bidding farewell to a customer so important?

Get ahead

1 Find out what legislation other than health and safety affects the way that you are able to work.
2 Find out how to check that large pieces of equipment, like tills, are working properly.
3 Find out which supplies take more than a day to arrive.
4 Make a point of actively asking each customer how they have enjoyed their visit, and make a note of their comments. You may want to discuss these with your supervisor later.
5 Find out what would be the difference between 'half board' and 'dinner, bed and breakfast' under the Trades Description Act.
6 Find out how many codes of practice your establishment has and how they relate to you and your job.
7 Write down all the formal communication routes within your establishment.
8 Find out what other laws relate to your place of work.
9 Find out what are the most common complaints which occur within your establishment, and why they occur.
10 List the nationality and complaint of your customers over a period of time. Is there a correlation between the things people complain about and the culture they come from?
11 Make a list of all the types of incident which occur which require you to contact people outside your establishment, such as the police. List those people that you would contact for each type of incident, and why.
12 When there is a serious problem, which you have to pass on to your supervisor, find out how your supervisor dealt with it and why your supervisor dealt with it the way they did.
13 Find out what are the most common legal problems which occur if you do not handle an incident correctly.
14 Some people have titles, like doctors and religious people. Find out how people with titles should be addressed.
15 Find out what are the most common mobility disabilities and what special facilities each type of disability needs to have provided.
16 See if it would be possible for you to learn another language, so that you could communicate with more people.

Create and maintain effective working relationships

This chapter covers:
ELEMENT 1: **Establish and maintain working relationships with other members of staff**

ELEMENT 2: **Receive and assist visitors**

What you need to do

- Find out what your responsibilities are as an employee, in respect of health, safety, equal opportunities and confidentiality.
- Identify the working structures of your organisation so that you can seek and obtain advice and support in difficult or serious situations.
- Become familiar with the correct procedures and communication channels should an incident, breach of security or difficult situation occur with customers.
- Recognise the importance of passing information on promptly and accurately within acceptable time scales to establish and maintain constructive working relationships.
- Identify why it is important to receive customers in a polite and professional manner and promote the products and services available within your organisation.

What you need to know

- What the company procedures are for dealing with awkward or aggressive customers.
- How to adapt methods of communication to suit the person you are dealing with.
- What the products and services of your organisation are. What your own job responsibilities are.
- Why you should comply with equal opportunities.
- Where, when and from whom you should seek information.
- Why it is essential to be discreet when handling confidential information.
- What are the most appropriate methods of communication when proposing change.
- What systems are in place for dealing with emergencies, incidents and breaches of security.
- Why it is important to operate paging systems effectively.
- Why you should receive visitors in a polite and professional manner.
- Why it is important to ensure, when using any form of communication, that the information is complete and accurate.

INTRODUCTION

As a receptionist one of your primary functions will be to deal with people. You may work within the same organisation with these people or they may be external, for example customers, suppliers' delivery people, maintenance personnel. The way that you deal with them will not only affect your relationships with them, but will also help them to form an impression of your company. Good people skills are not just about relationships, they are good for businesses too.

Dealing with people is a difficult skill because people are all individual. You will need to develop many skills to deal with people. These skills relate to communication, team work and attitude, as well as to developing your knowledge about procedures, policies, legal requirements, structures, systems, products, services, and the facilities of your organisation.

In order to maintain relationships there is a need to pay constant attention to behaviour. This is often easier to do with external customers, because you are aware of the relationship that you have with them as being service or product related. However, we seldom consider what our colleagues' or managers' needs are. They are your customers too – they also need a product or a service from you as a team member. Team work is vital to the quality of the service and product being delivered by your organisation. Everyone has a role to play.

ELEMENT 1:   Establish and maintain working relationships with other members of staff

---

WORKING WITHIN THE COMPANY STRUCTURE

Understanding your own job role is of great importance and in a well-structured company usually a written job description is available. This normally contains the key tasks and duties that you should perform along with details of your responsibilities to your immediate supervisor and colleagues. In certain situations the details may not be written down and if that is the case, it is important for you to have a discussion with your immediate supervisor to clarify your role and develop an agreed written job description.

Do this

- Obtain an organisational chart and identify your own job role within your organisation.
- Obtain a copy of your job description.
- Using an organisational chart draw lines showing links that you have within your organisation.
- List the people that you have to deal with in your organisation.
- Place all of the above in your portfolio of evidence.

TEAMWORK

What do you need from others to provide a service? What do others need from you to provide a product or a service? These questions are vitally important, as important as the relationships with external customers. In order to provide a quality product or service you will need the help of your colleagues. You must take the time to understand the pressures, priorities and schedules of other members of the staff.

The reception desk is at the heart of an organisation with communication as the life blood. When you work on the reception desk you will be dealing with many external customers or visitors who may require information relating to other parts of the organisation. It is important that you recognise the rest of the team, and although you are one of the primary points of sale, you are dependent on other areas to deliver the goods. It will therefore be important to have a good understanding of other departments in your organisation, the way in which they work, their internal structure and the individual people involved within those departments.

Other relationships within organisations are less apparent, for example the relationship between the housekeeping department and kitchen, or between the reception and kitchen. However, these links still exist. Every job role with any organisation is interdependent on other departments. These relationships are based upon communication. The channels of communication will vary from organisation to organisation; however, they fall into two basic types *formal* and *informal*.

Formal communication will take the form of standard operating procedures, organisational policy, procedures, legislative information, team briefings, memos, appraisal discussions, training sessions, coaching, telephone calls and letters.

Informal communication usually occurs in one-to-one conversations, face to face or in a brief telephone conversation.

Whether communication is informal or formal, the importance of a constructive exchange cannot be over emphasised. Some of the benefits that flow from effective communication are that it:
- helps you to improve the service
- strengthens the team effort
- informs both internal and external customers of the latest situations.

Good communication is the key to successful businesses. Everyone needs to be kept informed. Well-informed people know what to expect and what is expected from them and understand what they can contribute to situations. Wherever you work, good communication skills are necessary to achieve results. You need to know about appropriate communication channels, company structures, your role and the different situations that require contact with your line manager.

MEMORY JOGGER

There are two channels of communication. What are they?

COMPANY STRUCTURES

Your own role and the role of others is formalised in the company structure. All companies, large or small, have some hierarchical structure. Within all organisations there are levels which relate to job responsibilities. They indicate a line of command. For example as a receptionist your immediate line manager would be the head receptionist. In the absence of the head receptionist you would then report to the next level in the line of command, the front office manager.

The line of command is important to you because it indicates who you should contact if there is a situation that you cannot resolve.

A simple example of a hierarchical structure for a department might look like the example below:

| General manager |
| Departmental manager |
| Supervisors |
| General staff |

You can then add all other departments and the illustration then becomes for example:

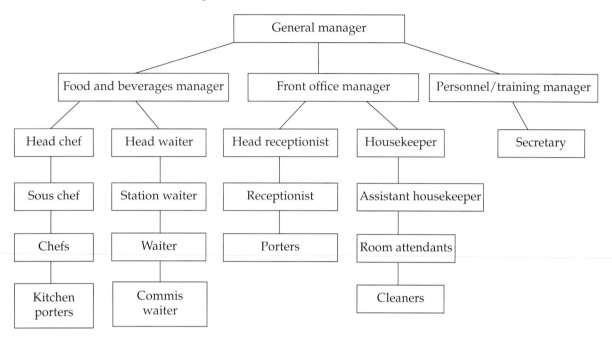

MEMORY JOGGER

All companies have hierarchical structures. What is the name of a common form of hierarchical structure?

This structure, when completed with all departments and names, forms a pyramid shape and is known as a *pyramid structure* or *hierarchical structure*. However, more and more companies today are taking away the levels of management to produce a flatter structure, where the responsibilities are shared. In this type of organisation the communication channels are also likely to be simpler because there are less levels involved and they may also rely more on informal communication rather than more formal memos and meetings.

Do this

- Using your establishment's organisational chart indicate:
  a who you report to
  b who requires a service from you and your department
  c who you require a service from.
- For the departments and people you communicate with list and state whether communication is formal or informal.

Keep this information in your portfolio of evidence.

YOUR OWN ROLE WITHIN THE ORGANISATION

You will have certain responsibilities wherever you work. Some of these you will be aware of, others will affect you without you realising that they exist. Many of these responsibilities are laid down in legislation. The following is intended to raise your awareness of some of legislation affecting you. The coverage is not exhaustive and additional reading material is recommended along with references to other units.

Common law rights and obligations

These rights and obligations affect both you and your employer. For the purpose of this unit a number of these have been identified that affect you. They are:

● *a duty to serve*. Which in simple terms requires you to be ready and willing to work to fulfil your contract.
● *a duty of competence*. Which requires you to carry out your job to a level expected within the organisation.
● *a duty of good faith*. The most important part of this relates to confidentiality. You must ensure that nothing is done to damage your employer's business. Information relating to the company's profits and/or to customers must not be divulged.

Essential knowledge

● Know what your role is within your organisation, where you fit, what you should do and the legislation affecting you.
● Know who your line managers are and how to contact them.
● Know in what circumstances you should refer problems to line managers.
● Know the most appropriate methods of communication within your organisation.

Equal opportunities policies

You need to be aware what your responsibilities are regarding equal opportunities. All companies should operate an equal opportunities policy which relates to the equal opportunity of every employee regardless of colour, gender, age, race, and ethnic or national origin.

However, it is less well known that it is illegal for hotels and other similar establishments to discriminate against anyone with whom they do business. You will obviously be affected by this law and must serve people in these categories unless there are other reasons, for example they are drunk or pose a threat to others.

You will also be affected by other legislation which is covered in other units and relates to:

● *Health and Safety at Work*. Which in general terms indicates that you must take reasonable care of yourself and others and that you must cooperate with your employer, so far as it is necessary, to enable them to comply with any duty or requirements of the *Health and Safety at Work Act* or associated Acts. (See pages 17–19.)
● *Hygiene*. Relating to both personal hygiene, the wearing of appropriate clothing and to your working environment. (See pages 2–9.)
● *COSHH*. Which relates to the safe use and storage of hazardous material. (See pages 20–21.)
● *Fire regulations*. (See pages 9–16.)
● *Reporting of accidents*. (See pages 24–27.)

To summarise this section you need to be aware that your employer not only has a responsibility to you, but that you also have responsibilities to your employer, and to internal and external customers.

Do this

Collect examples of the statutory law affecting you. Retain a copy of these documents in your portfolio.

COMMUNICATION SKILLS

People are the most important part of any business, whether they are internal colleagues, managers, external suppliers, visitors or customers. The way in which you communicate with them will make a difference to you, to them and to the business. It is important that when communicating with others you establish and build up a rapport.

The type of communication you use will depend upon who you are communicating with, what you need to communicate, why you need to communicate and the speed with which you need to communicate, i.e. is it immediate or can it wait?

There are three general types of communication:
● *verbal* – face to face (either one to one or within a group), over the telephone
● *non-verbal* – face to face (either one to one or within a group)
● *written* – letters, notes, memos, faxes, computer generated messages.

Non-verbal communication

If communication is face to face, non-verbal communication will also play a part. First impressions are formed in the first few minutes of contact and are based largely upon non-verbal communication, although stereotyping and prejudice will also play their part. Non-verbal communication is also known as body language. It is more likely to convey attitudes as opposed to verbal communication which conveys information.

Body language accounts for nearly fifty-five per cent of people's communication, so it is easy to see why it is so important to understand body language and also to see why some people prefer face-to-face contact, rather than contact via telephone, computer or fax machine.

Body language can convey a lot of messages and without realising it we all send out these messages. They are likely to be based upon:
● whether you like, or think you might like, the person you are dealing with
● how the person is reacting towards you
● the situation in which the meeting takes place
● other situations which may have conditioned you.

The whole of the body is used in non-verbal communication, hence the use of the term 'body language'. The most expressive part of the body is the face, which can convey many different emotions and feelings. Facial expression can include the use of the eyes and mouth, although the head is used as a whole when nodding to replace the spoken yes or no. The facial expressions used will be linked to other body movements and gestures which will also need to be read. The reality is that when

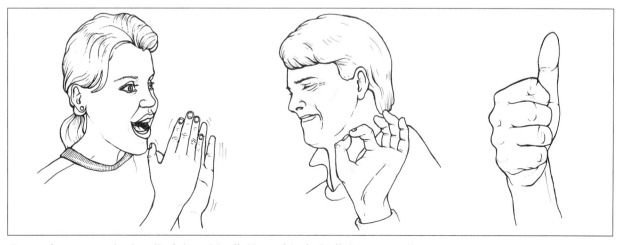

Face-to-face communication: 'Isn't it exciting!', 'Everything's OK!', 'No worries!'

you start to read body signals you must look at all of them to decide what they mean. Take any one in isolation and it can be misleading.

Do this

● Identify and list your own prejudices which may affect your body language and communication skills. (Recognising your prejudices will help you to avoid them.)

Verbal communication

Telephone contact

The use of the telephone as a means of communication is very common. It is immediate and often enables you to talk with the person that you need to straight away because you will know where to contact them. Care needs to be taken when using the telephone because calls can often be overheard by others, so if the information is confidential, the telephone may not be the best method of communication.

When you use the telephone as part of your job, as you do on reception, you need to make sure that:
● you speak clearly
● you establish who you are, who they are and what the call is about
● you give clear information, taking notes if necessary
● you action any points that you may have agreed during the conversation.

The organisation that you work for may also have certain procedures to follow when using the telephone, for example on how you should answer the telephone, how many rings the telephone makes before being answered, what you should say, how you should record the messages, when you need to pass the call on and how to pass the call on.

Do this

Find out if your organisation has any laid-down communication procedures. If they do, then obtain a copy for your portfolio of evidence. If they don't, write down what procedures you use and include examples of messages as well as a summary of how, when and why this method of communication was chosen.

Verbal communication difficulties

When communicating with people daily there will be occasions when there are barriers. The sorts of common communication barriers that we encounter relate to language. Difficulties can be caused by dialects, jargon and accents. If you have to deal with people with language difficulties you will need to check that they have understood you and that you have understood them. This is achieved by using questions and by observing their gestures to confirm the level of understanding,

Emotions are conveyed in language by pitch, tone and volume. You will use a variety of skills to interpret and react to the person you are dealing with. For example, if you encounter someone who is annoyed or aggressive, they will often use a raised voice. You must avoid shouting otherwise the situation is unlikely to be calmed down. You will also need to control your body language to avoid appearing to be a threat or aggressive in return. Many people go to the reception desk when they have problems which really relate to other departments. You need to balance the needs of the organisation and the customer, when you find the solution. Avoid blaming other people within the organisation, try instead to solve the situation and then later to find out what went wrong to avoid similar occurrences in the future.

Written communication

On reception written communication has many forms – letters, memos, notes, computer generated information, facsimile messages and so on. When using writing as a method of communication you must ensure that:
- the style is appropriate to the audience
- it is clear who it is from and what it is about
- it is well worded, spelt correctly and accurate.

It is also vital that all written communication is circulated only to the intended audience. It is therefore important to establish whether it is the most suitable method of communication and ensure that anyone who needs to see it does.

Confidential information needs to be handled discreetly and may require a combination of communication methods to ensure confidentiality is maintained.

Do this

Collect examples of written communication to a variety of people within your organisation. Include these examples in your portfolio.

EFFECTIVE WORKING RELATIONSHIPS

Communication is a tool used to establish and maintain relationships with internal and external customers within an organisation. It is important to keep other people around you informed about what is going on, what you need to be able to deliver the product or service, and any problems you have encountered. By using communication effectively the quality of the product and/or service of your organisation can be maintained and improved.

Different organisations will use different methods of communication to achieve results. You need to demonstrate that you have taken appropriate opportunities to discuss work-related matters using the correct communication channels.

There are some simple rules that you need to follow in order to maintain effective working relationships. They are:
- Always keep other people informed of the situation.
- Take care in selecting the method of communication, consider what you want to say, the best method of communicating it and how you phrase the communication.
- Always use the correct communication channels, based upon your organisation's structure.
- Always deliver whatever you have promised to others promptly.

MEMORY JOGGER

What action should be taken to ensure effective working relationships?

COMMITTING TO RESULTS

The success of any organisation is reliant on gaining the commitment of people who work within it. Establishing the role that each person within the organisation plays and appreciating how everyone fits together to form a team is vital. As part of a team your individual contribution to the organisation, other team members and external customers is all of fundamental importance to achieving results.

In addition to knowing your own job role, the role of others and the method of communication, you will also need to know about the products, services, standards of service and organisational policies. In order to achieve this you will reed to ensure that you obtain as much information about the organisation where you work as possible.

Case study

You have just joined the staff of a large London hotel, and are working nights on reception. Two hotel porters are in the habit of congregating in the reception area to talk and smoke during quiet periods. You feel this creates a poor impression of the establishment and have tried to raise the matter informally with the staff concerned, but to no avail. You need to resolve the situation, but need to balance the needs of the hotel and the customers as well as retain a working relationship with the night porters.

- *What should you do next?*
- *Who should you contact?*
- *What form should the communication take and why is this the best method of communication?*

What have you learned?

1 What is your role within your organisation?
2 Who is your line manager?
3 What are the most appropriate methods of communication likely to be when:
   a handling a disagreement
   b handling a conflict
   c dealing with a problem?
4 What are your responsibilities with regard to equal opportunities?
5 What is the importance of consulting others about change?
6 When and how should you consult other people about change?
7 Why is it important to be discreet when handling confidential information?
8 What different methods of communication do you use and when is it appropriate to use them?
9 Why do you need to adapt and use different approaches in different situations?
10 What are the three methods of communication?
11 As a percentage, how much does body language contribute to the communication we exchange with people?

ELEMENT 2:   Receive and assist visitors

RECEIVING AND ASSISTING VISITORS

Receiving visitors is one of the most important duties that you will perform for your organisation. However you deal with these visitors, whether they are internal, external, expected or unexpected, it is essential that you should always maintain a degree of professionalism to maintain standards and ensure security.

The visitors' impression of the organisation that you work for is created by the people as much as the environment. First impressions are considered to be the most important impressions that are left with us. Creating a good first impression is vital, especially on reception. Many companies have recognised the importance of creating a good impression and have developed detailed procedures for dealing with visitors.

All too often procedures become so familiar to you that you forget why they were created and what they are intended to achieve. You are the primary sales point for the rest of the organisation. The way in which you deal with people, internally as well as externally, can make all the difference. Greeting people is very important, as is assisting them. You need to balance their needs and see that they are matched with the appropriate person, product or service.

MEMORY JOGGER

Why is it important to create a good first impression when receiving and assisting visitors?

Most of the time the service we give and receive is adequate. If the service falls below expected norms a complaint may be made, if you are lucky. From a complaint it is possible to learn a lot and improve the level of service. Compliments come from service that exceeds expectations and must therefore be exceptional. Hence the fact that you are much more likely to receive letters of complaint than letters of compliment.

There are some simple rules that should always be followed to ensure that the service given to visitors fulfils both their needs and the needs of the organisation. All visitors should be:

● Greeted promptly.
● The nature of their business established.
● Directed to the appropriate people, products or services within the organisation promptly.
● Any difficulties should be acknowledged and assistance sought from the most appropriate person.

PROMOTING BUSINESS

It is important that you know about the products that your organisation offers. An example of this on reception would be to offer to book a wake-up call, breakfast, papers and a meal in the restaurant. Information about the restaurant's menu, specials, opening times should be to hand. Equally important is the need to direct visitors or customers to the correct facility or person. When someone arrives at your reception desk you will need to remember that they may not know your organisation; it is up to you to inform them of the products and services that are available.

Essential knowledge

● You need to be familiar with your organisation's procedures.
● You should be able to promote the facilities of the hotel by being familiar with what your organisation has to offer.
● You should have a knowledge of the local area, tourist attractions and transportation.

Do this

Describe or obtain copies of the procedures your organisation has in place for:
● Dealing with visitors.
● Routing visitors to other departments.
● Dealing with emergencies, including aggressive customers.
● Promoting the facilities of the organisation.

Promoting the services and products of your organisation is good for business. You should always recognise this when dealing with both internal and external customers. It is that business that keeps everyone in employment at all levels within the organisation. Knowing about the place where you work is good for business and also has many benefits for you, the organisation and the customer:

The benefits for you:
● It makes you feel part of the organisation that you work in.
● It allows you to act professionally.
● It creates good team spirit.

The benefits for your organisation:
● It creates a good impression for customers.
● It maintains security.
● It is cost effective.
● It promotes sales.

The benefits for the customer:
- It creates a good first impression.
- The external customer is likely to return, the internal customer is likely to be more helpful towards you when you need some help, information or a product.
- They are likely to return or contact you again.

Do this

- Write a description of your organisation's products and services. Include all the departments.
- Find out what the procedure is for the evacuation of external customers if there is a fire where you work.

COMMUNICATION

Choosing the most appropriate method of communication is very important when dealing with any person that you come into contact with. You need to chose the right method of communication, suited to the needs of that person. You will need to take into account:
- who they are
- what they want
- if they have any special needs, for example if they are foreign speaking, hearing impaired or in a wheelchair.

Routine enquiries

Most of the time the enquiries that you will be dealing with will be routine, those which form most of your working contact with people. One example of this would be routing people to other parts of the organisation. For this you will clearly need to know the layout of your place of work and the best way to reach different areas. You must also be aware of any routing policies that your organisation may have, for example if someone asked if Mr Smith was in room 36 what should you do? Confidentiality is very important; you must be careful not to divulge confidential information. If in doubt you should always check.

Complex enquiries

You are likely to have to deal with people in many complex situations; angry, upset, aggressive, drunk or distressed visitors. There may be procedures for dealing with problem situations, for example aggressive customers or emergency situations. You need to check whether there are such procedures in place and what the procedure or policy states you should do. Where they do not exist the following points should provide some guidance.
- Always try to stay calm.
- Try to move an angry customer away to a quiet area.
- If they are very angry, let them have their say – this time will allow you to think.
- Try to identify what their needs are.
- Don't argue – in fact try to speak softly, but be firm. This will have several effects; first it is likely to calm them down and second it is more difficult to argue with someone when they are speaking softly.
- Acknowledge your own difficulties as quickly as possible and seek help from the most appropriate person within the organisation.

Eventually the customer usually runs out of steam. Trying to judge if you can deal with the customer or require assistance is important to establish early on, otherwise the customer will have to explain the situation all over again, which is likely to make them even more angry or distressed, once you have put them in contact with an appropriate person.

Dealing with emergencies requires some basic knowledge of your company procedures. In the case of emergencies, procedures and policies often exist.

Do this

Find out if there are procedures in your organisation for:
- fire
- suspicious packages
- bomb alert
- unknown visitors
- dealing with aggressive visitors.

Essential knowledge

You need to know what your own responsibilities are, for example:
- What do you do if you find a package?
- What must you do if there is a fire or a fire alarm?
- Why should you challenge people who you might find wandering around your establishment? Who should you contact?
- When should you contact someone else in difficult situations? How can you contact them?
- What are your organisation's products and services?

PAGING SYSTEMS

Paging systems are used in many large organisations where people have to be contacted but there is no telephone extension near to where they are working. There are two types of paging system used:
1   An electronic bleep that simply identifies that the person is required and should report back to a central point of contact, often reception.
2   An audible message transmitted using strategically placed speakers. This type is usually used in reception areas and public rooms.

HEALTH, SAFETY AND SECURITY

Security is becoming an increasing problem for organisations. With fewer people employed, large areas are left unattended. Wherever you work, because it is visited by numerous people, it is very difficult to control access. Many catering organisations, e.g. hotels, have a large number of exits, so the maintenance of security is compromised again. It is therefore important that any person entering your place of work is challenged about why they are there and what they want.

You should make sure that you are familiar with any laid-down procedures, since in any of these circumstances you need to react quickly. Being familiar with the procedure helps because you do not have to think of a solution. Most of the time in these situations you will refer the matter to the appropriate line manager. However, there may be occasions when that person is not available. In this situation your knowledge of the company structure is vital, so that you can contact the next most appropriate person.

DEALING WITH EMERGENCIES

There are a few basic steps that you should try to follow in any emergency situation.

1 Do not panic, try to stay calm.
2 Try to think about the situation; if you feel it is beyond your control, contact someone who can help quickly, before the situation gets out of hand.
3 Always try to speak calmly, to avoid panic in others.
4 Try to use the procedures that your organisation has developed; they are there to help.

The best preparation is knowledge so you need to make sure that you know your job well and that you understand your role and how that fits with your and other peoples' responsibilities.

Case study

You are working on the reception desk of a small hotel which caters predominantly for conference guests during the week. A man has been sitting in the reception area alone for periods over a few days. You assume he is with a conference and do not take much notice of him. You do not pay any particular attention to him when he comes and goes, what he is wearing or which conference he appears to be with and do not challenge him because you assume he is a guest.

At the end of the third day you leave the desk unattended for a short time. When you arrive back at the desk the television and video in the lounge area have gone. It is later discovered that the person you have seen for the last three days was watching your movements and planning his opportunity to steal the television and video.

- *What should you have done?*
- *Who should you have spoken to about the man?*
- *What can you learn from this situation?*

What have you learned

1 What are the systems for security in place within your organisation?
2 What are the procedures in your organisation for dealing with:
   a aggressive visitors
   b emergencies?
3 What are paging systems and when might you use one?
4 Why is it important to allocate roles and responsibilities clearly via the organisational structure?
5 What products and services does your organisation have available?
6 What are your responsibilities when dealing with visitors?
7 What are your responsibilities in complying with equal opportunities in relation to visitors?

Get ahead

1 Find out which legislative laws affect your job role.
2 Find out what legal problems could occur if you did not handle an incident correctly.
3 Find out the names of all the companies that carry out work for your establishment and make a list, including the internal contact.

Operate organisational systems on behalf of customers

This chapter covers:
ELEMENT 1:   **Maintain customer records**
ELEMENT 2:   **Exchange service information inside the organisation**
ELEMENT 3:   **Explain products and services to the customer**
ELEMENT 4:   **Maintain service when systems go wrong**

What you need to do

- Ensure that all documentation is correct.
- Regularly update and check records.
- Make legible records which can be easily retrieved by others.
- Ensure that records conform to relevant statutory obligations regarding confidentiality.
- Correct factual mistakes in customer records.
- Report inconsistencies in customer records to the appropriate authority.
- Act promptly on any changes in current services/products.
- Send accurate, relevant, and complete service information.
- Act promptly to service information received from others.
- Monitor service problems passed to others and see that customers are kept informed.
- Supply prompt service information.
- Communicate any service-improvement suggestions to the appropriate authority.
- Share ideas and techniques to improve customer service with colleagues.
- Supply details of products or services on request.
- Suggest alternative products or services to meet customers' perceived needs.
- With the use of sensitive questioning, explore customer product and service needs.
- Suggest additional products and services to meet customer service needs.
- Update your own knowledge of products and services in response to customer feedback.
- Explain failures in service supply immediately to customers.
- Keep customers updated about service interruptions.
- Give information to customers to protect them from unnecessary worry.
- Offer practical help to colleagues to maintain customer service when systems go wrong.

What you need to know

- What products and services your organisation provides.
- Which documentation and records relate to products and services.
- How to complete, adjust and store records.
- Why documentation is used.
- When it is necessary to alter records and why.
- How to identify and what to do when reporting inconsistencies.
- Why procedures, policies and statutory obligations exist.
- What the procedures and policies relating to customer service are.
- Why it is important to review service provision.
- What communication channels exist within the organisation.
- How to develop team relationships.
- Why communication methods are important.

- How to monitor service problems.
- The procedures and policies relating to customer service.
- Customers' statutory rights.
- How to explain and simplify products and services for customers so that they will understand and appreciate them.
- What questioning techniques to use.
- The sorts of things that can go wrong with service supply in the organisation.

- How communication channels relating to systems can go wrong.
- Which methods of communication to use.
- Why it is important to maintain constructive relationships with colleagues.
- How to provide creative solutions.
- What are the statutory obligations in relation to emergencies and service failures.

ELEMENT 1:   Maintain customer records

CUSTOMER RECORDS

Customer records play a very important part in any organisation. As well as being used at the time of enquiry, registration and during the period of service, they can also be very useful at a later date. The records can be manual or computerised.

Records should be accurately recorded, be easy to read, and regularly updated to ensure continued accuracy so that they do not become incorrect, or 'stale' and of no further use, e.g. a customer has moved address or died.

Enquiry information

Information should be recorded at the time an enquiry is received, and can be retrieved again if a reservation is made. (See page 116 for more about how this is done.)

Your organisation will probably use an enquiry form to log who made the enquiry, when the enquiry was made and what the outcome of the enquiry was. To convert the enquiry into providing a service is obviously the goal, but you will want nevertheless to retain these enquiry details for statistical information. (See page 132.)

Reservation information

Once a reservation is taken, all relevant information is recorded on a reservation form and then entered into your reservation system. Each reservation will be given a reservation number, and this can be useful when tracing a booking you wish to amend or cancel at a later date.

Registration information

In all hotels registration information has to be recorded by law from every guest who arrives who is aged 16 and above and the collected information retained for a minimum of six months. The police may request to see these records at any time. Non-British guests have to provide fuller details than British guests (see page 153). This information is confidential.

Billing and guest service information

Dockets used to prepare accounts, summary sheets, invoices, paying-in books, cash and trading accounts have to be readily available for query by customers and management. All this information has to be kept for six years for the Inland Revenue and VAT Inspector.

Guest history information

Most information retained on customers staying in a hotel is recorded in guest history files which again can be manual, e.g. on a card index system, or computerised and could contain the following information:

● Name and address of guest.
● Dates and length of stays.
● Rooms occupied.
● Prices paid.
● Special requests.
● Details of any comments or complaints.
● Possible dates of birthdays/anniversaries.
● Preferred newspaper.
● Any other preferences, e.g. special table, allergy to feathers.

The length of time you keep these records will depend on your organisation and its policy.

Essential knowledge

You must be able to locate and store information about your organisation's products and services. Some information must be retained for a minimum of six years.
● It is a legal requirement that invoices and accounts and other trading records are kept for six years for VAT and income tax purposes.
● These types of records would go into long-term storage and the information is confidential

---

MEMORY JOGGER

Why is it important to report inconsistencies in records immediately?

Inconsistency in records

You may find when processing records that the facts appear incorrect. You may know that a particular address does not exist or that a guest has registered in one name but paid with another name and credit card details. Any discrepancies should be reported to your supervisor. It may be a processing error or a fraudulent attempt to gain services without paying.

As you work more and more with customer records you will become more familiar with discrepancies.

Do this

● Gather examples of all your establishment's documentation for your portfolio.
● Design an enquiry form.
● How important is it that all documentation is filled out clearly, and what would be the consequences if you were unable to read the details clearly?

Correspondence

Correspondence will be retained for some time, usually for a year in the main filing cabinets and then transferred to other storage areas.

Correspondence could be on the following:
- Letters of enquiry.
- Confirmation letters.
- Complaints.
- General topics, e.g. filed A to Z.
- Brochures and price lists.
- Contracts.
- Taxation matters.
- Personnel records.
- Customer records.
- Reports.
- Accounts.

Your organisation may also hold all or any of this information on disk and keep a back-up paper copy depending on its importance and relevance.

SYSTEMS

Recording methods

Within your organisation there will be standardised documents to record information. They have been designed to act as a check list for you to ensure that all required relevant information has been recorded.

As a reservation progresses through your organisation you may discover that an error has been made. It is at this point that all records, systems, and information circulated have to be amended to ensure that information is accurate. The amendment may be a customer's name incorrectly spelt, a different arrival date, a change of numbers, etc.

Many systems are now computerised so that large amounts of data are held on disk with a back-up disk made in case the first disk becomes damaged or lost. As you can imagine, this saves tremendously on storage space where once paper was used. Information on disk can also be used in conjunction with paper records.

In some organisations such as hospitals, whole rooms, floors and buildings are used to store patient records. The information contained in these records is confidential.

There may come a point in time when your organisation no longer has space to store the required records and the records then become archived onto microfiche or sent to another area, building or site to be stored with a retained index in case retrieval should be required at a later date. Records treated in this way are seldom required for reference. Once a storage system is set up to retain records it is important that the following procedures are maintained:

- Everyone should be clear on how information is retained and should recognise the importance of retaining information.
- Recording and regular filing of this information should take place or the information will not be where it should be and cannot be accessed.
- Anyone taking away information from its usual place, e.g. from a customer file, must leave a note to reference where it is now temporarily located in case someone else also requires that information.
- Any file removed should be returned to filing and not passed directly to someone else unless the filing details are amended to say where the file is now located at the time it is passed over.
- Records should be updated regularly.

MEMORY JOGGER

What happens when you no longer have space to store your records but they still have to be kept?

Do this

- Look at the customer records that your organisation holds. How are they filed and are they easy to retrieve?
- Who has access to customer records in your organisation?
- If you noticed an error in customer records, who should you inform? Are you permitted to make an amendment?
- How, when and by whom are records updated in your organisation?

FILING METHODS

There are many methods of filing documents. They can be filed:
- Alphabetically by the customer's name – A to Z.
- Chronologically.
- By date of arrival.
- By record number.
- By subject matter, e.g. complaints.
- Geographically by area.
- Decimally, e.g. Dewey system found in libraries.

There may be subfiling within a system, e.g. first by date of arrival and then alphabetically.

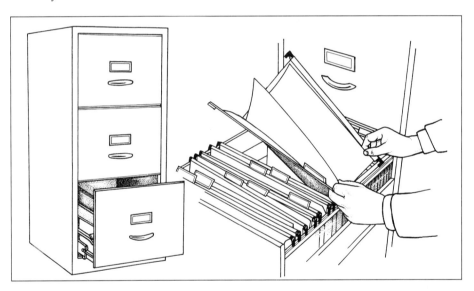

A filing cabinet and example of a suspension file

File information can be kept:
- On index cards.
- In box files.
- In concertina files.
- In suspension files kept in filing cabinets or cupboards.
- On microfiche.
- On computer disk.
- On CD ROM.

RETRIEVAL METHODS

All filing methods require you to be familiar with the system in operation in order for you to be able to retrieve documents you require and you should follow the system described on pages 100–102.

Computerised records

Each time a customer makes contact you can, if you have the relevant computerised program, ask for their name and postcode, and the computer will instantaneously bring up other information, such as an address, which you can check with the customer to save them having to give you their details every time they wish to purchase a service. Other information recorded about the customer will also be retrieved at this time such as the date of their last stay, etc. This presents the opportunity to amend details if they have been incorrectly recorded. New customers can also be entered at this point onto the system.

Any system used should not be accessible to unauthorised people and should be kept confidential and locked away when not required.

Case study

The police arrive trying to trace a particular guest and wish to know whether they have been in residence or are currently staying. You know that all information about customers is confidential and should not be divulged.
- *What do you do, and what is the legal position?*

What have you learned

1 Why is it important that all customer data are correct?
2 What would be the result if records are illegible?
3 Why does filing play an important part in maintaining customer records?
4 State seven methods of filing.
5 What types of storage are used in filing?
6 For how long must registration information be stored?
7 Who may want access to registration information and for what purpose?
8 What is a reservation number and when is it used?

ELEMENT 2: Exchange service information inside the organisation

The service provision that your organisation provides will be regularly reviewed by your managers acting on information received from customers and you will be informed as to any changes.

Other changes come about when customers request service change related to date, time, numbers, etc., after information has already been circulated within your organisation. You will have to amend customer records and inform internal departments in this situation.

INTERDEPARTMENTAL COMMUNICATION

MEMORY JOGGER

Which records would you check to see if a room is occupied?

Arrival lists are circulated daily to all departments so that a proficient service can be provided – so that the chef will know how many meals to prepare, the housekeeper will know how many rooms to prepare for arrival, etc. Special requests are included on these lists so that these can be prepared in readiness.

In return all departments will notify reception of any changes or discrepancies in these figures so that reception records and systems can be amended.

A good example of such a discrepancy is that the housekeeper may notice that what should be an occupied room has been vacated, and reception should be notified immediately. There could have been an error on the arrival and house lists, or the customers could have left without paying their account. This is known as a 'walk out'. If it is a walk out, reception will notify the manager, the police and other organisations and sister hotels to warn them with any description of the customers.

Do this

- Find out the types of communication your organisation circulates to distribute information.
- Find out how this is carried out.

Essential knowledge

- You need to know how information about products and services is distributed within your organisation and how and when this is done.
- Information may be circulated daily, weekly, monthly or annually in any format.

Communication systems

Word of mouth
Spoken instructions and messages one to one or to a group of people.

Meetings
Meetings are a good way of getting information across to one or more people and can be with staff or customers.

Memo
A memo is a written communication system used internally. It is a formal message put on paper and circulated to one or more people.

AA *   *Hartington Hotel*   *RAC*

18 Broad Walk
Buxton
Derbyshire
SK17 6JR

FAX TRANSMISSION

TO: Mr Simmons   FROM: Tracey Brown
FAX: 0181 123 4567   DATE: 12th June 1996
TEL/FAX: 01298 22638
NUMBER OF PAGES INCLUDING THIS ONE 2
IF YOU DON'T RECEIVE ANY PART OF THIS FAX PLEASE 'PHONE BACK

MESSAGE

In response to your fax I am now pleased to confirm that I have reserved the following accommodation for the night of Saturday 15th June, 1996 at the bed breakfast rate of £80.00 inclusive of VAT at $17\frac{1}{2}$%.

I note that you request a taxi to be booked for Sunday 16th June at 6.a.m. to take you to the airport. This will be ordered for you and the price confirmed to you on arrival.

A map showing our location is enclosed.

We look forward to welcoming you.

A fax message

Letter

Letters are posted or given to staff and customers and give information about services and products.

Noticeboards

These are used to display information for everyone to see and read. A staff rota would be pinned on the noticeboard and health and safety information, etc.

Leaflets

Leaflets are ideal for stating opening times and prices.

Pay Slip Envelope

All members of staff receive a pay slip envelope on a weekly or monthly basis and any changes in services or systems can be included to reach all staff and management.

Tannoy

This is a voice message transmitted through loudspeakers announcing information to staff and customers. Messages can be coded specially in an emergency so that staff are alerted to an emergency situation and customers do not panic so allowing staff to get to evacuation points.

Lists

Lists are used in many situations: stock sheets, arrival lists, departure lists, credit control, laundry lists, store and stock requisitions, etc.

Message board

A message board is often situated in a reception area so that customers can see it. A message board can use special letters that are pressed into a special board or electronically controlled. Message board systems are used for short messages, selling a service, or for stating information, e.g. a conference room venue.

Pagers/bleepers

Pagers, or bleepers, are worn whilst on duty to enable you to receive messages when you would not normally be able to, say when you are working in a room with no telephone. Different signals signify urgent and non-urgent messages.

Internal television channel

Used to inform customers about messages and service provision.

Tele-conferencing

Meetings can be held via satellite link across the world or within your organisation's local branch offices without delegates having to travel to a meeting point.

E-Mail

This stands for *electronic mail*. To be able to receive electronic mail you need a computer and messages are sent to your computer from another terminal. The computer can tell you when you have messages by bleeping at you. This can be extended to allow you to see the person sending you a message if they have a video camera on their terminal.

Whatever kind of system is used the communication received must be dealt with promptly and acted upon quickly. Lack of or poor communication in whatever form can bring an organisation to a standstill as no one has the required information to do their job.

Do this

- List the communication systems used in your organisation. There may be more than those listed above.
- State how effective they are in getting information through.

SERVICE PROBLEMS

It is when communication systems fail that problems arise. If a request for flowers and champagne is not passed on and the customer arrives, then they are disappointed with the service provision in the first five minutes of their stay.

Why has there been a breakdown in communication? Did someone forget to order the flowers? Was room service/bar not informed to supply the champagne suitably chilled? Was this request, made during the reservation, not noted or passed on?

In such cases reception will receive the complaint and have to deal with it. You must try to organise flowers and champagne as soon as possible to pacify the customer, who has every right to be disappointed and angry. How can this error be prevented in the future? If service is to be improved this type or error in communication should not happen again.

Some service problems are easier to remedy. Should an ordered taxi fail to arrive you can order another immediately. If the situation is urgent, perhaps you or one of the employees could take the customer to their destination if it is not too long a journey and you can leave your duties for a short time.

Service Report Book		
16/2/96	Room 109	Jacuzzi not working. Job given to TS. Reported by Jayne. Room temporary 000.

You may not have experience to deal with service problems, but your colleagues and supervisor will, and you can learn how to solve problems quickly and help each other out.

You learn about service problems through customer complaints, customer comments and guest questionnaires. We need to know when something goes wrong and put it right as soon as possible.

Case study

The housekeeper notifies you at reception that her arrival list does not tally with her manual room count. Room 203 has been occupied and vacated, and is not occupied as your list to her states.
- *What could be the reason for this difference?*
- *Which of your records can you check?*
- *Who should be informed?*
- *Why is it important to act quickly?*

What have you learned

1 Why is it important that your service provision is regularly reviewed?
2 Who decides changes to service provision and on what basis?
3 What is a 'walk out'?
4 List the types of communication used in your organisation.
5 What would happen if information was not circulated within your organisation?
6 How are service problems monitored?

ELEMENT 3: Explain products and services to the customer

It is your job to explain products and services to customers when information is requested, so you must have a good knowledge of the goods and services that your organisation provides. This is called product knowledge.

To gain this information you can read and learn your promotional literature and you will be trained to give this information in your organisation's accepted manner. Once you have this knowledge you will be able to 'sell' for your organisation. Selling is an acquired skill. Very often because organisations and their services are complex, and prices and services are constantly changing, it may not be possible to learn the product knowledge comprehensively. In this case you will need reference material close at hand to give correct, up-to-date information.

Many sales are lost because of the manner of the receptionist, so you should be warm, friendly, and genuine in your description of goods and services. Any false warmth and lack of courtesy can be spotted immediately by the customer, and not only will you lose that potential sale, they will tell other people of their 'bad' experience and other potential sales may also be lost.

Very often customers do not explain what they really want and so you have to be confident and willing to ask questions to 'tease out' their exact requirements by asking open questions that begin with 'where, what, when, who and why' so that the customer gives you more information.

Essential knowledge

It is important that you talk to customers to find out their exact requirements and be able to suggest suitable products, services or alternatives.
- Your impression of helpfulness and friendliness can help your organisation do business.
- Information you give must be accurate.
- Even if you are unable to provide the required service, if you make a good impression customers will have no hesitation in returning to your organisation for further business.

Do this

Compose a dialogue. The customer says, 'I want a reservation for Saturday night.' What will you say, and what questions should you be asking to ensure that you have all the relevant information and can match the customer's perceived needs?

Even when you have found out the customer's requirements it is not always possible to offer the exact service required. Rather than lose the sale you must offer an alternative, another type of room, another time for a dinner reservation, another date, another hotel. However, do not offer too many alternatives or you will confuse the customer into being unable to make a choice. Remember, even if you do not make the sale, the customer will remember you as being helpful and may use your services another time.

MEMORY JOGGER

What could be the results of giving wrong information?

If you can obtain the customer's name during the conversation continue to call them by their name throughout the conversation.

Any descriptions of services and prices must be correct and fairly described. Any incorrect information can lead to prosecution under the *Trades Descriptions Act*.

Do this

- List the prices of the services that your organisation provides.
- Check within your organisation when and if a new pricing structure will come into operation.
- Ask your colleagues or supervisor to test you on your product knowledge.

What have you learned

1 How do you ask open questions?
2 If you are unhelpful and unfriendly what is the knock-on effect to your organisation, your job and your colleagues?
3 If the requested service or product is unavailable, what should you offer?
4 If you are uncertain as to whether you have the required skills, how can you improve? How can colleagues help?
5 Where can you obtain information on your products and services?

ELEMENT 4: Maintain service when systems go wrong

Unfortunately, there are times when your organisation will be unable to provide a service even though they have promised to do so. Very often this happens when circumstances are beyond their control.

You are at the centre of the organisation and will have to explain what has happened and when services can be expected to return to normal.

Take the example of a power cut. Your organisation is computerised and you cannot access your computerised systems, the establishment is very cold because the central heating is not working, the catering facilities are all electric, etc.

There is very little that you can do. You have to keep calm, apologise and inform your customers about what has happened if they are unaware. Contact will have been made with the electricity supplier to find out when services can be expected to be resumed. Provide alternative services where possible and arrange for the customers to be well looked after.

If enquiries are made about future reservations explain that the computer has gone down in the power cut, and that you will contact the customer as soon as the computer is up and running again so that they will have the first opportunity of access.

MEMORY JOGGER

How can information about delays in service provision be given to customers?

If the telephone system has also failed, there could be a rush of customers to reception to find out what is happening. This is when other colleagues could be of assistance to you to help deal with the large numbers of people involved. If there was time and free staff, they could tour the establishment giving up-to-date reports, and this would be informative. There is nothing worse than being on a train which suddenly grinds to a halt. You know that the train has stopped, but you want to know why and for how long, and how you will be affected, and whether you will miss your next connection, etc.

Do this

- Think of three other types of failure in service and how they can be resolved.

It is important that the customers are not subjected to unnecessary worry during periods when services are unavailable, and that they are kept in touch with how the situation is progressing.

In a crisis situation even the most difficult of colleagues will rally round to assist for the benefit of the organisation, and it is important that you should work as a team to improve the situation. If some colleagues go one way, and some another, it will not help the difficulties already being faced. Every effort must be made to resume service without additional problems being caused by a lack of team work.

Customers cannot be charged for services and facilities they have not received, so if there is a failure in service they must be compensated either by payment or with the offer of another opportunity to use services and facilities. If a pop star was ill and unable to sing at the concert you had tickets for, you would expect the return of your money or free tickets for another performance. In some circumstances customers may be liable for compensation as well.

Do this ✔

Ask colleagues about occasions when service provision was interrupted. Ask what it was necessary to do before normal service was resumed.

Case study

Mr and Mrs Wainwright are arriving today on honeymoon and are staying in the Honeymoon Suite. They have booked the 'Honeymoon Special' which includes a suite, four-poster bed, jacuzzi, champagne, flowers and chocolates. Unfortunately, the jacuzzi has been reported to you this morning as being out of order.
- *What can you do about this?*
- *Will you be liable for compensation if unable to provide the complete advertised package?*
- *Who else should be notified to provide the additional services that have been requested?*
- *How can you prevent or minimise their disappointment?*

What have you learned?

1 How do you know when service provision has gone wrong?
2 Why must products and services be fairly described?
3 How can customers be informed of a service failure?
4 Why should customers be kept informed of a service failure?
5 Why is it important not to worry customers about service failures?
6 Any failure in service or product may require you or your colleagues to step into the breach and provide help. Who will benefit from this extra effort?

Get ahead

1 Given the opportunity of a free day, it would be very useful for you to attend one of the national exhibitions where you can see the very latest communication systems.
2 The English Tourist Board has developed a range of customer care programmes called Welcome Host, Welcome International and Welcome Manager. All these day courses provide underpinning knowledge for NVQs and focus on customer service provision.

Deal with bookings

This chapter covers:
ELEMENT 1:   **Deal with booking enquiries**
ELEMENT 2:   **Confirm, cancel and amend bookings**

What you need to do

- Deal with customers' enquiries in a polite and helpful way at all times.
- Identify customers' requirements and give accurate information.
- Invite customers to make a booking.
- Request customers to confirm their bookings with a deposit if appropriate.
- Provide customers with confirmation of their booking according to the law and house custom.
- Identify unconfirmed bookings, check, chase and amend booking system.

- Ensure that all booking amendments and cancellations are followed through so that booking systems and records are up to date.
- Prioritise your work in an organised and efficient manner taking account of laid down procedures and legal requirements.
- Inform other organisations of availability of services and facilities.
- Deal effectively with unexpected situations and inform the appropriate people when necessary.

What you need to know

- Why confirmations and deposits are required from customers.
- Why it is important to give accurate

verbal and written information to customers.

INTRODUCTION

All establishments require some kind of a booking system to record bookings for accommodation, functions, conferences, exhibition rooms and restaurant reservations.

A booking system can be manual, for example, written in a book, charted on paper or computerised. More and more establishments are moving towards computerisation.

ELEMENT 1:   **Deal with booking enquiries**

MANUAL BOOKINGS

Bookings can be taken in many ways but are generally made:
- by telephone
- face-to-face by personal callers
- by customers who have already used your establishment (repeat bookings)
- by written communication either by letter or fax.

Whatever method is used you must show good customer skills and efficiency. Show

MEMORY JOGGER

What are the three main types of manual booking system?

interest in the enquiry and try to sell and promote the services and facilities available. Smile when talking to a customer.

Manual booking systems

Whatever manual booking system you use, it is best at first to take details of the reservation on a reservation form. This will act as a check-list when entering the details in your booking system which could take the form of either of the systems explained below. (See illustration on page 113.)

Bedroom book
This is a simple book similar to a page-a-day diary. This system is only suitable for small establishments up to about 20 bedrooms. It has a page per day and a line per bedroom. Customers' names have to be entered each day that they are staying. If staying a week, a fortnight or longer, it can be quite a chore for you to enter their names on each page for every day of their stay. Also, if there were more than 20 rooms the book would have to be very large to have a line for each room. (See illustration on page 114.)

Conventional chart
This is filled in by pencil. Use 'arrow' type lines to show the length of stay with the customer's name written over the top. The arrows show length of stay making it unnecessary to put the customer's name down on every date. Underneath the line you can also put the number of people occupying the room, if different from normal, for example, one person in a double room.

Care must be taken to be exact in drawing the arrows which should start from the middle of one column to the middle of the column for the final day of the customer's stay. A half-way point is chosen because an establishment day runs from midday to midday: the traditional check out time. (See illustration on page 114.)

Do this

- Using a sheet of lined paper make up a page for today's date with space for twenty bedrooms. Put today's date on the top and the bedroom numbers 1-20 down the left hand side.
  There is a simple code that is used to identify the type of room:
  S = single
  SB = single with bath
  T = twin
  TB = twin with bath
  D = double
  DB = double with bath
  TR = triple
  TRB = triple with bath
  F = family
  STE = suite.
  Learn this code by heart.
- Using your example of a bedroom book enter today's date and the following bookings:
  Mr and Mrs Jackson: double with bath for two nights
  Mr and Mrs Bryant: suite for one night, honeymoon
  Mr Wilson: single with bath for seven nights
  Miss Ellis and Mrs Gregory: twin with bath for four nights
  Mr J Brown: single for one night
  Mr S E Brown: single with bath for three nights
  Mrs Chester: single with bath for two nights
  Mr and Mrs Simpkin: double room for one night
  Mr Blake and Mr Smith: twin for one night from tomorrow
  Ms North: twin with bath for one night.

This system can be confusing but is faster and more efficient than the bedroom book.

Package tours may also make block bookings for weeks on end beginning and ending on a particular day, for example, Saturday to Saturday. This means that as one party leaves, another party arrives. The rooms are continuously booked for weeks on end maximising occupancy. This is known as back-to-back booking.

Density chart
This system is different again. You do not book a particular room but a type of room. It shows at a glance whether space is available but not whether a particular room number is free. It is used in large establishments and usually there is space on the chart to overbook, to make sure that maximum revenue can be obtained.

```
RESERVATION FORM              DATE: . . . . . . . . . . . . . . . . . . . . . .
NAME: . . . . . . . . . . . . . . . . . . . . . . . . .
ADDRESS: . . . . . . . . . . . . . . . . . . . .    Tel No: . . . . . . . . . . . . . . . . . . . . . . .
                                                    Ext: . . . . . . . . . . . . . . . . . . . . . . . .
Booked By: . . . . . . . . . . . . . . . . . . . .   Room No: . . . . . . . . . . . . . . . . . . . . .
Date of ARRIVAL: . . . . . . . . . . . . . . . .   Time of ARRIVAL . . . . . . . . . . . . . . .
Date of DEPARTURE: . . . . . . . . . . . . . .
```

ACCOMMODATION REQUIRED: TERMS OFFERED:

En-Suite Double		En-Suite Twin	
En-Suite Single		Basic Single	
Basic Double		Basic Twin	
Triple		Disabled	
Ground Floor		No. of Children	
		Age of Children	

BB [ ]   DBB [ ]

Rate Quoted

Special Requirements
Bath [ ]   Shower [ ]
Front Room [ ]
Vegetarian [ ]
Other [ ]

```
Payment Method  . . . . . . . . . . . . . . . . . . . . . . .
Card No . . . . . . . . . . . . . . . . . . . .   Exp. Date . . . . . . . . . . . . . . . . . . . . .
Confirmation Requested [ ]   T/Agent . . . . . . . . . . . . . . . . . . . . . .
Guaranteed Res: [ ]          Guarantee No . . . . . . . . . . . . . . . . . .
6 p.m. Release [ ]           Cancel No . . . . . . . . . . . . . . . . . . . . .
US TO CONFIRM [ ]            BEEN BEFORE [ ]
SOURCE . . . . . . . . . . . . . . . . . . . .    BOOKING FEE £ [ ]
```

ROOM Nos	BEDROOM BOOK FRIDAY 13TH SEPT '96		ROOM Nos	BEDROOM BOOK SATURDAY 14TH SEPT '96	
		NUMBER OF NIGHTS			NUMBER OF NIGHTS
TB1	Jones	2	TB1	Jones	
DB2			DB2		
S3			S3		
D4			D4		
F5	Mr/s Wilson	7	F5	Mr/s Wilson	6
T6			T6		
DB7			DB7		
S8			S8		
DB9	Mr/s Jenkinson	1	DB9	Mr Simpson	4
TB10			TB10		
S11			S11		
T12	Miss Blake & Miss Smith	2	T12	Miss Blake & Miss Smith	1

Do this

Using the Conventional chart shown below:
- enter Mr and Mrs Wall in a double room with bath for three nights from 18th September
- enter Ms Woods in a single room for the night of the 14th.

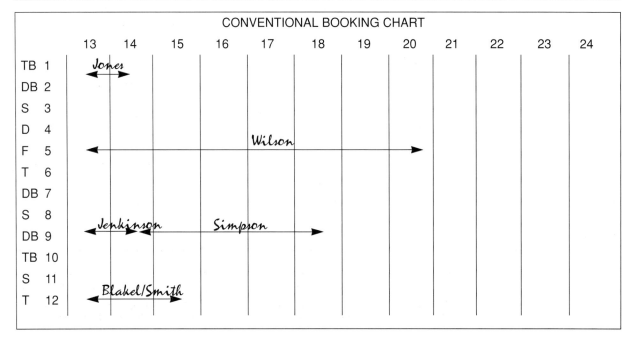

DENSITY CHART

	13th	14th	15th	16th	17th	18th	19th
S	⊘⊘⊘⊘⊘⊘	⊘⊘⊘⊘⊘⊘	⊘⊘⊘⊘⊘⊘	⊘⊘⊘⊘⊘⊘	⊘⊘⊘⊘⊘⊘	⊘⊘⊘⊘⊘⊘	⊘⊘⊘⊘⊘⊘
	⊘⊘⊘⊘⊘⊘	○○○○○○	⊘⊘⊘⊘⊘⊘	○○○○○○	⊘⊘⊘⊘⊘⊘	⊘⊘⊘⊘⊘⊘	⊘○○○○○
	□□□□□□	□□□□□□	□□□□□□	□□□□□□	□□□□□□	□□□□□□	□□□□□□
SB	⊘⊘⊘⊘⊘⊘	⊘⊘⊘⊘⊘⊘	⊘⊘⊘⊘⊘⊘	⊘⊘⊘⊘⊘⊘	⊘⊘⊘⊘⊘⊘	⊘⊘⊘○○○	⊘○○○○○
	⊘⊘⊘⊘⊘⊘	⊘⊘⊘⊘⊘⊘	○○○○○○	⊘⊘⊘⊘⊘⊘	○○○○○○	○○○○○○	○○○○○○
	□□□□□□	□□□□□□	□□□□□□	□□□□□□	□□□□□□	□□□□□□	□□□□□□
T	⊘⊘⊘⊘⊘⊘	⊘⊘⊘⊘⊘⊘	⊘⊘⊘○○○	⊘⊘⊘⊘⊘⊘	⊘⊘⊘⊘⊘⊘	⊘⊘⊘⊘○○	⊘⊘⊘⊘⊘⊘
	⊘⊘⊘⊘⊘⊘	⊘○○○○○	○○○○○○	⊘⊘⊘⊘⊘⊘	○○○○○○	○○○○○○	⊘⊘○○○○
	□□□□□□	□□□□□□	□□□□□□	□□□□□□	□□□□□□	□□□□□□	□□□□□□
TB	⊘⊘⊘⊘⊘⊘	⊘⊘⊘⊘⊘⊘	⊘⊘⊘⊘⊘⊘	⊘⊘⊘⊘⊘⊘	⊘⊘⊘⊘⊘⊘	⊘⊘⊘⊘⊘⊘	⊘⊘⊘⊘⊘⊘
	⊘⊘⊘⊘⊘⊘	⊘⊘⊘○○○	⊘⊘⊘⊘⊘⊘	⊘⊘⊘⊘⊘⊘	⊘⊘⊘⊘⊘⊘	⊘⊘⊘○○○	○○○○○○
	□□□□□□	□□□□□□	□□□□□□	□□□□□□	□□□□□□	□□□□□□	□□□□□□
D	⊘⊘⊘⊘⊘⊘	⊘⊘⊘○○○	⊘⊘⊘⊘⊘⊘	⊘⊘⊘○○○	⊘⊘⊘⊘⊘⊘	⊘⊘⊘⊘⊘⊘	⊘⊘⊘⊘⊘⊘
	⊘⊘⊘⊘⊘⊘	○○○○○○	⊘⊘⊘⊘⊘⊘	○○○○○○	○○○○○○	⊘○○○○○	⊘⊘○○○○
	□□□□□□	□□□□□□	□□□□□□	□□□□□□	□□□□□□	□□□□□□	□□□□□□
DB	⊘⊘⊘⊘⊘⊘	⊘⊘⊘⊘⊘⊘	⊘⊘⊘⊘○○	⊘⊘⊘⊘⊘⊘	⊘⊘⊘⊘⊘⊘	⊘⊘⊘⊘⊘⊘	⊘⊘⊘⊘⊘⊘
	⊘⊘⊘⊘⊘⊘	⊘○○○○○	○○○○○○	⊘⊘⊘⊘⊘⊘	⊘⊘⊘○○○	⊘○○○○○	○○○○○○
	□□□□□□	□□□□□□	□□□□□□	□□□□□□	□□□□□□	□□□□□□	□□□□□□
F	⊘⊘⊘⊘⊘⊘	⊘⊘⊘⊘⊘⊘	⊘⊘⊘⊘⊘⊘	⊘⊘⊘⊘⊘⊘	⊘⊘⊘⊘⊘○	⊘⊘⊘○○○	⊘⊘⊘⊘⊘⊘
	⊘⊘⊘⊘⊘⊘	⊘⊘⊘⊘○○	○○○○○○	○○○○○○	○○○○○○	○○○○○○	⊘⊘○○○○
	□□□□□□	□□□□□□	□□□□□□	□□□□□□	□□□□□□	□□□□□□	□□□□□□

On a density chart rooms with their code for type are shown by a circle and once they have been allocated a slanting line is put through the circle to show that it is no longer available.

A square represents overbooking. This means that bookings are taken for more rooms than exist, in the hope that some of the bookings will not be taken up and so the squares can be transformed back into circles. (See illustration above.)

Overbooking

Unfortunately, in some establishments there is a high proportion of people who book rooms and do not arrive. This is known as a 'no show'. Money is lost when a room remains empty not just because the hotel has lost the revenue from the accommodation charge but because the revenue from meals and bar sales is also lost. Staff have been engaged and food bought in and prepared which will be wasted.

Do this

Using the density chart enter:
- a twin room for 7 nights
- a family room for 3 nights from the 15th.

It is important to try to fill every room every night. Cancellations, non-arrivals or no-shows prevent one hundred per cent occupancy being achieved and so many establishments overbook to try achieve it. Difficulties can arise if all the customers actually do arrive and some have to be booked out at another establishment.

It can be difficult to decide who to book out. This difficult and delicate situation needs very careful handling so that all customer satisfaction is not lost and should be handled by your superior.

COMPUTERISED SYSTEMS

There are many types available and these speed up the handling of enquiries and booking of accommodation considerably.
● At the touch of a button you can see whether there is the required type of room available for a particular date.
● If there is, you can then key in the reservation. This will act as a reservation form and will record all the necessary information.
● The computer will recognise if the customer has stayed before as soon you key in the name and it will bring up all the other information, such as address, telephone number, car registration, date of visit and any special preferences.

Not only will it do this, but it will also print out the customer registration forms, daily arrival sheets, print-outs of bookings and an analysis of any information you require, such as the daily takings, annual takings or average spend.

Whatever system is used, the idea is to maximise room occupancy so that every room is occupied a hundred per cent of the time and any spare rooms which are empty for a period of some days can be filled more easily.

Do this

● What type of booking system does your establishment use? Find out the advantages and disadvantages of this system for you as the operator and for your organisation.
● What is the most usual way in which your establishment gets its reservations: by telephone, face-to-face bookings or repeat bookings?
● Find out how your customers heard of your establishment. Keep a record for one week and then prepare a graph to show how most of your customers first became aware of your establishment.

Tourists checking in

OTHER SOURCES OF RESERVATIONS

There are other different sources from which bookings can come as well as those discussed above.

These can be from:
● booking agencies, travel agents and tourist information centres
● repeat bookings from regular customers
● customers who have used specific guide books, published, for example, by the AA, RAC, ETB and BHA
● customers attending functions, conferences and exhibitions.

Tourists

Tourists will require information on where to visit and how to reach tourist attractions. They will want to know what special events are taking place during their proposed stay at your hotel. They will probably request special rates such as 'Bargain Breaks' and may stay only for a few nights. The information you provide may influence the length of their stay at your establishment.

Business people

A conference table

Business people will require to check in and out quickly and a quiet room where they can work in the evening. They may need an electric point to use a computer, back-up secretarial facilities and the use of a fax machine. It will be necessary for them to have easy access to a telephone if they do not have their own portable. Price of accommodation may not be too important to them as their company will be paying the bill. But they will require a comfortable room with all the necessary facilities and you might be able to sell other services in the form of meeting rooms and conference facilities.

This type of customer is known as a CIP (a Commercially Important Person) because, if they are pleased with the facilities and services, their personal recommendations may bring further business.

Families

Families may want to know if you have family rooms where they can all sleep together or adjoining rooms with a connecting door. They may also ask if you have facilities such as cots, high chairs, special menus for the children and a baby sitting service.

Older children and teenagers will want leisure facilities such as a swimming pool, a games room, and horse riding. You will need to know which nearby places you can safely recommend to them (a happy child makes a happy adult!). Make sure that any facilities reserved for families such as cots or high chairs will be available and in place when the family arrives. If your establishment has only a limited number make sure they have not been double-booked.

Credit Card Details

The above section is to be imprinted by hotel

Please complete in BLOCK CAPITAL LETTERS and drop, together with your room key into the QUICK CHECK-OUT BOX.

Please note: Check-out time: NOON

QUICK CHECK-OUT

Valid only if it has been imprinted with your Credit Card.

If you DO NOT require an itemised Hotel Statement, complete this box only:

Room No	*Date*	*Check-out Time*

Signature

If you DO require an itemised Hotel Statement, complete this box **also**:

Name:
Company:
Address:

QUICK CHECK-OUT is a service which will handle your Hotel Bill in advance.
Just fill in the card and have your credit imprinted in advance.
Our reception staff will be happy to tell you more about the **QUICK CHECK-OUT** system.

FORUM HOTEL LONDON

Cromwell Road, London SW7 4DN
Telephone: 0171-370 3757

A quick check-out card

Guests at reception

Do this

● Find out what special facilities, if any, your establishment offers to business people and families.

MEMORY JOGGER

Why is it important that the customers' requirements have been identified?

Disabled customers

Disabled customers will ask you the following questions:
● do you have ground floor bedrooms
● will I be able visit all parts of the establishment in a wheelchair
● are there are any steps up to the entrance and if so is there a ramp
● is there an adjoining room for a carer
● is the bedroom big enough for a wheelchair to turn around in (a turning circle of 120 cm x 120 cm is required)
● is the bathroom big enough and suitably equipped for a wheelchair user?

A lift to an upstairs room might be acceptable but would be highly dangerous in a fire when a lift must not be used. The disabled person would then be trapped upstairs. One of the best equipped establishments for disabled customers is the Copthorne Tara Hotel in London which offers every possible facility to make the stay comfortable and enjoyable for the customer, however disabled. Remember there are different degrees of disability which can range from a broken leg to total paralysis from the neck down which means the customer needs twenty-four hours a day care. Every disabled customer is different and needs different kinds of care to make them comfortable. Some people look perfectly healthy but in fact may be disabled by a heart complaint or have a terminal illness or an artificial limb. You must be aware of their possible needs and anticipate their requirements without embarrassing yourself or the customer.

If a customer with hearing difficulties, for example, makes an enquiry, think how you would deal with him or her and what special arrangements you would make. Obviously you would speak clearly and slowly making sure that you did not turn your back to them for they may only be able to understand you by lip reading. If the enquiry is made by telephone, you will have to speak louder than normal and ensure that the customer can hear all the information, repeating the details of the booking to ensure that it is correctly understood.

Whatever type of disability you encounter you could be sympathetic and caring. Obviously try to match the prospective customer with the right facilities for their needs. A customer in a wheelchair would not be happy to be allocated a top floor room while an elderly customer may be happier nearer the lift as they will not have so far to walk.

Essential knowledge

- Any information given about available facilities should be fairly described and priced correctly. Incorrect or misleading information, such as saying that the establishment is five minutes from the sea when, in fact, it is ten minutes away, could lead to prosecution under the *Trades Descriptions Act* and will damage both customer relations and the establishment's reputation.
- Providing accurate information is also important in maintaining security and customer goodwill.

Do this

- Act out the following scene with a colleague. A partially deaf customer arrives in reception and enquires about a room for the night. Make a booking for tonight, register the customer and give out a key. Remember do not turn your back to the customer.
- Working in pairs, take it in turns to be blindfolded and led by your partner around the establishment or campus. Note how difficult it is to arrive at a strange place, totally unaware of any dangers ahead of you in the form of obstacles, like steps and furniture.

TELEPHONE SALES

We have dealt in some length with how the telephone should be answered but remember that the customer cannot see you or your organisation so that the first impression the customer has is of your voice on the telephone. How you sound is all important.

With the correct attitude and charm you can turn the enquiry into a booking which will make money for your establishment.

Essential knowledge

- Customers will expect complete confidentiality during their stay and may not want any information about their stay or preferences disclosed to a third party. This could include selling lists of customers' names and addresses to mail order companies.
- Customer history information should be totally confidential.

PERSONAL CALLERS

Personal callers expect an even more efficient service from you and will make an immediate judgement about your establishment based on your personal appearance and the tidiness of the reception area. Customers, may of course, make a further booking for a future stay as they leave the establishment. Then, you must give them as regular customers special attention to make sure of their continued goodwill.

Make sure that any special requests that they have made during their stay have been noted and entered on a customer history card or computer. They could then be offered the same room if they wish for their next visit. If they have asked for extra pillows or any additional item make sure that this item is ready for them when they arrive next time. Try to remember even if it is only their choice of newspaper. This makes them feel special and these little things add to customer satisfaction.

Ask all personal callers if they have a preference for a particular room. If you can leave the reception area you could actually show them some bedrooms and the facilities that you have to offer, such as a swimming pool, lounges, bars, restaurants and other public rooms. Take time and you will make a sale. If they ask for a standard double show them a superior double as well, particularly if the stay is for a special occasion when a higher charge may well be acceptable. Perhaps your establishment can offer additional items such as flowers and champagne in the room on arrival.

FACILITIES REQUIRED

People making enquiries about bookings, by telephone, letter or in person will be anxious to know that you have the facilities they require before they commit themselves.

The available facilities are equally as important as price to a prospective customer and you must know what you have to offer.

OTHER BOOKING METHODS

Booking agencies

Agencies that book accommodation on behalf of a client usually request a fee of not less than ten per cent, paid for by the establishment. This is called a commission charge. Travel agencies and establishment booking services are the main businesses that will contact you and make a booking in this way.

Tourist information centres

These are known as 'TICs' and they operate a scheme called 'Book a Bed Ahead' known as BABA. The TIC rings you to see if accommodation is available and makes a booking on the customer's behalf. The customer pays them ten per cent when the booking is made, and they are given two copies of the TIC booking form. When they arrive at the establishment they give you the top copy so that you can deduct ten per cent from the first night of the bed and breakfast price of their account.

The benefit to the customer is that although they paid ten per cent at the time they made the booking this is deducted from the bill by the establishment on departure making this a free service.

Customer group bookings

A group of people reserving accommodation will request a discounted or special deal rate in return for their business and usually free places for the coach driver or party leader.

When deciding to accept a group you must consider the following factors:
- size of party
- type of accommodation required
- time of year

- days of the week
- length of stay
- terms required, for example, B and B, DBB or full-board
- marketing mix. Will the group fit in with your existing customers?
- price you can offer. Should you discount if you are always fully booked for this period?
- is there any special event in your area?

The group could be friends, students, walkers, conference delegates, climbers, a football team, a choir, an orchestra, a reunion, a pop group, a family, photographers, golfers, painters, OAPs, tourists, journalists or dancers.

The group may also be attending an exhibition, a conference or a function. Some of these customers may only require use of the establishment's facilities for the day, the evening, overnight or for a period of days and nights for training and meeting purposes. Whatever type of business, the customers requirements need to be recorded so that suitable arrangements can be made and the required facilities made available.

In a large establishment conference, exhibition and function business may be handled by a department other than reception, such as the conference and banqueting department. It is from here that other departments in the hotel are notified of their requirements and, if overnight accommodation is required, this will include reception. A rooming list detailing accommodation available may be sent out to the organiser of the party in advance so that suitable rooms can be allocated before arrival.

Many establishments have strict deadlines for cancellations or reductions in length of stay otherwise cancellation charges are made. This is so that other bookings are not turned away because accommodation is being reserved for a large booking, which is then cancelled at the last moment.

Essential knowledge	● It is important that any information you give either verbally or in letter form is totally accurate to ensure customer satisfaction and increase sales.

UNEXPECTED HAPPENINGS

Be aware of anyone sounding drunk who may not be in a fit state to be received. You have the right to refuse a customer who has had too much to drink. If you take in someone in this condition it is more than likely that there will be trouble.

It may be difficult to persuade a personal caller who is drunk to leave but tell them that the establishment is fully booked and get help to make sure that they are escorted off the premises before there is a nasty scene.

Take care when accepting bookings from customers who have sent confirmation by fax and whose bills are to be settled by account at a later date. This booking could be in the name of a company which does not exist and the address could be false. Always check with your superior before accepting this method of payment to ensure that credit checks have been carried out on the company.

Confirmation by letter or fax and a deposit is encouraged in some establishments so that customers will honour their bookings.

A 'no-show' customer may turn out to be one who arrives later than planned. Do not be tempted to release accommodation to another customer when someone is late arriving or you may have to deal with a very tired and cross customer with nowhere to stay.

If there is an error in a booking and the establishment is proved to be at fault, the customer may reserve accommodation at another more expensive establishment and claim any difference in price.

Be aware of couples with little luggage who arrive early in the morning wanting immediate access to their rooms. Experience shows that they may only want to occupy the room during the day. Later in the afternoon they may go out, apparently for a stroll, but not return. This is called a 'walk out'. Walk outs usually only occur from amongst those who arrive without a reservation as a 'chance' booking and so to prevent this happening many establishments now ask for full payment on arrival or take an imprint of a credit card.

Remember the following points

- Work in a quiet, tidy and efficient manner prioritising jobs and completing one task before moving on to the next.
- Ensure that you are following health and safety regulations and that you report any dangerous equipment, trailing wires or safety hazards that you notice to your superiors.
- The way in which you carry out specific tasks must be according to the custom of your establishment. All staff on whatever duty at any time of day or night should complete all the necessary work so that there is never a muddle left for the next group of staff on duty.
- Never miss an opportunity to sell the services of your establishment, whether it be accommodation, meals or conference business. Find out what the prospective customers require in way of facilities and price and, if at all possible, offer the service or an alternative to them. If in doubt ask your supervisor.
- Any receptionist can sell a bedroom, but can you create a sale, or persuade the customers to spend more than they intended, in the form of food and beverages, upgraded rooms or extra nights? The possibilities are endless.

Do this

- Make a list of all the extra facilities you could sell to a prospective customer.
- Practise, in a role-play situation, with or without a scripted dialogue, how you could do this. Base this information on the product knowledge that you have gained from the establishment where you work, or from your college or placement.

Case study

A party of ten people failed to arrive yesterday who were due to occupy ten single rooms which makes up a third of your rooms, and so as a result occupancy was only two thirds last night even though you had turned other business away. On checking the reservation, no confirmation or booking fee had been received, and the reservation had been made three months prior to this date.

- *What steps could you have taken to ensure that the party would arrive?*
- *What is the legal position for non-arrivals?*
- *How can you prevent this happening again?*

What have you learned

1. List and briefly describe the methods of recording reservations.
2. How can reservations be made and what remains the most popular method?
3. Why is it important that prospective customers do not see systems in operation?
4. Why do some establishments overbook?
5. List the different mix of customers that might book accommodation or have a meal at your establishment.
6. State their particular needs for a comfortable stay.
7. How should telephone enquiries be handled and what alternatives should be offered if you are unable to accommodate the customer?
8. What steps can be taken to ensure that the customer will arrive at your establishment, and what can you do in the event of their non-arrival?
9. How should you deal with a customer who appears to be drunk on arrival and requests accommodation?
10. What signs should alert you, when customers arrive, that there may be something amiss?

ELEMENT 2:   Confirm, cancel and amend bookings

BOOKING DETAILS

However the booking is made it is essential that the customer is dealt with in a polite and helpful manner using the correct form of address: 'Sir' or 'Madam'. Remember the customer is not interrupting your work but is the reason for it. Booking details as mentioned earlier (pages 111–112) could be recorded on a booking form if a manual system is used or recorded straight on to the computerised booking form. The advantage of a computerised system is that it will automatically retrieve any previous bookings or information about the customer.

The booking form acts as a checklist so that all essential information is obtained from the customer.

Below is a checklist of the customer details you need:
● customer's name, title and initials (this is especially important if the reservation is made using a credit card as its use will then guarantee payment)
● address including postcode
● telephone number
● type of accommodation required
● number of rooms
● day, date and time of arrival
● day and date of departure
● terms required
● price
● confirmed booking or provisional
● deposit requested
● special requests
● credit card number and expiry date (if appropriate).

Do this

● Find out what type of method your establishment uses to record reservations.
● Design a form that would be suitable for recording the information or practise filling one in if your establishment already has one.
● Using similar information draw up a conference checklist that you could use to record the booking information for a conference organiser.

CORRESPONDENCE

As explained later in Unit 2NA3: *Deal with communications and book external services*, the efficiency and speed of your reply is all important to clinching the sale. The prospective customer will probably have contacted more than one establishment in your area and will accept the best letter giving clearest information and full booking details.

The letter must sound friendly and welcoming to encourage the customer to make a booking.

Bookings made by correspondence may follow this pattern:
1 letter of enquiry received
2 establishment replies enclosing brochure and tariff
3 customer writes again requesting a specific date and room
4 establishment replies offering this or an alternative
5 customer replies accepting or refusing this offer

6 establishment may reply confirming accommodation has been reserved according to house custom.

Bookings made in this way can take some considerable time to finalise, even as long as three weeks from the date when the first enquiry was received until final confirmation was made, using first class post. However, the process can be speeded up by the use of a telephone call to confirm availability of accommodation on required dates. Therefore it is not at all surprising that most bookings, including from those overseas, are now made by telephone since it is so easy to check facilities, price and availability by this means. If the 'lead time' is short (the length of time from when the enquiry is made to the arrival date) then confirmation can be sent by fax and received the same day.

Confirmation by letter or fax and a deposit is encouraged in some establishments so that customers will honour their bookings.

Should the customer not arrive and the accommodation not be relet, the hotel can bill the customer for two thirds of the cost as compensation. However, they cannot be charged the remaining third which is for food they have not consumed. Obviously, customers who do not arrive, or cancel their booking at the last minute, lose business for an establishment and every effort should be made to ensure that this does not occur.

Essential knowledge	● A contract can be verbal or written. It is better that the contract is written, if possible, in case a claim for compensation is made. A written contract is easier to prove. ● Once an offer of a booking has been accepted it is a legally binding contract and cannot be broken without penalties, unless both parties agree to change the conditions or cancel the booking.

Do this

● Write a letter to an establishment requesting a brochure and tariff. Note how long it takes to reach you.
● Compose, then type or word process, a reply to a letter of enquiry requesting a brochure and tariff for your establishment, that will encourage the prospective customer to make a reservation at some future date.
● Once you have mastered this, try to make up a letter in another way which follows the AIDA formula. This stands for:
A = attention
I = interest
D = desire
A = action.
The first paragraph of the letter is written to get their attention, the second paragraph should get their interest, the third paragraph should make them want to visit your establishment and the final paragraph should prompt them into action such as actually picking up the telephone and making a booking. This is not easy, but see what you can come up with. Read your letter to your colleagues at work or fellow students in class to see who has the best ideas. Decide which letter would prompt you into making a booking.

CONFIRMATIONS AND DEPOSITS

Many establishments have computerised reservation systems, which provide an instantaneous confirmation letter at the touch of a key taking the details from the completed booking form.

With manual systems, you have to prepare individually typed or word processed standard letters, inserting the customer's name, address and booking details manually.

Some establishments request a deposit to ensure that the customer will arrive and take up their reservation. A receipt is issued to the customer when the deposit is received. The deposit is subsequently deducted from the customer's account.

A deposit can be made by cash, cheque or credit card when the booking is by telephone. When a credit card deposit is taken you would include the credit card slip and the usual receipt. (See example on pages 173–174.) A deposit can only be taken by telephone and credit card if your establishment has signed an agreement with the credit card company to do this.

GUARANTEED RESERVATIONS

If the 'lead time' is short (the time from when the booking is made to the arrival time), for example, the same day, many establishments now request that the customer guarantees the reservation with a credit card. This discourages a 'no show' booking but still allows the customer to cancel their reservation up to 6 p.m. on the day of arrival.

To take a guaranteed reservation:
- take the customer's full name including title, first names and surname and full address
- ask for the credit card number and expiry date
- quote a reservation number to the customer and state the accommodation will now be held later than the 6 p.m. release and retained for them for twenty-four hours, but they may still cancel up to 6 p.m. on the expected day of arrival without incurring a charge.

In these circumstances no charge is made to the credit card unless the customer fails to arrive. It is only then that you would complete the credit card slip and charge the customer for the full cost of one night's accommodation.

Essential knowledge	● It is important to give accurate verbal and written information to customers to maintain customer satisfaction. ● Written confirmation of a booking is desirable so that the law of contract can be upheld in case of any dispute. Telephone bookings can be difficult to prove in case of non-arrival or cancellation.

What have you learned	1 If no bedroom index exists you could make an example based on just one bedroom and later add to this and update it when alterations are made. You could visit the room or look at a floor plan to get the information. 2 Can you describe, step by step, how a reservation is made at your establishment? 3 Once made, what happens to the record that you have just completed? 4 Prepare a confirmation letter to a customer according to your house custom. 5 How is a deposit entered into your system? 6 How is a deposit handled at your establishment? 7 If there is a query about a reservation how could you check your system? 8 What steps can be taken to ensure that the customer will arrive at your establishment, and what can you do if they fail to arrive? 9 What does AIDA stand for and when should it be used? 10 What are the benefits of a guaranteed reservation to the establishment and how is a guaranteed reservation taken over the telephone?

A booking system needs constant monitoring and updating as customers make and cancel bookings otherwise you are unable to get a true picture of what accommodation is available.

BOOKING CANCELLATIONS

The problem of cancellations can be very difficult to overcome, especially if they are made at short notice. This is why large deposits are often taken for functions such as wedding receptions, conferences and exhibitions.

If your establishment receives a cancellation for accommodation which you are unable to relet, you may charge the customer two thirds of the cost. The remaining one third is not charged because this is for food which has not been consumed.

Whether you decide to charge the customer will depend on the circumstances of the cancellation and whether you are hoping to receive further valuable business from the customer.

Many restaurants are now suing customers who cancel their reservation at the last minute or fail to arrive to compensate themselves for the loss of business.

Hotels and other establishments are also becoming tougher in their approach to last-minute cancellations since they too cannot afford to lose revenue in this way.

Remember to always amend your reservation system immediately when you have a cancellation.

MAKING AMENDMENTS TO THE RESERVATION SYSTEM

It is important that you make any alterations to a reservation immediately you become aware of any changes in the customer's requirements. This means your records will always be up to date and you can seize any opportunity to take other bookings in place of a cancellation.

You may be asked to make any of the following changes:
- change in the services or facilities required
- change in the date or time required
- change in a customer's personal details
- change in the number of people wanting the reservation
- booking cancellations.

The booking amendment may be made by telephone, face to face or by letter or fax.

Essential knowledge

- If it is house custom, it is important that you give a telephone caller a cancellation number. Ask the caller to give you the reservation number, if they have been given one, so that you know that it is not a hoax call.
- As bookings are received you should be constantly checking on a daily basis to make sure that all provisional and unconfirmed. bookings have been confirmed. This can be done on the next day's reservations, next week's, or on those for two weeks ahead. You should chase unconfirmed bookings with a telephone call.

MAXIMISING OCCUPANCY

To enable you to reach the ultimate goal of one hundred per cent occupancy you must let other organisations or agencies know of any vacancies as soon as they occur.

Which other organisations should be informed of availability of services and facilities?

Amongst the agencies you could contact are travel booking agents, your own central office or the local TIC which you can get in touch with quickly by phone, fax or computer terminal.

It is usual for you to get in touch with other local establishments and sister hotels daily so that you are all aware of availability and can direct business to each other if one of you is fully booked.

Do this

- At work, prepare a typed or word processed list of the functions that you expect to cater for over the next month.
- Once this is prepared find out which members of staff should receive a copy and which other departments you should send a copy to.

UNCONFIRMED BOOKINGS

All expected arrivals should be checked daily and at least two weeks in advance to make sure that all the facilities requested by the customers are in place and that the bookings are confirmed.

If you find any discrepancies you can telephone the customer and enquire whether they wish to retain their booking, and, if so, ask them to confirm them as soon as possible in the normal way.

UNEXPECTED HAPPENINGS

Occasionally you will find that a customer has given a false name and address. This could be because the reservation is meant to be a surprise for someone else or because, for some reason, the customer wants to remain anonymous.

Should the customer still arrive even though you have been unable to trace him or her at the address or telephone number you were given, it would be good practice to ask them to settle their account on arrival in case there is any intent to defraud your establishment.

EFFICIENT WORKING PRACTICES

It is good practice to monitor your reservation system constantly. You should work efficiently, looking out for errors and carefully noting any alterations so that possible sales are never lost and every opportunity can be used to obtain maximum occupancy.

Case study

It is 18.05 and your establishment has achieved 100% occupancy.
Mr and Mrs Williams arrive to check in and you have no accommodation left available. They show you their confirmation letter. You check the booking system and see that they have not been entered.
- *What should you do?*
- *What is the legal position?*
- *Does their time of arrival explain why there is no room?*
- *If you are at fault what can you do to make amends?*

What have you learned?

1 State how a booking amendment is made in your establishment.
2 Why is it important to immediately amend your system?
3 What other organisations could you contact if you have space available so that you can reach maximum occupancy?
4 Have you experienced any unexpected situations? How did you deal with them?
5 Why should you constantly monitor and update your booking system?
6 How can the number of cancellations be minimised? What proportion of the cost of the accommodation can be charged to a customer who never arrives?

Get ahead

1 As you become more proficient in handling booking enquiries you will find the work easier and will start to learn how to sell other facilities too. Follow the example set by your more experienced colleagues. How many enquiries do you convert to a sale?
2 If you work for a large organisation there will usually be a separate sales and marketing department. Ask if someone from this department would be prepared to give you further training in selling to customers.

Deal with communications and book external services

This chapter covers:
ELEMENT 1: **Deal with incoming telephone calls**
ELEMENT 2: **Make telephone calls**
ELEMENT 3: **Handle mail, messages and written communications**
ELEMENT 4: **Book external services**

What you need to do

- Answer calls promptly and clearly.
- Deal with calls in a polite and helpful manner, and identify the callers and their requirements.
- When dialling out, obtain the correct telephone number and ensure that the purpose of the call is clearly conveyed.
- Give only accurate and disclosable information.
- Write down any messages accurately and clearly, and relay them promptly to the appropriate person.
- Collect, sort and distribute written communications to appropriate people or locations.
- Deal with uncollected written communications according to laid down procedures.
- Secure written communications so that unauthorised people do not have access to them.
- Book external services appropriate to customer needs.
- Give only accurate written or verbal details of bookings and of relevant alternatives available.
- Deal effectively with unexpected situations and inform the appropriate people when necessary.
- Prioritise your work in an organised and efficient manner, taking into account laid-down procedures, and legal requirements.

What you need to know

- Why it is important to give out only accurate verbal and written information to customers.
- What information can be given to callers.
- Why it is important to relay messages promptly.
- How to leave a clear and accurate message.
- How recorded delivery and registered mail are received and recorded.
- Why confirmation and deposits are required from customers.
- Why it is important to make sure that unauthorised people do not have access to documents and information.
- Why suspicious items should be reported immediately.

ELEMENT 1: Deal with incoming telephone calls

The telephone plays a very important part in communications in reception work.

You will deal with many areas:
- external calls
- internal calls
- transfer calls
- enquiries

- confidential information
- taking and leaving messages
- unexpected situations such as obscene calls and bomb threats.

Part of the reception area at a large hotel

ANSWERING THE TELEPHONE

External calls

MEMORY JOGGER

How should the telephone be answered to an external call?

When answering a telephone call you are the first point of contact that the customer has with your establishment. The impression that you give is very important.

- Sound confident and pleasant. The smile on your face will transfer to your voice.
- Answer the telephone if possible within three or four rings. The caller cannot see that you are busy and may think that there is no one on duty.
- If necessary excuse yourself from personal callers at the desk to answer the telephone promptly.
- Speak slowly and clearly.
- Each establishment will have its own method of answering and style which you need to follow.

Take the caller's name, their reason for calling and the name of the person to whom they wish to speak. If taking a message note the date and time the call is received. Address the caller by name throughout the conversation. Do not use slang words, for example, 'OK', 'Cheers', 'See you', 'Hang on a minute', 'Okay Doke', 'Love' or 'Duck'.

Internal calls

Internal calls are sometimes answered in a different style, usually simpler with a shorter greeting, but still with a smile. (See the illustration on page 131.) If you are answering on a switchboard or exchange which is computerised you should be able to tell, when the call comes in, whether it is an external or internal call, and give the appropriate greeting. Customers staying at your establishment will be impressed if

A receptionist answering the telephone

you use their name when you answer the telephone. Keep the house list by your side if your telephone exchange is not already programmed with this information.

Transferring calls

When transferring calls remember the points set out below.
● First ask the caller's name.
● Check that the person they wish to speak to is available and actually wants to speak to the caller.

A receptionist handling calls at the switchboard

- Should the person, for whom the caller has asked, not wish to speak, ask what they wish you to tell the caller or whether you may take a message.
- Connect the call telling the caller that you are, 'Putting you through now' or 'Trying to connect you'.
- Should there be any delay, try to return to the caller about every thirty seconds, giving information on the call. Your switchboard may automatically try to reconnect the call for you. If the line is busy tell the caller, 'The line is busy. Would you like to hold or call again later?', or, 'May I take a message for you?'. Offer to call them back. However difficult the caller may be, remember to keep smiling, and sound pleasant.
- Always have a pen and paper available to take a message. (See the illustration on page 131.)

Do this

- Visit your switchboard, and watch and listen to the operator.
- Find out the way in which calls are answered in your establishment. Make a note of this for future reference.
- Practise the greeting first of all with a smile and then without a smile. What difference does it make? Try this at home too, when answering the phone.
- Check the way three establishments answer the phone. Which greeting do you like best? Is the greeting too long? The record for the longest greeting stands at twenty two words and the shortest at eleven. According to the Northern Editor of the *Hotel & Caterer Magazine*, Bob Gledhill, both are held by Forte Hotels. These are the two greetings:
1 'Good afternoon. Thank you for calling the Forte Posthouse, Stratford-upon-Avon, formerly the Swan's Nest. Gail speaking. Can I help you?' (twenty two words).
2 'Forte Travel Lodge room-line. Where would you like to stay?'
- Make a list of slang words that you must not use. 'OK' is the hardest one not to use.

Handling enquiries

Callers may ask you many different questions.
- How can I find your establishment when I reach your town/city?
- What attractions are there in the area to visit?
- What is the cost of a double room with breakfast?
- Tell me about your restaurant.

Any information you give must be accurate. Make sure you have the answer to hand. This is called 'product knowledge'. You will be able to find out the information from a variety of sources. These should be readily available and located at the switchboard for easy reference. They may include some of the following:
- house list of all customers currently in residence with room numbers
- extension numbers of all key staff and departments
- emergency telephone numbers of police, fire and ambulance and a doctor's number, as well as the 999 emergency number
- site and floor plan or diagram of building
- current tariff or price list
- details of special offers currently available
- a local newspaper
- a daily newspaper
- local guide book
- street plan of your town or city
- an Ordnance Survey map of your area
- local telephone directory
- national telephone directories
- dialling codes directory
- a dictionary
- foreign dictionaries with useful phrases

- London Underground map
- AA and RAC guide books
- other guide books giving information about places to visit in Britain
- Fodor's *Guide to Europe*
- national and local train and bus timetables
- Whitaker's *Almanac* (which gives names and addresses of associations, societies, government offices and national institutions)
- a copy of *Who's Who*, which gives the names of distinguished people
- a copy of Burke's *Peerage* which gives information about the rules of social precedence
- telephone numbers of reliable taxi firms.

Obviously if you had all this information available to you the area would be rather cluttered so be selective and keep your reference section tidy.

Do this

- From the list above, highlight the reference sources which you have available to you in order of importance.
- Make a typed list of local attractions and how to get to them. Note down opening times and approximate cost.
- Find out details about the local places of worship; what denomination, or religion, they belong to, how you get to them and the times of services.
- Find out the opening hours of the shops.
- Find out where the nearest chemist is and what the opening hours are.
- Find out the telephone number of local hospital, doctor and dentist.
- Find out which local banks and building societies there are with cash dispensers, and how to get to them.

Confidentiality

Some information is confidential and should not be given to callers, so take care when giving out information.

- Never confirm whether a customer is in residence at your establishment or give out a room number without first checking with the customer and/or your supervisors.
- Staff home numbers are also considered to be confidential except in an emergency. Even then you should still get authorisation before giving them out.
- Rather than give out the number, take the caller's name and telephone number (and extension number if appropriate) and contact the member of staff or customer first. They can then decide whether or not they wish to return the call.

Essential knowledge

- It is important that you only give out accurate information to callers. Wrong information will lead to customer dissatisfaction.
- Incorrect information could seriously inconvenience the caller and lose business for the establishment. Inaccurate distances or directions could, for example, make the customer late for an appointment, or miss a train or plane.
- Make sure that any information you are giving out can be disclosed and is not confidential. A customer may not wish it to be known that they are in your establishment or not wish to be disturbed.
- Making false claims could be against the law under the *Trades Descriptions Act* if, for example, you claim that the establishment is five minutes walk from the sea, when, in fact, it is a ten minute walk.

MEMORY JOGGER

What information should be recorded when taking a telephone message? Why?

Taking and receiving messages

Remember to write down the time and date of any message you take. This may be very important in some instances and will also show the person receiving the message whether they need to reply. They may have already spoken to that person since you took the message.

Always have a pen or pencil and a telephone message pad available. The telephone message pad will act as a prompt as to what questions you will need to ask.

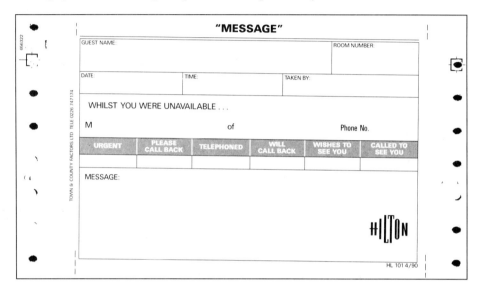

Messages are best taken in duplicate. In case of any dispute you can confirm that a message was taken at a particular time, date, by whom and for whom.

Repeat the message to ensure accuracy. Think how easily a simple message can be misunderstood if only heard once. The message can then be:

● attached to the customer's key so that he or she will see it immediately they return to the establishment
● put in the customer's pigeon-hole if the key is out
● taken into the customer's room or another message pinned on the bedroom door stating message awaiting and whom to contact
● brought to a customer's attention by a 'message awaiting' sign on the TV screen if the establishment has suitable technology.
● brought to a customer's attention by a personal pager which is sometimes lent to important customers.

When you finish your shift or day's work you must be sure that all messages have been passed on. If there are any special circumstances make sure that the next shift member on duty is aware of these so that they may be dealt with.

Sometimes it may be necessary for you to be the bearer of bad news. For example someone close to a customer or to a member of staff may have died or had an accident. Giving this type of message requires great tact and diplomacy. This type of message should be handled by your supervisor or the management team and delivered personally.

It can also be a problem when customers cannot be contacted because they have left the establishment for the day or checked out and need to be traced urgently. Other people, for example, customers or staff, may be able to give you clues as to the customer's whereabouts. If customers have not checked in using their own name and you have no record of their name on the house list the task will be even more difficult.

In this instance you should:
- be patient with the caller, explaining the problem in tracing the person to whom they want to speak
- never promise that you will get through as you may be unable to do so
- only agree to try to make contact and, if appropriate, to contact the caller with a progress report.

Do this

- Find out what greeting your establishment gives an internal caller.
- Design the layout for a message pad for your establishment to record telephone messages that will act as a check list so that you can note down all relevant information. Obviously it must have the name of the caller on it but decide what other information is needed. Try using the message pad with the next message you take. Does it act as a prompt for you to get down all the necessary information?
- Find out what information is confidential and should not be given out to callers. Find out why not and make a note.
- Learn the extension numbers so you can connect calls without hesitation, and the names of all staff and their departments.
- Practise taking and making internal calls and taking and leaving messages.
- Using a tape recorder, test how you sound on the telephone.
- Get a friend to call you and see if you can answer his or her questions.
- Phone your establishment and leave a message for yourself. See how long it is before you receive the message, whether it is correct and at what time it was received.

Obscene calls and bomb hoaxes

Obscene callers enjoy causing you distress.
- Stay calm, and do not scream.
- Take the telephone and quietly put it down. Then get help.
- If you feel you can, keep the caller talking so that the call may, if possible, be traced.
- Report the call to your superiors.
- Whether it is an obscene call or a bomb threat, listen carefully for background noises which may give you a clue as to the caller's whereabouts and could prove useful information for the police.
- Try to detect any type of accent or dialect. Note whether the caller is male or female, young or old.

Bomb hoax calls need very special handling and the following steps should be taken:
- keep the caller talking for as long as possible but only after they have repeated the message so that you can write down their exact words and where the bomb is located
- keep the caller talking so that the call can be traced
- listen for background noises and traces of an accent and note whether or not the caller is phoning from a call box. Note down the time at which the call was made.
- ask if there is a code word
- warn the caller that there are people in the building.

The BHA (*The British Hospitality Association,* formerly *the BHRCA British Hotels, Restaurants and Caterers Association*) recommends that you try to find out the answers to questions set out below.

When it will go off?
Where is it?
Where do we look?

Where are you?
What does it look like?
Why are you doing this?
Who are you?

When the caller hangs up:
- dial 999
- state 'bomb threat'
- inform management *immediately*
- follow the house custom emergency instructions for fire and bomb scares. These may require you to contact extensions to other departments especially where large numbers of people are present, such as restaurants and meeting rooms so that they can be evacuated as quickly as possible.

When emergency services are summoned you must:
- leave the building for the assembly point taking with you details of customers so that you can check that they have safely left the building and any cash not locked in the safe
- never go back in to the building until the all clear is given
- keep the guest/diners' list, an essential record, available and safe.

Do this

- Remember that you can practise an emergency evacuation of the building in a class or work situation but you should take great care when making telephone calls to ensure that the calls reach the correct extensions otherwise chaos will result. Therefore in pairs and under controlled conditions, that is, with supervision, make and receive bomb threat telephone calls, noting the above information and listing it.
- Draw up a list of people in order of priority in your establishment to contact in this event.
- Next time your establishment has to evacuate the building, make a note of the time it takes from receiving the call until everyone has left the building and *stay calm*.
- Familiarise yourself with the nearest emergency exit and all emergency exits through-out the building.
- Make sure that you are prepared for emergency situations such as a fire or a bomb threat and that you know what to do in the event of an emergency. (See page 135.)
- Do you know what part you should play if the fire alarms sound? Is it your responsibility to dial 999 and phone the fire brigade or does your fire alarm system automatically summon emergency services?

Most fire alarm systems and fire zone boards are located at the switchboard. If management are not immediately available you may have to decide what action should be taken and whether the hotel is to be evacuated

Answer phones

If your establishment has an answer phone, to take messages outside business hours, it is important that any recorded messages are dealt with as soon as possible to show the caller that you are an efficient organisation. Remember to play back the messages as soon as you arrive at work and turn off the machine taking care not to wipe off any of the messages.

Do this

- Compose a lively and interesting message for an answer phone machine which will encourage callers to use this service and leave an understandable message.

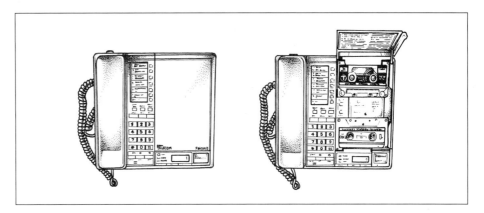

An answer phone

EFFICIENT WORKING PRACTICES

Remember these points:
- Keep your working area tidy at all times.
- Keep a pen or pencil plus a spare always available for messages.
- Do not work under a pile of papers so that you have to search for the telephone when it rings.
- Sound confident and smile.
- Remember you are the first point of contact with your organisation and the impression you give is vital to the customer and can make or break the sale.
- The telephone is the main communication link and you are the person answering the phone and connecting all calls within the establishment. Your competence is on the line and your job, and the job of everyone else in your establishment if you lose business through incompetence or rudeness.

An untidy reception desk

Case study	*A telephone enquiry is received which requests confidential information about a guest in residence.*
	● *How can you deal politely and promptly with the caller without disclosing any information?*
	● *What would happen if you give out the confidential information requested?*
	● *What repercussions would this have?*
	● *What is your establishment's policy and what training have you had to deal with this type of situation?*

ELEMENT 2:   Make telephone calls

HOW TO MAKE A TELEPHONE CALL

When making a call, take care when dialling so that the correct number is used to get through the first time. If you should misdial or have been given the wrong number, apologise and redial the correct one. Sometimes operator assistance is required to obtain a correct number or to get a reply. Operator assistance is also required to make a timed priced call, especially for international numbers (called an ADC call which means Advice of Duration and Charge). This is when the British Telecom operator will connect you and then later phone you back with exact details of the number dialled, length and charge of the call. Many establishments now use telephone loggers which automatically record telephone charges, and in some cases post them directly onto the bill. When contact is made introduce yourself and your establishment before explaining the reason for calling.

Make sure you always work according to house custom.

If you have to leave a message on an answer phone do not panic. Clearly state the date, time, your name, telephone number and establishment and the message so that your call can be returned as soon as possible.

Do this

● Look up, copy out and learn the main area codes and local codes that you are likely to need to make calls, for example, London 0171 and 0181. (The code is dialled before the number to get the correct area.)

● Look up, copy out and learn the main overseas codes, for example, those for France and the USA.

● Find out the numbers you need dial for operator assistance and keep them close by the telephone. Better still, learn them by heart.

● Find out how to:
  contact the operator
  make an ADC call
  report your telephone out of order
  obtain Emergency Services
  make an international call.

<table>
<tr><td>Essential
knowledge</td><td><ul><li>You must be able to maintain customer satisfaction by providing the required service in a reasonable time.</li><li>You must retain the establishment's reputation for service by responding quickly and efficiently to customer requests.</li><li>You must not disclose confidential information in any of your telephone calls or messages.</li><li>Do not break the law by making calls to arrange any service that will bring the hotel into disrepute.</li></ul></td></tr>
</table>

Whatever type of call you are making whether connecting an external business call, or internal calls to customers or staff, all calls should be dealt with in a professional manner. They are all important.

Some establishments try to save money by making as many business calls as possible after 6 p.m. You may have been instructed to ask whether telephone calls you put through for staff are personal or urgent and could be made later in the day at a lower cost.

Unexpected situations

If you are unable to get through to a particular number it may be that the telephone line is out of order and should be reported as soon as possible so that repairs can be put in hand.

Perhaps the person you wish to contact is no longer available at the number you have been given and you should therefore try to trace them by asking questions, consulting a telephone directory or through directory enquiries.

You may dial a number only to discover that it is incorrect or not ringing because the code or telephone number has been changed, for example, an extra digit added by British Telecom. You may have to seek assistance.

Dialling 999: Fire, police and ambulance

As a switchboard operator it will probably be your responsibility to telephone for the emergency services, if and when required, using the 999 code. Some fire detection systems have an emergency call built in so that when the alarms sound the fire brigade is automatically alerted but, if you have to make this type of call, remain calm and speak slowly and clearly, giving as much information as possible so that emergency services can arrive without delay.

In some establishments it is the house custom to alert management first, by way of an announcement or telephone call, before evacuating the premises. To avoid panic the initial announcement or call is very often coded. This allows house systems to be put in to operation and the evacuation controlled before the customers are aware of the emergency.

ELEMENT 3:   Handle mail, messages and written communications

---

HANDLING MAIL

As soon as the mail has arrived, it is usually sorted and placed in pigeon-holes or delivered to the appropriate departments according to house custom. If possible, deliver bulky items such as parcels. Otherwise telephone the member of staff or customer telling them that there is a parcel awaiting collection in reception. Use a stamp to date all mail received for customers, then check it against the house list to ensure that they are in residence. Place mail in their pigeon-hole with their room key. If electronic keys are used and no keys are kept at reception or in pigeon-holes, deliver the item or a written message stating that a letter has arrived (giving time and date) to the customer's room. (See the section on message taking on page 134.)

Staff mail can be pinned to the staff notice board for collection at the end of shift or when the relevant member of staff is next on duty, or given to the shift leader for distribution.

A registered post label displaying the serial number

When registered post is received, it must be signed for and entered into a record book (known sometimes as a remittance book) with details such as who received it, date and time. Practise doing this.

Special deliveries by courier or Datapost should be dealt with immediately, as should fax or telex messages.

If the customer has checked out by the time the letter is received, it is usual to obtain the customer's home or business address from the details taken at registration or from a customer history file. The letter is then posted on to the customer the same day.

Confidentiality

Confidentiality is ensured by destroying any documents no longer required by using a shredding machine. This cuts the paper into very thin strands which are impossible to piece together and read. This paper can then be recycled. Take care not to shred any documents without the proper authority.

Each day's mail should be answered the same day and, if possible, posted out the same evening. This will give an impression of an efficient establishment.

Fax and telex messages should be replied to within the hour if the required information is available. The reply can be sent by fax or telex at any time of day or night if there is a fax or telex in the relevant office or home to receive the document or message and if it is switched on.

Essential knowledge

- You must make sure that all communications received by the establishment are protected from unauthorised access. This is to prevent theft, loss or damage and to maintain confidentiality.
- Suspicious items should be reported immediately as they may contain bombs or explosives and you should make no attempt to tamper with these,

---

Fax machines

A facsimile machine, known as a 'fax', scans a document and sends an encoded signal down the telephone line to the receiver's machine where it is decoded into document form and printed. In order to receive a document a fax machine must be loaded with paper and switched on. Each fax owner has a number similar to a telephone number which is keyed into the machine and then the document or documents are fed through, encoded and sent down the telephone line to their destination. The fax machine will confirm whether the message has been received. The original document remains in one piece for the sender to keep for reference.

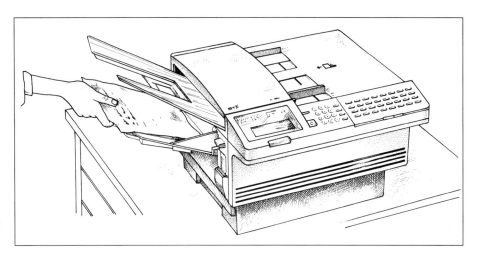

A fax machine. This machine can also make photocopies.

Telex

The telex machine was invented before the fax machine and could only send a message not whole documents or plans. It is no longer used in many establishments and is being replaced by the more versatile fax machine.

Do this

- Visit your administration department or post room, if you have one, to discover how the mail and deliveries are dealt with in your establishment. In some establishments the postman delivers to reception.
- If you do have a shredding machine find out where it is located in case you are sent to destroy unwanted confidential information.
- Find out who authorises the destruction of documents in your establishment.
- Find out the difference between a letter and a memo and when each should be used.
- Find out the difference between a fax and a telex message.
- Find out the time of the last collection of post to guarantee delivery the next day.

SPECIAL TREATMENT OF CUSTOMERS

From time to time, in many establishments, very important customers will come to stay, known as VIPs. A VIP can be anybody, from a visiting head of state to a pop star. These customers and their messages and mail will require special treatment and possibly special security. A VIP could be a target for terrorists or pestered by fans. Any parcels and letters received for them should be very carefully checked. Report anything suspicious to your superior. When VIPs are staying it is also specially important that no information is given to callers, either personally or by phone, about which room they are occupying or their whereabouts at the time of enquiry. This is especially so if they have given strict instructions not to be disturbed or are staying at the establishment for a complete rest to get away from pressures of work.

Obviously any messages or mail for VIPs should be given top priority.

Make sure you know what to do in the event of an emergency. Be on the look out for suspicious bulky letters and packages and unattended parcels and luggage. Report any strange happenings immediately to your superior. Letter bombs and explosives are covered in full detail in Unit NG1.

ELEMENT 4:   Book external services

ADDITIONAL SERVICES

There are many additional services which can be provided for customers. The range and availability will depend on the type of establishment in which you are working.

Listed below are some of the more usual services which are later described in some detail:
- car hire
- taxis
- flowers
- secretarial services
- theatre tickets
- airline tickets
- car parking
- hairdressing
- in-house movies
- laundry
- mini-bars
- room service
- pony trekking
- golf
- cycle hire
- guided tours
- visits to attractions
- further accommodation reservations
- restaurant reservations.

Your establishment may offer some of these services in-house. In order to ensure that the customers are aware of their availability, they can be listed in a customer services directory and placed in the information folder in the bedrooms.

Sometimes customers will want you to make the booking for any extra services they require. The establishment may even pay for the service they book and charge this to the customer's account as a VPO (see page 167).

(see page 167)

Essential knowledge

- Customers will be dissatisfied and inconvenienced if they receive incorrect directions and information. They may miss important meetings, rail connections, flights or arrive at a tourist attraction to find it closed.
- Incorrect descriptions could lead to prosecutions under the *Trades Descriptions Act* 1968.

Car hire

Customers travelling without their own transport, particularly if they have arrived at a local airport or station, may want to hire a car. Hiring a car gives the customers freedom to travel when and where they wish and is much more convenient.

National companies are available with fleets of vehicles to hire at airports. Also larger establishments often have contracts with them and some even a car hire desk.

As an additional service some establishments may provide a free service (usually known as a courtesy service) to airports, sister establishments or the beach.

Taxis

Sometimes customers will want you to make the booking for the extra service they require. As already mentioned, establishments may even pay for the service and charge this to the customer's account as a VPO.

Booking a taxi is one of the most frequent requirements of a customer. You must ensure that the taxi arrives in time to get the customer to their intended destination.

Unless your establishment has a special arrangement with one particular taxi or car hire company, it is a good idea to obtain prices from several companies for comparison especially if the taxi is to be hired for a long period or the journey is a long one.

If your establishment has double-booked a customer who arrives to find no accommodation available, it is usual to provide a taxi free of charge to take the customer to another establishment where you have obtained accommodation for them. Remember to say that your establishment will pay for the taxi when placing the order. Do this in accordance with house custom.

Some accommodation bookings include a taxi order. This is called an A & TO (Accommodation and Taxi Order) and it is included in the price charged.

Many taxi companies now provide a freephone service in the lobby to ensure that any enquiries reach them directly.

Flowers

Flowers for a special occasion are another customer requirement. Some establishments offer 'Romantic or Special Occasion Breaks' which include flowers in the room and sometimes champagne as well.

Flowers for an anniversary or surprise present can be ordered by reception from a local reputable florist and again charged to the customer's account as a VPO. A large establishment may have a resident florist to provide this service.

To ensure that the customer is satisfied with the service it is important that you know how much the customer wishes to spend, their preferred type and colour of flower, for example, red roses. It may be your house policy to ask the customer to write down the details of their request. Always repeat the request to the customer to make sure that all the details are correct.

Secretarial services

Establishments which cater mainly for 'business' type customers offer secretarial services to prepare documents, send faxes, and do photocopying. This is an extra service for which an additional charge is made. The work is usually carried out in a separate office away from the reception area. The work can be handed in and collected later or delivered to the customer's room or suite or to the exhibition and meeting rooms for conference delegates.

A pager

Where this service is not available on the premises an external secretarial service can be contacted to carry out the required work.

As an additional service, personal pagers can be loaned to customers so that they receive important calls and messages promptly wherever they happen to be in the establishment. This avoids disturbing the other customers by the use of the public address system to give out messages over the tannoy such as, 'Will Mr Smith please come to reception, where there is an important message waiting.'

When you do use a public address system, ensure that you speak clearly and slowly, repeating the message at least twice. Make sure that you do not mumble the message.

Courier services

These can also be provided for customers for fast delivery of documents and parcels. These may include motor bike couriers for local deliveries or national carriers for large or long distance deliveries.

Theatre tickets

Booking theatre tickets is another service required by customers, specially by those staying in establishments in the London area and others within a reasonable travelling distance of a good theatre or opera house. Tickets for shows can be purchased on behalf of the customer and added to their account as an additional service. They are also offered as a package called a 'Theatre Break' which combines accommodation with the show of their choice.

If there is a choice, ask the customer where they would prefer to sit, such as stalls, circle, upper circle or the gods, as the prices will vary greatly. Remember to check the date and the time of the performance they wish to see.

Flight tickets

Large London establishments have special airline desks where customers may collect their flight tickets. Other establishments near airports also offer a ticket collection service for their customers.

In some London hotels, such as the Forum, it is possible to have an automatic check-in service for luggage at the hotel. The luggage is then taken directly on to the plane and the customers have simply to collect it when they reach their destination.

Make sure that the luggage is correctly labelled before accepting it.

Some of the above services will be carried out by the concierge rather than a receptionist but this will depend on how large your establishment is and how it is staffed.

Car parking

In some establishments, customers leave their car at the entrance where their luggage is unloaded and porters 'car jockey' the cars to the establishment's car park or garage. The car keys can be kept by the porters until the customers wish to go out again when the car is driven back to the main entrance. This service is provided to increase customer satisfaction. It is also used when car parking space is limited because the cars can be parked closer together since it is only porters who need access to the cars.

MEMORY JOGGER

How can you be sure that an external service you have been asked to arrange, such as booking theatre tickets, will match the customer's requirements?

Holiday luggage

Off Street Car Parks No. 103871			City of Newcastle upon Tyne		
OVERNIGHT PARKING **PERMIT** VALID FOR ONE NIGHT ONLY	Day of Issue	Day	Day	Month	Year
			16	AUG 1992	
Authorises this vehicle to be left in this Car Park in accordance with the Off Street Parking Place Order 1980	Valid for One Night only commencing Day of issue	From	4.30 p.m. On date of issue		
		To	9.30 a.m. on following day		
For Parking Conditions see Overleaf	Vehicle Reg. No.		E986 VKU		
OXFORD CAR PARK This side of permit must be displayed inside windscreen					

A parking permit

The concierge's desk at a large London hotel

Hairdressing

Larger establishments may have a hairdressing salon in the building or arrangements with a hairdresser who will come to cut and shampoo the customer's hair in their room. This is another popular service, particularly if the customers are attending an important function.

In-house movies

Before the advent of Sky Television many establishments offered, and some still do, a movie channel. The customers can select this channel in the bedroom and the charge is added automatically to their account.

To advertise this service, notices in the foyer and bedrooms show which movies are on at particular times.

Laundry services

Customers away from home often require some laundry to be washed or dry cleaned. To cater for this, many establishments, either on the premises or in conjunction with a local laundry, will offer a 24 hour or same day service, in addition to providing a trouser pressing service. Many establishments now provide presses in the bedrooms and fold away ironing facilities.

Luxury establishments may employ a valet (a gentleman's gentleman), who will press clothes and lay out a set of clothes, especially for black tie functions when evening dress is worn.

MANCHESTER AIRPORT

GUEST SAME DAY LAUNDRY & DRY CLEANING SERVICE

Place completed laundry card and garments into bag provided. Please notify Housekeeper between 7.00 am and 8.30 am for return by 6.00 pm.

Name   Room No.   Date

	Price	Guest Count	Control	£	p		Price	Guest Count	Control	£	p
DRY CLEANING						**LAUNDRY**					
Suit-2 piece	£9.75					Shirt	£4.25				
Suit-Ladies	£9.75					Blouse	£4.25				
Jacket	£6.25					Dress	£6.95				
Trousers	£5.75					Skirt	£5.25				
Overcoat	£9.00					Trousers	£5.75				
Raincoat	£9.00					Nightdress	£3.75				
Sweater	£3.95					Pyjamas	£3.75				
Cardigan	£3.95					Slip	£1.75				
Jeans/Cords	£5.75					Vest	£1.50				
Dress-Day	£6.95					Pants	£1.75				
Skirt	£5.25					Socks	£1.50				
Skirt-Pleated	£6.25					Bra	£1.50				
Shirt/Blouse	£4.25					Handkerchief	£1.50				
Tie	£2.50					Jersey	£2.80				
Waistcoat	£3.50										
PRESSING						**PRESSING**					
Suit from	£5.00					Skirt from	£2.50				
Trousers	£2.50					Jacket	£2.50				
Dress	£2.50					Blouse/Shirt	£2.00				
		Sub-Total						**Sub-Total**			
								TOTAL			

SPECIAL INSTRUCTIONS..
PRICES INCLUSIVE OF V.A.T.

Please note: The Hotel cannot be held responsible for shrinkage or colour fastness.
In cases of loss or damage, the Hotel must be notified within 24 hrs.
The Hotel restricts any claims on items to 5 times the value of cleaning prices.

A hotel laundry list

It is usual to find a laundry list in the wardrobe of each bedroom, which details the services available, for the customer to complete. The additional charges are added to the customer's account.

Pony trekking

Nearby there are usually centres where horses can be hired for a day's pony trekking. If required, the services of a local guide can also be hired.

Golf

Many customers wish to play golf while away from home and you will need local knowledge as to where the golf courses are, how many holes they have and whether unaccompanied non-members can play a round of golf.

Cycle hire

Customers may also wish to go cycling on cycle trails often found on disused railway tracks. They offer a delightful day out in the countryside.

Guided tours

Cities and heritage centres often offer tours of the city or an area of historic interest in an open-topped bus, with a guide giving a running commentary, or guided walking tours to places of particular interest.

Guided tours by bus are found in cities such as Oxford, where it is possible to purchase tickets which allow you to get off at any stop and, when you are ready to move on, take the next bus. Check that the guides are fully licensed before recommending the tour.

Tourist information centres offer 'Blue Badge Guides' who conduct local walking tours at set times throughout the day in peak season.

Local attractions

Tickets can sometimes be purchased from reception for local attractions in the area. Many establishments are able to offer discounted rates for customers through a deal made with the management or administration of the attraction to encourage more visitors.

Mini-bars

These are small cabinets placed in bedrooms from which customers can select alcoholic and soft drinks and light snacks such as crisps and peanuts, at any time of day or night when the establishment's bars are closed. Some systems automatically record a price when a flap is lifted and the selection is made. Others operate an honesty system, where customers state what they have consumed.

A mini-bar

Room service

Larger establishments offer room service for food and drink, in some cases at any time of day or night, although during the night the service may be limited to certain items.

Breakfast is the meal served most often in the customer's room. Many establishments provide a menu on which the customers mark their requirements. They then hang the menu on the door handle outside their room before going to bed. The

A room-service trolley

breakfast is delivered to the room or suite at the required time, allowing the customer extra precious moments in bed or preparation time for that important meeting or an early departure.

Accommodation

Customers often require you to make bookings for accommodation for their next overnight stop and will ask advice and for your recommendations as to where to stay. If you have a sister establishment in the required location you will recommend this one and make an onward booking for them, first checking the type of accommodation required, date, number of people, price range and arrival time. Check your house policy.

There are some discount schemes available to customers, such as the AA 'Country Wanderer'. A customer purchases vouchers at the beginning of their holiday and has the first night pre-booked at an establishment operating within the scheme. As a condition of acceptance the establishment where they stay overnight has to make the next onward booking free of charge.

Restaurant

Sometimes customers may need to make a reservation for the establishment's restaurant if it is very popular. You may be asked to do this, specially if the restaurant is not open at the time when the customer wishes to book.

Do this

- Find what is on at your local theatre this week, the price of seats and starting time of the performances.
- Find out if these times fit in with your restaurant times or are special arrangements necessary to encourage customers to dine with you before or after visiting the theatre?
- See if your establishment can be put on the theatre's mailing list so that your information is always up to date.
- Design a leaflet, setting out the additional services that your establishment could provide, including things like tickets to local attractions, flowers or taxis, which could be sent out with the replies to letters of enquiry. The leaflet could also be displayed at reception to encourage an increased spend by each customer.
- In which cities are establishments likely to offer airline tickets?
- Find out if your establishment offers a laundry service and how soon items can be processed and returned to the customer.

HOW TO BOOK EXTERNAL SERVICES

- Address the customer by name or as 'Sir' or 'Madam'. This applies when dealing with all customers at any time.
- Identify yourself and your establishment when making a booking.
- Ensure that you are certain of their exact requirements. If you get the requirement wrong they will not be satisfied with the service they are purchasing and will complain to you or your superior.
- Check that the service is available and also check the price. If possible, report back to the customer to ensure that the price is acceptable to them before booking unless, of course, they have already told you that price does not matter to them.
- If the customer will be out all day, ask him or her to tell you how much they are willing to pay and to list alternatives, in case their first choice is not available.

Theatre tickets

- Remember some services may be a surprise present for a husband, wife or travelling companion, so do not mention these services as customers check in with a comment like 'Oh yes, Mr Jones the flowers are in your room just as your secretary ordered'. This kind of comment could completely ruin someone's romantic weekend for two. So be tactful.
- Treat any request as a challenge and make a positive response like, 'Oh yes, we can do that for you'. With a little time and effort you can.
- Suggest alternatives if their first choice is not available.

Unusual requests

However, a word of caution: do not book or attempt to book any services which would bring the establishment into disrepute. If in doubt, check with your superiors. This could include services such as escort services or stripper-grams.

If the service required is one which you cannot provide, contact an external establishment which can, stating:
- your name
- the name of your establishment
- service required
- customer's name
- date and time required.

Check the availability and cost and, if acceptable, place an order.

Essential knowledge	● Do not make arrangements for any service to be provided which could bring your establishment into disrepute or break the law as you could be prosecuted. ● It is essential to be accurate in describing the price and the facilities you are booking to maintain customer satisfaction and to preserve the reputation of your establishment. ● Give written quotes to the customers, whenever possible, for the service they require.

Do this 	● Make a list of any services which customers might ask for at your establishment, college or placement. These will depend on how close it is to facilities such as airports or theatres. ● Find out the approximate costs of these services and when they are available so that you can confirm whether it is possible to arrange this facility and check whether it is within the customer's price range. ● Type or word process your information, date and initial it. When new information and charges become available, update it. ● What alternative arrangements could you provide if, for example, a booked taxi failed to arrive?

Case study	*Customers have asked you to book some theatre tickets for this evening, and have now gone out for the day. You are unsure now which theatre and production was requested.* ● *What can you do?* ● *How can you be sure that you match customers' exact requirements on future requests for guest services?* ● *If you do manage to eventually purchase the tickets or any other service, how must the customers be billed?*

<table>
<tr><td>What have you learned</td><td>

1 List services which could be requested.
2 Are you fully aware of the external services that can be provided for customers at your establishment? Make a list and ask your supervisor to check it.
3 How much do these services cost and at what times of the day, night or week are they available?
4 Where can you find information about these services to pass on to interested customers?
5 When obtaining information, why is it important that it is accurate and within the law?
</td></tr>
</table>

<table>
<tr><td>Get ahead</td><td>

1 Make a point of visiting local tourist attractions, such as the theatre, and use the external services yourself, if appropriate, so that you then can give first-hand information to your customers.
2 Learn the telephone alphabet:
</td></tr>
</table>

A for ALFRED	N for NELLIE
B for BENJAMIN	O for OLIVER
C for CHARLIE	P for PETER
D for DAVID	Q for QUEEN
E for EDWARD	R for ROBERT
F for FREDERICK	S for SAMUEL
G for GEORGE	T for TOMMY
H for HARRY	U for UNCLE
I for ISAAC	V for VICTOR
J for JACK	W for WILLIAM
K for KING	X for X-RAY
L for LUCY	Y for YELLOW
M for MARY	Z for ZEBRA

Deal with the arrival of customers

This chapter covers:

ELEMENT 1: Deal with the arrival of customers without advance bookings

ELEMENT 2: Prepare for and deal with the arrival of customers with advance bookings

---

What you need to do

- Greet customers in a warm and welcoming way correctly identifying their requirements.
- Access and check availability of services and facilities, identifying alternatives if a first request is unavailable.
- Try to ensure that the customer makes a booking.
- Prepare the documentation and other items for registration in advance for the arrival of customers.
- Ensure that registration documentation takes place and details are entered into the booking system.

- Give accurate information about charges and facilities to match the customers' requirements.
- Promote other services within the establishment.
- Distribute details of arriving customers to all departments.
- Deal effectively with any unexpected situations and inform the appropriate people when necessary.
- Prioritise your work in an organised and efficient manner taking into account laid-down procedures and legal requirements.

What you need to know

- Why registration documentation must be correctly completed by the customer.
- Why correspondence relating to the booking should be readily available.

- How rooms are allocated within your organisation.
- Why it is important to give accurate information to customers.

ELEMENT 1: Deal with the arrival of customers without advance bookings

---

INTRODUCTION

Customers who arrive without making a booking in advance are known as 'chance customers' or 'walk ins'. Obviously no advance preparations have been made for them and so the steps to be taken by the receptionist are slightly different and have to be taken with more speed than for those customers who have pre-booked.

First impressions

If the reception area is untidy and looks chaotic it creates a bad impression of you and may also cast doubt on the efficiency of the rest of the establishment, for

MEMORY JOGGER

Why is it important that customers are greeted warmly and their requirements identified?

example, the kitchen. Keep your reception area tidy at all times and work in an organised and tidy manner. Finish one job and clear away before starting another.

Give a smiling and appropriate greeting to everyone who approaches your reception desk: 'Good morning, Sir/Madam. May I help you?'. Remember customers are *not* an interruption to your work. Without them you would not have any work to do or even a job. It is the customers who pay your wages even if indirectly!

REGISTRATION

When a customer arrives without an advance reservation there are certain procedures you should follow.

- Check your reservation system to see if you have the required accommodation available.
- Describe to the customer the accommodation that you do have available, assessing their needs according to the type of customer, the price and for how long it is available.
- If it is acceptable to the customer, obtain the customer's details and enter them into the system, either manually or on computer, depending on the system at your establishment. If you have a computerised system, the name and address will be recognised and the computer will automatically display full details on the screen.
- If what you have available is not suitable, offer alternative accommodation, price or dates or contact any sister establishment to check whether the customer's first choice is available there.
- If they accept the accommodation you have available or the alternative ask the customer to complete registration.

If the customer has stayed at your establishment before you may be able to print out this information automatically from the customer history cards or customer database and the customer will only be required to sign to confirm it as correct.

- Give customers a key-card confirming the price and room number and either show them to their room or send a porter with them according to house custom.
- Inform all departments that further customers have arrived.
- Open an account for the customers identified by the room number allocated to them.

Do this

- Imagine that an extra twenty customers have booked into your establishment and you have forgotten to tell other departments. Who should you have informed, and why? What would have happened?

Chance customers

Some establishments insist on getting an imprint of a credit card or asking for full payment in advance for customers without a prior reservation. This should be handled tactfully so that the customer is not upset by this request and, of course, regular customers would not be asked to do this. Say something like, 'Would you mind letting me have an imprint of your credit card?' or 'I am sorry Sir, but full prepayment of the first night is required for customers who have not booked in advance.'

Do this

- Using the example of the registration form shown on page 153 fill it in with your personal details. What other information could be obtained and for what purpose do you think this would be used?
- What other questions could you ask on the form?
- Design a registration form which would ask for this further information.

Καλωσορισατε **Viteite Bienvenue**
歡 迎 **Bemvindo** أهلا وسهلا **Welcome**
Välkommen Salamat datang 歡 迎
Welkom Bienvenido Willkommen

ROOM NUMBER	
RATE	
ARRIVAL DATE	
DEPARTURE DATE	

RECEPTIONIST ☐   CHECKED BY ☐   CR ☐   WI ☐

CHECK-OUT TIME 12 NOON

Forum Hotel London

ACCOUNT NUMBER	ARRIVAL DATE	DEPARTURE DATE	ARRIVAL TIME	NO. OF ROOMS	ROOM TYPE

DAILY RATE	NO. OF GUESTS	ADVANCE DEPOSIT	ROOM NUMBER	PACKAGE PLAN

SIX CONTINENTS CLUB MEMBER   YES ☐   NO ☐

DEPARTURE DATE: _____ NEXT DESTINATION:_____

PLEASE COMPLETE THIS BOX IF THERE ARE ANY CHANGES IN THE INFORMATION PRINTED ABOVE

FAMILY NAME: MR. MRS. MS   FIRST NAME: SELF SPOUSE

HOME ADDRESS:
STREET: CITY:

COUNTY/STATE POSTAL CODE: COUNTRY:

COMPANY: POSITION:

NATIONALITY: PASSPORT NUMBER: ISSUED AT:

METHOD OF PAYMENT: CASH ☐   PERSONAL CHEQUE ☐   A/C TO CO VOUCHER ☐   CREDIT CARD ☐   ☐ ☐ ☐ ☐ ☐   DEPOSIT ☐
BY ARRANGEMENT ONLY   ACCESS AMEX DINERS VISA JCB

IN THE EVENT OF THE PAYER INDICATED ABOVE FAILING FOR ANY REASON TO PAY ANY SUMS CHARGED TO ME I ACCEPT FULL PERSONAL RESPONSIBILITY THEREFOR. THE LIABILITY OF THE FORUM HOTEL LONDON FOR VALUABLES LEFT IN ROOMS IS LIMITED. SAFE DEPOSIT BOXES ARE AVAILABLE FREE OF CHARGE. I AGREE THAT MY USE OF SAFE DEPOSIT BOXES WILL BE IN ACCORDANCE WITH THE HOTELS DEPOSIT RULES AVAILABLE ON REQUEST AND AS SET OUT IN THE ROOM CARD

GUEST SIGNATURE:

BIRTHDAY: / DAY MONTH

A registration form from the Forum Hotel, London

MEMORY JOGGER

Who must register? What information must be obtained from a non-British citizen?

Essential knowledge

A registration form must be completed on arrival for several reasons.
- By the *Immigration (Hotel Records) Order* 1972 it is a legal requirement that every one over the age of sixteen who books sleeping accommodation in return for payment completes a registration form giving full name and nationality.
- Customers who are not British subjects have to give additional information such as passport number, place of issue, their next destination and full address if known.
- Information given at this time can be used later if there is any query.
- Customer accounts can be accurately made up.
- The registration form helps internal audit purposes.
- The information given helps the sales and marketing departments in their work.
- In case of an emergency it is important that you have an exact record of all customers.

```
                MANCHESTER AIRPORT

                      HILTON


        GUEST _____


        ROOM NUMBER _____


        RATE _____
        (INCLUSIVE OF VAT)


        CHECK-OUT DATE _____


        SIGNATURE _____


                PLEASE KEEP THIS CARD
                WITH YOU AS PROOF OF
                      RESIDENCE

                      THANK YOU
```

A hotel key-card

Types of customer

Different types of customer will have different needs in terms of accommodation and facilities required. Most establishments cater for many types of people such as businessmen or women or people on holiday. This is known as the marketing mix, although one type of customer might be more in evidence than another depending on the type of establishment and where it is situated.

The types of customers likely to arrive can be quite varied.

Family groups
Make children especially welcome. This creates a very good first impression and as mentioned earlier, 'a happy child makes for a happy adult'. What is more these are the customers of tomorrow.

Crying children make the parents feel tense and wonder if they should have come away at all. Some establishments give a welcoming pack to children (a goodie bag) which will keep them happily occupied while the formalities of checking in to the establishment are completed.

Customers with communication difficulties
A customer with a communication difficulty could be deaf and have poor speech or have a stammer, or come from a foreign country and be unable to speak English very well. They may not be able to make you understand what exactly they want. You

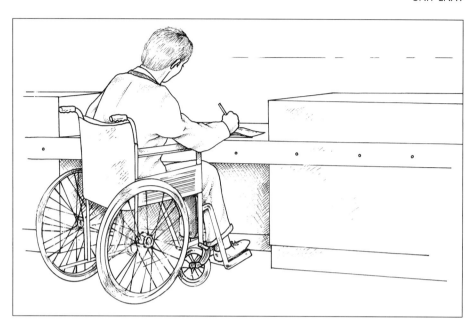

A customer in a wheelchair completing the registration form

should not become flustered by this. Remain calm and patient, repeating slowly what you have to say and, if necessary, use sign language and printed literature to illustrate the point you are making. If the customer is deaf or partially deaf do not turn your back to them or mumble your words. Never laugh or giggle even if you are tempted to do so because you feel nervous or are unsure of what to do in this situation. If you really are unable to communicate call your supervisor who will be able to help.

You or other members of staff may be able to speak a foreign language and this will be useful when dealing with foreign customers.

Disabled customers

Disabled customers should be greeted in the same way as any other customer and should not be 'talked down to' or patronised. If there is a section of the reception office counter which is at wheelchair height check in any customers in wheelchairs at this section or otherwise give them the registration documents to complete in their wheelchair. Other disabled customers who find standing for any length of time difficult should be able to complete their registration documents sitting down.

The room allocated to disabled customers should be suitable for their needs. The room should be on the ground floor or near a lift. Is it easily accessible in a wheelchair? Can the wheelchair get into the bathroom and bedroom and turn around?

Not all disabilities are easy to detect as perfectly healthy looking customers can be disabled by a whole range of illnesses and disabilities such as heart disease or an artificial limb. Look for signs such as shortness of breath or slow walking and try to put yourself in the customer's position.

New customers

New customers may be feeling apprehensive about approaching the reception area and will be looking for signs of reassurance. Give them a warm welcome. Provided they are satisfied with how they are treated in respect of service and accommodation they will become regular customers.

Regular Customers and VIPs

Regular customers will expect you to remember them, give them a specially warm welcome and arrange for them to have all their special requirements without them having to remind you. You may be able to obtain this information from a customer history form if one is held on computer. This will make a good impression as people like to be remembered.

A VIP will require a very special and speedy service and check-in facilities. Perhaps it is your custom to have a special area for them to check-in or they may be shown straight to their room.

Non-British passport holders
These may require help in understanding the information you give to them and help in completing the registration formalities.

Unexpected happenings

Anyone arriving at reception asking for accommodation must be in a fit state to be received and have the means to pay. If a drunk arrives requesting accommodation you would be unwise to accept the booking.

State politely that the establishment is fully booked. If the person is reluctant to leave or starts to cause a disturbance summon help from a porter or from your superior.

Should anyone arrive at reception without the means to pay their bill they too should be advised that there is no accommodation available.

Blacklists

Customers who have stayed before and caused trouble or damage are unlikely to be accepted again under any circumstances. They may be on a blacklist of customers who must not be offered accommodation. This is confidential information and can usually be found in the customer history records, whether computerised or manual. Do not take a booking from anyone who is on the blacklist.

Do this

- Check with your supervisor to see whether you have a blacklist.
- Make a note of what type of customer usually arrives without a reservation. Is there a pattern in the type of customer you can expect on particular days or periods, for example, at weekends?

Case study

A party of eight Japanese visitors check into your establishment without prior reservations.
- *Who should be informed of their unexpected arrival?*
- *What special requirements may they have?*
- *What would happen if you failed to notify various departments or enter their arrival onto the reservation system?*

What have you learned

1 Who must register on arrival?
2 What minimum information must be given by the customer?
3 What other information could be given and for what purpose?
4 What information should a non-British passport holder give?
5 List the types of customers, how they should be welcomed on arrival and what special arrangements should be available for them.

ELEMENT 2: Prepare for and deal with the arrival of customers with advance bookings

INTRODUCTION

Customers who have made an advance booking are somewhat easier to welcome and check in. You will have had time to prepare for their arrival and to ensure that everything is ready for their stay.

Before arrival

Arrivals for the day should be checked for accuracy and special requests to make sure that all details are correct. Key-cards and registration forms can be prepared to speed the check-in procedure and once completed the customer has only to check for accuracy and then sign the registration form. This can be done whenever there is a quiet moment. Some smaller establishments may still use a registration book or visitors' book which the customer signs on arrival, and no advance preparations can be made if this method is used.

Registration can be carried out by three methods:
● a visitors' book
● a registration form
● by computer.

The visitors' book
A visitors' book was traditionally used before other methods came into being. Each customer signed the book on arrival giving their required details. The visitors' book was usually very large, leather bound and after some time, depending on how large the establishment was, became dog-eared before the end of its use. If a large number of customers arrived at once they had to queue to sign the register and could, whilst registering read all the other entries. The receptionist could not process any of the customers' information until this formality had been completed, and if many customers arrived at once would have to wait until everyone had signed the register.

The registration form
This is a piece of paper or card often combined with a key-card which can be prepared before arrival for an advance reservation and given out individually to each customer as they arrive. It is confidential and can be filed after use. A more expensive but cost-effective method.

Computerised registrations
Computerised advance reservations details can be printed out in advance for the convenience of the customer, requiring the customer only to check the details for accuracy and sign their name.

Naturally, all departments within the establishment will need to know the arrivals for each day so that arrangements can be made, for example, for food, staff, laundry and restaurant reservations.

MEMORY JOGGER

How can details such as price and room number be conveyed to the customer?

ON ARRIVAL

● You must be able to retrieve the booking from whatever system your establishment uses.
● Once retrieved, confirm the details to the customer in this way: 'Oh yes, Mr Jones, a double room for two nights. Would you like to register for me please?'
● While the customer is registering, you have a few minutes to see if he or she

might need the reservation amending. Ask yourself if they are elderly or disabled and if you have allocated them a suitable room. If not, this is when you can ensure customer satisfaction by possibly changing the room to one more suitable for their requirements.

● Give the customer the registration form to check and complete and ask them how they intend to settle their account. Make sure that they have completed all the required details and if not ask them to do so. Non-British customers have to give passport details. Your establishment could get into trouble with the police if this information is not obtained.

● You also need the details of each customer staying in the hotel in case there is an emergency evacuation. You will then need to know the exact number of customers and their names. You will also need this information to draw up the arrivals list which must be issued to all departments.

● Then issue the room key and key-card and have them shown to their room or give them directions according to house custom. Remember to ask them at this point if they will require a table reservation for lunch or dinner, or, for example, coffee or afternoon tea. In this way you can sell the services and facilities you have available. This is a created sale which the customer may not have thought they wanted, but may in fact buy. If any amendments have been made to the booking you will have to change all the booking details within your system and notify all departments again so that all information throughout the establishment is totally up to date and accurate.

Do this

● List the advantages and disadvantages of all registration methods in terms of security, cost and ease of use.
● List the additional services and facilities you could sell to a customer who has just arrived in your establishment.

Essential knowledge

Registration is a legal requirement. If the customer has an advance booking, registration documents can be prepared in advance. This helps to keep the room occupancy figures of the establishment accurate and up to date, and provides an additional service to the customer.

Unexpected happenings

One of the worst things that can happen is for a customer to arrive believing that they have a reservation to find that you are not expecting them. This is called a 'no trace' booking, and can be handled in two ways:
● you can own up to having no record of a reservation
● you can pretend that everything is fine.

This second method will only work if you actually have space. If you do not the customer may become very angry at this point. If they can prove that the error is on your part you must provide suitable accommodation for them elsewhere at an equal or better standard of establishment. You have to pay any difference in price and provide transport to get there if required.

Check through your reservation records for the customer's name, to see if there is any record of a booking being made. Check also under other dates or months and look to see if the reservation has been wrongly filed under another name such as a company's name or secretary's name.

Telephone bookings are the most difficult to trace and, to overcome this, many establishments and central booking offices give a booking number when a reservation is made. This can be quoted to confirm that contact has been made between the customer and the establishment and is easier to trace in case of dispute.

Another unexpected happening is when the customer does not arrive even when they have made a reservation. This is called a 'non-arrival'.

Breach of contract law

If a customer does not arrive or cancels a booking at short notice, the law says that an establishment may charge two thirds of the total cost (the other third is for food not consumed) if the accommodation remains unlet. This goes some way in recouping the loss of revenue, but can be difficult to prove if the booking was made by telephone and not confirmed in writing. The customer would have to be contacted and billed for the outstanding amount only after the booking period was ended to make sure that the accommodation could not be relet for the whole or part of the period and the account adjusted accordingly.

If the customer refuses to pay the compensation the matter has to be taken to the small claims court and the proceedings may take some time. Restaurants too have begun to charge compensation for non-arrivals and loss of revenue as some unscrupulous people book tables in several restaurants for the same night and decide on the day which one to go to leaving the others with empty tables.

Other difficult circumstances

It can be a problem when customers arrive and you can see that they would not have been accepted for a variety of reasons if they had not pre-booked. They may, for example, be drunk or on your blacklist. In these instances inform your supervisor and the security officer, if you have one, so that they can handle this difficult situation. Warn other departments in case of any incidents.

6 p.m. release

One way of reletting short notice bookings is to only hold them until 6 p.m. of the day of arrival. This gives an opportunity for the rooms to be re-allocated after this time. However, very often, you may find that you have turned away business all afternoon only to discover after 6 p.m. that you had space all the time.

Guaranteed reservations

Asking a customer to guarantee a booking with a credit card is a more certain way of ensuring that they will arrive. You can, moreover, charge them for the first night of the stay whether they arrive or not.

The customer must be given a reservation number at the time of booking and details of his or her full name, address, credit card number and its expiry date must be taken. The customer may cancel the booking up to 6 p.m. on the evening they are due to arrive without incurring any charge. Even though credit card details are known, you must take an imprint of the credit card on arrival to confirm details as correct. If you are at all suspicious, you can contact the credit card authorisation centre to check out the customer.

Do this

- Role-play in a class or work situation what you would say to someone who arrives with a no-trace booking when you are fully booked. Write down the dialogue first, including the steps you should take if you are at fault or if the customer is at fault.
- Mr Dane, a no-trace booking, has arrived. You can allocate him a room. What is the procedure for checking him into your establishment.
- Complete a registration form, using the sample on page 153, for Mr Dane who is partially sighted.

There are many difficult and sometimes amusing circumstances surrounding the arrival of customers with and without advance reservations. As you become more and more confident you will be able to handle check-ins calmly and confidently. Like any new job your first check-in will be the most difficult but, after that, it will soon become routine. Each establishment has its own procedure but the aim is to be welcoming, efficient and competent to answer any queries the customer may have about the tariff or facilities.

Do this

- At registration you could obtain other information useful in sales and marketing. Think of other questions which could be included on the reservation form to help in the increase of repeat or new business.
- Suggest these to your supervisor.
- What other little-used services at your establishment could be promoted to customers when they register? How could this be done?

CONFERENCE, FUNCTION AND EXHIBITION BUSINESS

Conferences

> ### MEMORY JOGGER
>
> What other services within your establishment could you promote?

Many establishments have a separate booking system for conference, function and exhibition business. In a large establishment this would be arranged by a separate department from reception but in a smaller establishment this is another part of your work.

Conference business may only last a day during which the delegates will arrive, be checked in, and stay for all meals then leave in the afternoon. Delegates may, however, stay overnight, a weekend, a few days or longer.

A group booking of any type, especially a conference booking, will mean that a speedy check-in is required. The ideal solution is to set up a separate check-in area, away from the main reception desk to avoid congestion, or pre-register the customers before arrival, eliminating this part of check-in. If the establishment still uses a book-type register a long delay can occur at the check-in while everyone queues

Conference delegates checking in separately from other guests

to sign the book. If registration forms are used these can be distributed and everyone can complete them at the same time. This enables you to complete the administrative tasks, give out the bedroom keys and key-cards as the completed registration forms are handed back rather than waiting for everyone to sign the book.

Functions

This type of business involves large numbers of people arriving at the establishment to attend a function such as a luncheon, dinner or a wedding reception.

The organiser of the function will be welcomed by you and, depending on your establishment's practice, shown the facilities which have been provided. Some of the customers attending the function may have booked an overnight stay so will be required to check in as they arrive, before the function begins, to allow them to change their clothes.

People such as the organiser, a bride or a groom may have been given free accommodation for the occasion as a thank you for bringing the business to your establishment.

If the occasion is a wedding do not disclose the room number of the bride and groom or even confirm that they are staying at the establishment. This is to prevent the wedding guests from playing any pranks on them which may be harmless but could damage the room, spoil the couple's stay and annoy other customers.

Exhibitions

Exhibitions can bring many people into your establishment who might not otherwise visit and it is an opportunity to sell items, especially meals and beverages.

All exhibitions or similar events should be clearly signposted on the information boards otherwise you will be constantly asked directions. Details of all conference, function and exhibition business should be circulated to all departments well in advance detailing the exact requirements and numbers attending so that the necessary arrangements can be made. Ideally a monthly sheet should be sent around with this information. You may be asked to prepare this.

Do this

● If your establishment does not already prepare one, make a list of forthcoming events and type or word process it. Ask permission from your supervisor first. Give it to your supervisor to check to make sure there are no errors or spelling mistakes and then deliver it to all departments. If you do not cater for this type of business, prepare a list detailing the number of customers staying overnight for the next month.

Case study

A customer arrives and you can find no trace of their reservation even though they insist that it was made last evening. You were on duty last evening, you log all your enquiries and you are sure that a reservation was not made in their name.
● *What can you do in this situation?*
● *What is the legal position?*
● *Does your establishment give customers a reservation number at the time of their reservation for purposes of confirmation?*
● *Can you offer accommodation to them anyway?*

Get ahead	I	Visit your banqueting department, conference or exhibition department and see how they monitor and record their bookings. If your establishment does not have these departments, visit your library and look in food service books to find examples of banqueting booking forms and memoranda which you could adapt for your establishment.
	2	At registration try to obtain other information useful for selling and marketing.
	3	What other little-used services at your establishment could be promoted to customers on arrival and how could this be done?

Prepare customer accounts and deal with departures

This chapter covers:
ELEMENT 1: **Prepare and maintain customer accounts**
ELEMENT 2: **Deal with the departures of customers**

What you need to do

- Always greet the customer in a warm and welcoming manner.
- Regularly prepare and update customer accounts in your accounting system in preparation of their departure.
- Keep a record of each charge entered on the account which must be readily available in case of dispute.
- Be aware of credit limits of each customer. (This is the amount of money they can charge to their account before making payment.)
- Keep customer accounts confidential and do not allow unauthorised access.
- Accurately record any account adjustments amending customer bills.
- Retain and file documentation details.

- Explain and allow the customer to check their account.
- Ensure that you have collected the bedroom key and other equipment belonging to the establishment.
- Complete departure documentation using correct account and booking systems.
- Keep a record of customer complaints, comments and suggestions and inform your supervisor.
- Be able to cope with unexpected situations effectively and inform appropriate people if and when necessary.
- Work in an organised and efficient manner.
- Prioritise your work in an organised and efficient manner taking into account organisational procedures and legal requirements.

What you need to know

- Why it is important to regularly update customer accounts with charges and adjustments to ensure accuracy.
- Why verbal and written information should be given to customers.

- Why customer accounts must be kept confidential.
- How to record complaints and comments and why they should be fed back to the appropriate people/department.

ELEMENT 1: **Prepare and maintain customer accounts**

INTRODUCTION

As soon as a customer arrives at your establishment it is usual to open an account or bill in their name or company. There will be a charge for accommodation if staying overnight. This charge may include breakfast or may be for the room only. If the charge is room only then breakfast will be charged as an extra. Other items ordered will be entered on the account. These might include food and beverages, such as morning coffee, luncheon, afternoon tea, dinner, sandwiches, drinks from the bar and wines. These items could be taken in one of the restaurants or coffee shops or served directly in the customer's room by room service.

Charging items to a customer's bill is known as 'posting' and it is done at least once a day throughout the customer's stay.

Charges may be not only for food and drink but could be for other items such as the use of leisure facilities, theatre tickets, flowers and hire of rooms for exhibitions and banquets. (The cost of any telephone calls will also be added to the account.)

The main charges on the bill will be the charge for accommodation and meals and can be entered onto the bill either manually, by machine or by computer depending on the custom of the establishment.

The charges for accommodation and food are generally decided in advance unless you are giving the customers a specially reduced price on the day. You can find the correct charge known as the rate from the tariff. This is a list of charges which must be displayed at the reception office and listed in the brochure. The rate to be charged which may be different for each customer, is given to them on arrival in the form of a key-card. The rate would be notified to them in a letter of confirmation if they have booked earlier.

Essential knowledge	It is a legal requirement that each customer receives *written confirmation* of the rate they are to be charged and what facilities and services are included. Prices must also be displayed in the entrance to the establishment including value added tax (VAT) and any service charges. This is a requirement under the *Tourism (Sleeping Accommodation Price Display) Order* 1977.

KEY-CARD

The key-card plays an important part in the accounting system as not only does it confirm *in writing* to the customer the rate they are being charged and the facilities available to them, it also allows them to charge items to their room when they produce it. Therefore they can pay one account at the end of their stay instead of paying for such items as bar drinks and food in the restaurant at the time of purchase. The key-card identifies the customer and confirms their room number. Without this it could be possible for anyone to enter the establishment, give a room number and charge items to that room.

Do this	Before progressing further it is necessary that you understand and learn by heart the various terms used for accommodation and food provided for customers:
	● room only – charge for the room with no meals included. This is also known as the *European plan*
	● room and breakfast – bed and breakfast. This is also known as the *Continental plan*
	● half-board – room, breakfast and another main meal, lunch or dinner. This is also known as *demi-pension* and *modified American plan*
	● full-board – room, breakfast, luncheon and dinner and sometimes including afternoon tea. This is also known as *en-pension* and the *American plan*
	● all inclusive rate – very similar to full-board but includes use of all the establishment's facilities such as a swimming pool or a golf course.

Customer Name *Mr M. A. Anthon*

Room No *608*

Hotel *Newcastle*

Date of Departure *11ᵗʰ Aug 92*

Tariff *£75*

To ensure that you fully enjoy your stay, please
refer to the Guest Services Directory in your
room, where you will find a detailed guide to
everything that the hotel can offer.

Please present this card when collecting your key or
whenever you wish to charge hotel services to your account.

A hotel key-card

CUSTOMER ACCOUNTS

Once you are sure that you know all the various terms we can move on to a simple account for an individual room.

We will begin with a manual system which will start with a simple account. (See page 166.) Any charges are added to the bill which is totalled each evening. The charges are for bed and breakfast in this example, but can be for room only, half-board or inclusive rate. The customers have had two dinners and a bottle of wine and these items have been added to the account making a total charge of £99.90.

Any items not paid for by the customer at the time they were ordered are entered on a slip of paper (with a duplicate or second copy) and signed for by the customer. This is known as a 'docket'. The receptionist receives a copy of this from any department in the establishment in which the customer has run up a charge, for example, in a bar or restaurant. These charges are then posted onto the bill.

Essential knowledge	● Obviously it is very important that any items put onto the bill are correct and that the final totalled account is accurate. There should be no errors in the bill when it is presented to the customer, so that the customer's last impression is as good as his first.
	● The customers use their key-card for identification purposes. Do not, however, confuse this type of key-card with the electronic key-card, which unlike a traditional key is computerised and unlocks their bedroom door. (See the illustration on page 167.)

Other useful terms are listed below.
● *Deposit* – an amount of money prepaid to secure the booking which is later deducted from the bill.

RECEPTION

Hartington Hotel & Restaurant
Broad Walk, Buxton, Derbyshire SK17 6JR
Licensed · AA · RAC · BHRCA

Tel: Management Buxton 22638 Visitors: Buxton 23105

M _V ✓ Mrs Smith_

Room No: _106_

VAT Reg No: 157 5766 26

A REMITTANCE IS REQUESTED UPON PRESENTATION
Visitors are respectfully informed that Cheques cannot be taken in Payment of Accounts

Proprietors: **Mr & Mrs M Whibberley**

10th Nov 19 93	£	p	£	p	£	p	£	p	£	p	£	p	£	p	£	p
Brought forward £																
2 Room & Breakfast	66	00														
Board or Incl. Terms																
Apartments																
Room Service																
Servants' Board																
Morning Tea																
Baths																
Breakfast																
Luncheon																
Afternoon Tea																
High Tea																
2 Dinner	24	00														
Supper																
Tea & Coffee																
Ale, Stout etc																
Minerals																
Wines	9	90														
Spirits																
Cigars & Cigarettes																
Laundry/Dry Cl'ng																
Telephone																
Newspapers																
Garage																
Sundries																
Paid Out																
Carried forward £	99	90														

Inclusive of VAT @ 17½%

 **Printed on Recycled Paper**

166

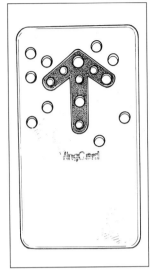

An electronic key

- *EMT* – early morning tea.
- *Docket* – a slip of paper detailing an item charged to the customer's room number signed by the customer.
- *VPO* – visitors paid out – an amount of money paid on behalf of the customer for such items as theatre tickets and flowers which is later added to the bill.
- *Allowance* – an amount deducted for a charge added in error, for example, for an overcharge or reduction in price to settle a complaint.
- *Discount* – an amount deducted for a special offer, for example, ten per cent when the booking is made through the Tourist Information 'Book a Bed Ahead' (BABA) scheme.
- *Refund* – given when overpaid for services. For example, a customer who has prepaid departs earlier than arranged.
- *Prepayment* – customer pays the bill before arriving at the establishment.
- *Transfer* – made when customer moves rooms or has an item put on a different account, for example, a ledger account to which the account is sent after they have left the establishment.
- *Brought forward* – a running total of money from customer accounts up to the day before.
- *Carried forward* – the amount of money from customer accounts up to the previous day which, when added to the current day's figure, gives the total takings to date.

It is important that you are familiar with these terms also so that the correct charge can be made.

■ ■ ■
FORUM
HOTEL
L O N D O N

PAID-OUT

No 50860

Guest Name _____   Room _____

EXPLANATION

_____

_____

_____

_____   _____
APPROVAL   GUEST SIGNATURE

A&G 005-07/84

A hotel paid-out form

Do this

- Refer to the tabular ledger sheet (on page 169) with the account for Mr and Mrs Roberts already entered and carry out the following customer bill exercise on the blank bill form on page 182. Use the details set out below.
  A double room with bathroom (DB) Room No. 201 has been reserved for Mr and Mrs Roberts, who arrive requiring bed and breakfast at £70.00. They go into the bar and order two gin and tonics at £3.50, which they charge to their room, showing the key-card for Room No. 201 as proof of residence and sign a bar docket.

The Excelsior Hotel

Customers in residence

Mr and Mrs Roberts (DB) double with bath at £70.00 BB Room No. 201. Mr Padstone (SB) single with bath at £50.00 full-board Room No. 205. Mr and Mrs Singleton (FB) family room with bath at £90.00 BB Room No. 207. Miss Pemberton and Mrs Sullivan (TB) twin at £95.00 inclusive rate Room No. 210.

Terms

EMT – £1.00 per person.
Breakfast – £7.00 per person.
Lunch – £10.00 per person.

Enter all the rooms on the tabular ledger sheet taking care to put charges opposite the appropriate item.

7.30 All customers have early morning tea at £1.00 each.
9.30 All customers have breakfast. Place a tick in the breakfast column and enter an amount of £7.00 for each customer. This separates the food takings from the accommodation (pension) element.

2.00 All customers have lunch. Only Mr and Mrs Roberts and the Singleton family are charged, because all the others are on inclusive charges.
2.00 Mr and Mrs Lambert arrive, require DB and are allocated Room No. 202. Open a new column for them.
2.15 Bar drinks of £7.80 for Mr Padstone.

Balance tab by adding up and down and across. This figure should be same added down and across. (When you have completed this exercise check your tabular ledger sheet with the one shown at the end of this unit.)

Learn the following terms by heart

SB – single with bath
TB – twin with bath
D – double
DB – double with bath
TR – triple
TRB – triple with bath
F – family
FB – family with bath
STE – suite

Cash takings from the bar and chance sales for meals and beverages would also be shown in separate columns called 'bar' and 'chance'. Any function business would also be shown on the ledger, itemised and added into the daily tabular ledger sheet.

Essential knowledge	<ul><li>It is important that customers' accounts are regularly updated with charges and adjustments so that when required they are readily available.</li><li>Once the customer's bill has been prepared and totalled a record must be kept of their bill and all the other bills for customers in residence that night. This shows a complete break down and analysis of all the sales of that particular day and enables you to see clearly the total takings and also the takings for particular areas such as accommodation and the bar.</li></ul>

ROOM No.	201										
NAME	ROBERTS MR + MRS ②										
RATE	£70 RB										DAILY TOTAL
B/F											
APARTMENTS	56	00									
PENSION											
BREAKFASTS	14	00									
LUNCHEONS											
AFTERNOON TEAS											
DINNERS											
EARLY TEAS											
BEVERAGES											
WINES											
SPIRITS & LIQUEURS	3	50									
BEERS											
MINERALS											
TELEPHONES											
V.P.O.'s											
TOTAL											
CASH											
ALLOWANCES											
LEDGER											
BALANCE C/F											

Osborne 0298 6224

CREDIT LIMITS

When a customer checks into the establishment a credit limit is usually set up. If no previous reservation had been made, many establishments now ask for full prepayment for the accommodation or take an imprint of a credit card to be sure that the customer will not leave without paying. If the customer should manage to obtain services and accommodation without payment they are known as a 'skipper' or 'walk out'. Obviously this should be avoided at all costs.

Long-term customers will be asked to pay their account at regular intervals, usually weekly, to make sure they are able to pay and to provide the establishment with a constant flow of money to pay their own bills. This is known as the 'cash flow'.

If customers are settling their account by credit card you will have to check with the credit card company to obtain authorisation. This will confirm that the sum of money (the amount of their bill) does not exceed their total credit limit. This is done by ringing a clearance telephone number, giving the customer's name and credit card number, the establishment's merchant number, the amount of money to the nearest pound and expiry date on the card. The company will then give an authorisation number which is entered on the credit card slip.

A credit card slip

With the latest technology credit limits can be programmed into computerised systems eliminating the need for telephone authorisation calls.

Establishments which do not have this facility would have to telephone for authorisation.

Difficulty arises when the authorisation is refused and you have to ask for another payment method. You may be requested to retain and then destroy the card which may be on the cancelled/invalid list. These occasions require tact and diplomacy.

Copies of credit card slips, after banking, as well as dockets, are carefully stored for easy access in case of any account query.

Do this

In a role-play situation, practise telephoning the credit card company to gain confidence, speed and accuracy.
The following steps should be taken.
- Ensure all this information is to hand:
    credit card
    docket and bill
    customer's card.
- Have a pen ready.
- Dial authorisation number:
    give customer's number
    your merchant number
    amount (to the nearest £)
    expiry date.
- Speak clearly and slowly and be prepared to write down the authorisation number on credit card slip.

LEDGER ACCOUNTS

Sometimes customers do not settle their accounts on departure but with prior agreement the bill is sent on for settlement later. This is usually in the case of a company account. Care should be taken to ensure ability to pay and credit references should be obtained from the customer's bank and other traders they have accounts with to confirm that they pay their accounts promptly.

The advantage for the customer is that they do not have the bother of settling the bill on departure. For the establishment it means that the customer may be encouraged to spend more money on other services and bring repeat business to your establishment rather than elsewhere. The disadvantage for the establishment is that payment will be slower as it can be a month or more before payment is received.

Credit limits of ledger customers as well as in-house customers need a careful eye kept on them otherwise the cash flow (the amount of money the establishment has available in their bank account to use for their payments) could be seriously affected.

If an account has not been settled promptly or credit limits have been exceeded it may be necessary to discontinue the account.

ALLOWANCES AND DISCOUNTS

There are many occasions when the published tariff (known as the rack rate) is not actually charged to a customer.
- This may be because an allowance has been made for poor service or facilities as compensation for disappointment.
- The customer may qualify for a discount, for example, a group rate.
- The customer may be taking advantage of a special offer, such as two for the price of one, a weekend or leisure break.
- The establishment has chosen to reduce rates to encourage more business.

Do this

- What special rates do you have in your establishment and who is able to claim them?
- Choose an establishment in a national chain and find out their rack rate. (This is the full published tariff rate without discount, that is, the highest rate for a room.) Then compare this to a special offer such as weekend break rate. How much is the saving to the customer?

Forum Hotel London

DEDUCTION/ALLOWANCE
No.100125

Guest Name _____   Date _____

Room/A/c NR _____

EXPLANATION

	Amount

CODE £   SIGNATURE

A hotel allowance form

REFUNDS

A refund is given when the full amount is refunded to a customer for cancellation of a prepaid booking or when services received and paid for were not satisfactory. A refund can be either partial or total. (A refund to a customer can go some way to satisfying a complaint.)

When a refund is given it must be clearly shown on the customer's account and in your accounting records otherwise your takings will not balance when this amount has been refunded.

It is important that whatever way the customer originally paid for the services that they are refunded by the same payment method, specially if they paid by credit card. The refund will show on their credit card statement and you will issue them a refund

Have you imprinted the summary with your Retailer's Card?

Bank Processing copy of Summary with your Vouchers in correct order:

1 Summary
2 Sales Vouchers
3 Refund Vouchers

Keep Retailer's copy and Retailer's Duplicate copy

No more than 200 Vouchers to each Summary

Do not use Staples, Pins, Paper Clips

Printed by Ritchie Print Pack, Kilmarnock
22124 (9/89)

	Items	Amount
Sales Vouchers		
Less Refund Vouchers		
Date	Total	
	£	:

VISA ACCESS MasterCard

Retailer's Signature

Retailer Summary

Complete this summary for every Deposit of Sales Vouchers and enter the **Total** on your normal Current Account paying-in slip

A paying in slip

A refund slip

voucher and bank this with your other credit card payments. (See the illustration above.) If the customer paid by credit card and the refund was made in cash then you would pay a commission charge for money that you have not received.

DEPOSITS AND PREPAYMENTS

Very often to make sure that the customer takes up their booking and actually arrives at your establishment you may, if it is your house custom, request a deposit at the time the reservation was made or full payment in advance known as a prepayment.

A deposit can be taken on a credit card over the telephone (see the illustration below) at the time the reservation is taken or paid by cheque and sent through the post, or it may be your house custom to request a deposit or full prepayment on arrival from any customers who arrive without prior reservation.

Naturally, whichever way you receive a deposit or prepayment you will issue a receipt and record this payment on your accounting system. You must of course remember to deduct the deposit or prepayment from any further accounts that you prepare for a particular customer.

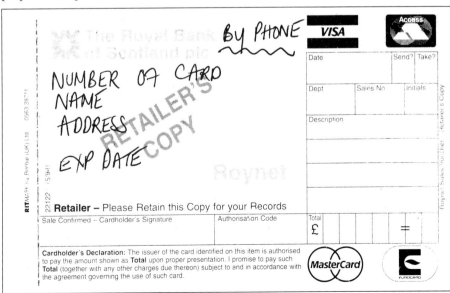

A slip recording a credit card payment made over the telephone

No _720_ _____ 19 ____

Received from _____

_____

the sum of _____

_____

£ _____

A receipt

Do this

Using the bills shown on the opposite page do the following exercises.
● Prepare an account on a manual system for two nights' bed and breakfast at £49.50 per night for Mr and Mrs Suburb and deduct £50.00. Use yesterday's date.
● Prepare an account for Mr and Mrs Brown who have prepaid one night's bed and breakfast at £49.50 but have had two dinners at £14.90, a bottle of wine at £12.40, two coffees at 80p, two liqueurs at £1.50. How much do they now owe?

Essential knowledge

● Whatever accounting method is used or method of payment taken, it is essential that all information remains confidential and is kept out of the way of public access. Customers may tamper with their own account or see confidential information.
● Unscrupulous staff, if able to tamper with the accounts, may either make 'adjustments' for friends and relatives or take cash payments which are not yet entered into the system.
● The night auditor, accountants, head office or management, will be constantly checking accounts and doing spot checks to look for errors and fraud.

UNEXPECTED SITUATIONS

Some business customers ask for their account to be adjusted to show an incorrect breakdown so that they can charge items, such as wine and drinks, to their account as accommodation or other allowable items which they can later claim back from their company.

Do not permit unauthorised staff to enter your reception area at any time to prevent access to accounts, details of takings and cash held in the safe. You may be held responsible for any errors or missing money.

Sometimes a customer may not have the means to pay. This is not always intentional for they may have lost their wallet or had their credit cards stolen. Consult your supervisor.

Hartington Hotel & Restaurant
Broad Walk, Buxton, Derbyshire SK17 6JR
Licensed · AA · RAC · BHRCA

Tel: Management Buxton 22638 Visitors: Buxton 2

MR. and MRS. Suburb

Room No: _____

VAT Reg No: 157 5766 26

A REMITTANCE IS REQUESTED UPON PRESENTATION
Visitors are respectfully informed that Cheques cannot be taken in Pa

19	£	p	£	p	£	p
Brought forward £						
Room & Breakfast						
Board or Incl. Terms						
Apartments						
Room Service						
Servants' Board						
Morning Tea						
Baths						
Breakfast						
Luncheon						
Afternoon Tea						
High Tea						
Dinner						
Supper						
Tea & Coffee						
Ale, Stout etc						
Minerals						
Wines						
Spirits						
Cigars & Cigarettes						
Laundry/Dry Cl'ng						
Telephone						
Newspapers						
Garage						
Sundries						
Paid Out						
Carried forward £						

Inclusive of VAT @ 17½%

 Printed on

Hartington Hotel & Restaurant
Broad Walk, Buxton, Derbyshire SK17 6J
Licensed · AA · RAC · BHRCA

Tel: Management Buxton 22638 Visitors

Mr and Mrs Brown

Room No: _____

VAT Reg No: 157 5766 26

A REMITTANCE IS REQUESTED UPON PRESENTA
Visitors are respectfully informed that Cheques cannot

19	£	p	£	p
Brought forward £				
Room & Breakfast				
Board or Incl. Terms				
Apartments				
Room Service				
Servants' Board				
Morning Tea				
Baths				
Breakfast				
Luncheon				
Afternoon Tea				
High Tea				
Dinner				
Supper				
Tea & Coffee				
Ale, Stout etc				
Minerals				
Wines				
Spirits				
Cigars & Cigarettes				
Laundry/Dry Cl'ng				
Telephone				
Newspapers				
Garage				
Sundries				
Paid Out				
Carried forward £				

Inclusive of VAT @ 17½%

Case study

A company account amounting to a large amount of money has disappeared from your bill tray. You can produce a further copy for settlement but consider the following:
● Who could gain access to this confidential information?
● How could the account be prepared again if a copy had not been produced?
● How would this account most likely be settled?
● What use could be made of the information contained in the stolen account?

What have you learned?

Do you really know what all these terms mean?
1 What does the American plan include?
2 What is another name for the European plan?
3 What is en-pension?
4 Give another name for the modified American plan.
5 What do you get on half-board terms?
6 Give another name for the Continental plan.
7 Can half-board include lunch?
8 If you were charging all inclusive rate would a customer have to pay extra for leisure facilities?
9 What does full-board include?
10 What is demi-pension?
11 What is the rack rate?
12 What is a discounted rate?
13 When would an allowance be put through?
14 Under what circumstances should a refund be made?
15 By what payment method should it be given?
16 What is the purpose of taking a deposit or prepayment?
17 List the methods by which this could be done.
18 How can a credit card payment be refunded?

ELEMENT 2: Deal with the departures of customers

INTRODUCTION

How you handle customers departing after settling their accounts is just as important as how you handle them on their arrival since a bad experience at this time could completely spoil a pleasant stay and discourage their return to your establishment.

Customers checking out do not expect to wait while their bill is being made up. If you know when they are expected to depart the account should be made up in readiness. There is nothing worse than a long queue at reception waiting to check out, with people getting agitated and making you flustered. Of course, there will be times when everyone is trying to check out at the same time, but you should be prepared for this.

Check that you have enough change in your till if customers are going to pay by cash (remember you will have asked them how they intend to pay when they registered). If you use a manual system make sure that you have a supply of credit card slips ready to be imprinted by the machine. Present the bill to the customer so that he or she can agree the total. If this is the case enter the amount on the slip and imprint in the machine. Pass the completed slip to the customer to check that the two totals tally. The customer will now sign and return the slip to you.

PREPARING THE ACCOUNT

Working from the dockets received from all departments within your establishment, you or a colleague will have prepared the account in readiness for presentation to the customer.

If a manual system is used the balanced and completed tab will ensure that there are no errors in the addition before presentation. However, this will not show whether you have overcharged or undercharged the customer. Remember to include extra charges such as telephone and mini-bar if not automatically logged.

Presenting the bill

Once the account has been prepared and has been requested, show it to the customer explaining the various items that have been charged to them. Some customers find the way in which an establishment's accounts are presented difficult to understand. There may be some queries, but if you are accurate in your work there should be no mistakes.

As discussed earlier the account can be handwritten, produced from a billing machine or computerised system, but any of these methods could contain errors arising from mistakes in posting charges. Therefore allow customers a few minutes to check and satisfy themselves that all is in order before taking the payment. Once payment has been accepted it is more difficult to correct an error.

Payments by customers can be a part payment or full payment. A part payment can be an amount paid on account leaving the balance to be paid later or sent to ledger. The part payment account could also be because a prepayment or deposit made has already been paid. The remaining amount may just be for extra items, for instance a tour operator may pay for the rooms and the meals, but all other charges are to be billed to the individual customers. When the account has been paid you must enter the payment on your system and give a receipt for the amount received.

At the end of your shift the total amount of the bills you have collected should be the same as the total value of cash, cheques, credit card payments in your till plus your float. If this does not match, you may have given the wrong change or undercharged or overcharged customers. This will have to be corrected. (You may have been told that you have given wrong change or noticed that you have overcharged or under-charged customers before the final balance.)

When you are sure that the customer has finally vacated the room and the account has been settled, remember to ask for the room key and other establishment property they may have hired, such as tennis rackets or cycles.

Do this

- In a class or work situation perform a role-play in which you present and explain the bill, collect payment and give a receipt.
- List the payment methods that your establishment accepts. Which one is most beneficial to the establishment?

CUSTOMER COMMENTS, COMPLAINTS AND CRITICISMS

It is a good idea when presenting the account to ask the customer if they have enjoyed their stay. This gives them the opportunity to comment or mention anything that was not satisfactory about their stay, in order that the service the establishment offers can be improved.

MEMORY JOGGER

Why is it important to record customer comments and complaints?

You should mention these matters to your superior who will pass them on to the relevant departments and the management. Ideally once a complaint has been received the problem should never arise again if handled correctly within the establishment.

Customers may also have customer comment forms in their bedrooms which give them the opportunity to list anything that spoilt their stay or suggest any further service or facilities which were not available to them. This is another way of improving customer satisfaction. (See opposite page.)

Remember that the comments, complaints and criticisms are not directed at you personally, but at the service offered by the establishment, so do not take these comments personally and become upset by them.

The vast majority of customers will be quite satisfied with their stay, but it is far better to check that everything is all right at this time rather than let the customer leave and then receive a letter of complaint. This is much more difficult to deal with once the customer has left. If they had complained during their stay then perhaps it could have been put right.

According to the custom of your establishment, the complaint could be entered in a complaints book, The person who logs the complaint should state exactly what is wrong. Give the date of the incident and then sign the book. You could also use the change-over book for this purpose. It is important that a record is kept and the matter dealt with on the spot or as soon as possible. It is not unusual to write later to the customer to apologise.

Essential knowledge

- Good customer relations and the elimination of complaints will increase sales within your establishment in the form of repeat business.
- Remedial action should be taken as soon as a complaint is received and the customer informed of what is to be done.
- It is good to pass on customers' compliments as well as complaints.

COLLECTION OF KEYS

It is very important that you collect the room key and any additional equipment that you have loaned to a customer. The loss of a key is very serious and may mean that a particular room will be out of action until a new lock is fitted. A new lock on a master key system can take up to six weeks to arrive and will make a lot of additional work for the housekeeper and his or her staff working without a pass key in certain rooms. Loss of any equipment will involve the establishment in replacing that item causing unnecessary additional expense.

When a key is lost or stolen the lock must be changed as soon as possible. If this is not done, the new occupants of the room could be burgled by the earlier occupant or someone else who has managed to obtain the missing key.

Types of key

There are four types of key which are listed below.
1. The Grand master which opens all doors and can 'double lock' a door to prevent entry if required, for instance, on the death of a customer or if for some reason you wish to prevent a customer from gaining access to their room, such as Right of Lien, if their account is unpaid. (See pages 180–181.)
2. The Master key which opens all doors.
3. The Floor key or Sub-master which will open a floor of rooms. This is carried by the room person to gain entry only to the rooms being serviced.

Reservations

How was your reservation handled?

😊 😐 😞
☐ ☐ ☐

.... Source

Arrival

How was your registration handled?

😊 😐 😞
☐ ☐ ☐

....

Guest Room

Was your guest room:

😊 😐 😞

☐ ☐ ☐ clean?

☐ ☐ ☐ comfortable?

☐ ☐ ☐ properly supplied?

Restaurant and Bars

	Service			Quality			Comments
	😊	😐	😞	😊	😐	😞	
Restaurant	☐	☐	☐	☐	☐	☐	....
Bar	☐	☐	☐	☐	☐	☐	....

Conference

How do you rate

😊 😐 😞

☐ ☐ ☐ service?

☐ ☐ ☐ facilities?

A customer comment form

4 The Room key carried by the customer.

The use of electronic keys is an advantage here as they are destroyed once the customer leaves the establishment and a new key is prepared for each new customer giving much better security. There are thousands of combinations and the key allocated can be reprogrammed for each new customer.

Do this

● Design a short customer comment form requiring boxes to be ticked and space for a few lines for a written comment.
● List the four types of key that are available and who would have access to them. State the steps to be taken should a key be lost.

MEMORY JOGGER

Why is it important to greet customers in a warm and friendly way when they are checking out?

BIDDING CUSTOMERS FAREWELL

This is as important as the 'Hello' and you should be sincere with your farewell greeting. Not all establishments wish to go along with the Americanism, 'Have a nice day!', but will have some farewell greeting, such as, 'Safe Journey', 'Thank you (name of customer)' and 'Goodbye. See you again soon'. Use whatever is your accepted custom. It is at this time that you have the opportunity to promote special events, other facilities within the establishment and further bookings. If you are able to leave the reception area and the customer states, for example, that they wish to return for their wedding anniversary later in the year, show them the best room you have available, pointing out its excellent features, price and any additional items available, such as champagne and flowers. Without you being too pushy they may make a further booking.

The reception staff saying goodbye to customers

UNEXPECTED SITUATIONS

Sometimes a customer may request their account to be transferred to another person or room number so that both accounts can be paid together. With any transfer of this kind you must amend your accounting system so that the rooms are linked from that time on and the earlier account is closed so that further items cannot be charged against it.

Sometimes a customer will settle their account by more than one payment method and as long as they are accepted by your establishment there should not be a problem.

On occasions you may be faced with departing customers who are unable to pay their account. They have lost their wallet or maybe they are not really who they said they were and had no intention of paying anyway.

To obtain food, accommodation and services without the means to pay is against the law and you can call the police. You are within your rights to confiscate any luggage they have, but not their vehicle. This is called the *'Right of Lien'* and if the account has not been settled after six weeks you have the right to sell their possessions after advertising them for sale.

A 'walk out' poses similar problems and you will be asked to give a full description of the customer when you notify the police, sister establishments and other establishments in the area to prevent this happening again.

In order to avoid a scene in reception any incidents like this should be handled in a private area and sorted out by your superior. Never leave the reception area unattended. If you are alone you should wait until help arrives.

Sometimes customers may want to alter the arrangements they have booked by extending or cutting short their stay. These are called 'stay ons' and 'early departures'. In both cases the bills will have to be amended and you will need to inform all departments of the change in the original booking arrangements.

In the case of early departures deposits and prepayments may be refunded at the discretion of management, but if the accommodation cannot be relet the customer could be charged for the period they are cancelling. Whether you chose to do this will depend on the circumstances of the cancellation.

Do this

- Make a list of circumstances when an early departure would be charged for cancellation and also when any deposits or prepayments would be refunded.
- How can the establishment protect itself against early departures?
- What does your establishment do if a customer is unable to pay for their stay?
- List the suspicious signs that would lead you to believe that a customer may leave without paying.
- What could you do to ensure that this does not happen in your establishment?

Case study

A customer, when presented with their account, states that they have no means to pay even though they had written information on arrival stating the likely cost.
- *Who should you inform?*
- *What can you do about this situation?*
- *Can you take steps to see that this does not happen again?*
- *If you are 'an inn' what property can you confiscate in lieu of payment?*
- *What is the Act called which allows you to confiscate property?*

<table>
<tr><td>What have you learned</td><td>1 Why is it important to maintain customer satisfaction?
2 How can you ensure that customers are happy with their stay?
3 What should you do if there is a complaint?
4 How can you encourage customers to make further bookings?</td></tr>
</table>

What have you learned	1 Why is it important to maintain customer satisfaction?
	2 How can you ensure that customers are happy with their stay?
	3 What should you do if there is a complaint?
	4 How can you encourage customers to make further bookings?

Get ahead	When you have the opportunity, visit a specialist catering exhibition, such as Hotech, Hospitality or Hotelympia to compare computerised accounting systems and recommend the most suitable and user-friendly version for your establishment.

EXCELSIOR HOTEL

19	£	p	£	p	£	p	£	p	£	p	£	p	£	p	£	p
Brought forward £																
Room & Breakfast																
Board or Incl. Terms																
Apartments																
Room Service																
Servants' Board																
Morning Tea																
Baths																
Breakfast																
Luncheon																
Afternoon Tea																
High Tea																
Dinner																
Supper																
Tea & Coffee																
Ale, Stout etc																
Minerals																
Wines																
Spirits																
Cigars & Cigarettes																
Laundry/Dry Cl'ng																
Telephone																
Newspapers																
Garage																
Sundries																
Paid Out																
Carried forward £																

Inclusive of VAT @ 17½%

 Printed on Recycled Paper

ROOM No.	201^{DB}		205^{SB}		207^{FB}		210^{TB}		202^{DB}						DAILY TOTAL	
NAME	ROBERTS Mr & Mrs (2)		PADSTOwE Mr (1)		SINGLETON Mr & Mrs (3)		PEMBERTON SULLIVAN MISSES (2)		LAMBERT MR/S (2)							
RATE	£70 RB		£50 INC		£90 BB		£95 INC		£70 RB						DAILY TOTAL	
B/F																
APARTMENTS	56	00	30	00	62	00			56	00					204	00
PENSION(700p)			20	00			95	00							115	00
BREAKFASTS	14	00			28	00			14	00					56	00
LUNCHEONS	20	00			40	00									60	00
AFTERNOON TEAS																
DINNERS																
EARLY TEAS	2	00	1	00	4	00	2	00							9	00
BEVERAGES																
WINES																
SPIRITS & LIQUEURS	3	50	7	80											11	30
BEERS																
MINERALS																
TELEPHONES																
V.P.O.'s																
TOTAL	95	50	58	80	134	00	97	00	70	00					455	30
CASH																
ALLOWANCES																
LEDGER																
BALANCE C/F																

Exchange foreign cash and traveller's cheques

This chapter covers:
ELEMENT 1:   **Exchange foreign cash**
ELEMENT 2:   **Exchange foreign traveller's cheques**

What you need to do

- Deal with customers politely and helpfully at all times.
- Check customers' identities. Accept and check the receipt of foreign cash or traveller's cheques.
- Inform customers of relevant exchange rates and commission charges.
- Accurately complete the exchange using appropriate exchange method and complete all documentation.
- Give correct money and receipts and check cash according to laid-down procedure.

- Only accept traveller's cheques in line with service operations.
- Receive and store cheques within establishment procedure.
- Ensure that the exchange point is secured from unauthorised access.
- Deal with unexpected situations efficiently and inform appropriate people as and when necessary.
- Prioritise your work in an organised and efficient manner taking into account laid-down procedures and legal requirements.

What you need to know

- Why it is important to give accurate information about exchange rates and commission.
- Why it is important that the identity of the customer must be established.

- How to access and calculate the exchange rates.
- Why exchange point must be safe and secured from unauthorised access.

ELEMENT 1:   **Exchange foreign cash**

FOREIGN CASH

Obviously if you can speak other languages it will be very useful when dealing with foreign customers making currency exchanges. It makes the customer feel at ease and solves any difficulties they may have in understanding the procedure.

As mentioned in other chapters you must deal with customers in a polite and helpful manner at all times, using the correct form of address with speed and efficiency.

Your establishment may not have easy access to a local bank or customers may wish to exchange or make payment with their money at times when the banks are not open, in the evening, for example, or at weekends.

You are providing a service for the customer and may therefore charge a little more than the banks for exchanging their money which is a common practice in establishments and recognised by customers.

Do this

- Visit your local bank and note the currency rates which are displayed for the convenience of customers.
- Write down the rates and also the names of the currency used in each country and learn these by heart.

When can exchanges be made?

MEMORY JOGGER

What must you remember to check when exchanging foreign cash?

Certain problems happen when exchanging currency. Very often the customer requires this service outside banking hours which means you are unable to contact your local branch to check the daily rate. You should do this whenever possible as the rates vary from day to day and you will have to be sure that you do not lose money on the exchange.

Remember you are trying to be quick and efficient. The next place for you to check is a national newspaper. Look in the financial pages under 'Currencies'. Here you will find listed the most common currencies with the daily rate, as well as some other more uncommon currencies.

Essential knowledge

When exchanging currency it is important that you give accurate information about the exchange rate and your commission charge so that the customer is quite clear about the transaction.

Do this

Below is a list of countries. Copy the list and write the currency used next to them.

Australia	Germany	Norway
Austria	Greece	Portugal
Belgium	Holland	South Africa
Canada	Ireland	Spain
Cyprus	Israel	Sweden
Denmark	Italy	Switzerland
Finland	Malta	Turkey
France	New Zealand	United States

Once you are familiar with the countries and their currency you can then learn to recognise the various bank notes that the customers will bring for payment or exchange. (Coins are not accepted.)

You will remember that an amount is added to make sure that the establishment does not lose by the deal. This is known as the 'commission' charge which will be a fixed rate probably one or two per cent for each time currency is changed. (This is called a 'transaction'.)

Foreign banknotes

It is handy if you have a calculator readily available so that you can quickly make the calculation once you have checked the exchange rate of the day. Do not forget your commission charge.

For example, a customer gives you 1000 francs. You have checked to see how much the rate is and it is 9.26 francs for every pound. You would then divide 1000 by 9.26 to find out how many pounds they can be given. This gives the answer of £107.99.

1% of this is £1.08 giving the answer of £106.91.

This is calculated in this way:
1000 divided by 9.26 = 107.99
1% of £107.99 (move the decimal point 2 places to the left) = 1.0799 (this is rounded up to 1.08)
107.99 minus 1.08 = £106.91

Do this

● To familiarise yourself with this process take ten of the countries listed above and suppose that you have been given 1000 units of each currency, for example, 1000 Deutsch marks or dollars. Work out these amounts in sterling. (British currency is known as sterling.)
● Remember to deduct the commission charge.

Before commencing the exchange

● Check that the customer is in residence.
● Ask to see their passport and make a note of their name and room number on the receipt that you will give them to confirm the amount of money they have given you in payment or to be exchanged.
● Tell the customer the exchange rate and commission charges before accepting their money so that they are completely satisfied.
● Count the foreign money in front of them and then count out the sterling in the same way. Do not put foreign money in the cash drawer until the customer is satisfied that the calculations are correct.

When you make up the cash for the bank, foreign currency must be entered on a separate paying in slip with a note of the customer's name and room number in case of any query.

Is foreign currency a welcome method of payment?

Although foreign currency is a good method of payment in that the establishment does not lose money by accepting it (as you do when accepting, for example, credit cards), there is the danger that if you are not used to handling foreign currency you may not recognise forged notes. Always check with your supervisor if in doubt or when dealing with large sums of money.

Customers travelling from abroad may want to settle their account in money from their own country or exchange this into British currency (sterling).

You may find that your establishment has a limit to how much currency it will and can exchange at any time. This may sound odd but remember you will have to carry large amounts of cash to satisfy large requests making it a security risk to have such large amounts on the premises.

- It is important that currency exchange is carried out in a secure and secluded area away from other customers. This is to avoid the risk of the client or the hotel being robbed. Doors and windows in this area should be barred and ideally it should be within easy reach of the hotel safe where the foreign notes and sterling can be deposited and sterling brought out.
- Take care not to leave your till unattended or unlocked. You may have a secret panic button which you can press, without the customer knowing, which will alert someone who will come to your assistance without alarming the customer.

Do this

- Make a list of any other security measures that could be used to make sure that any transactions are carried out in absolute safety.

Unusual happenings

We have mentioned the risk of possible forgery and unless you are very experienced in the handling of foreign notes this could be difficult to detect. However, if there is a spate of forgeries around, your establishment will usually have been warned by the police about what to look out for. Also, if there have been any incidents locally, sister establishments or other local establishments will warn you to be on the look out.

If at all suspicious or worried about the person exchanging the currency, or the currency itself, call your superior to check this out for you and be on your guard as there are a lot of confidence tricksters about. So if in doubt, check it out.

What have you learned

1 What is the usual commission charge for currency exchange?
2 What is the purpose of this charge?
3 What is the first thing to check before conducting an exchange?

ELEMENT 2: **Exchange foreign traveller's cheques**

TRAVELLER'S CHEQUES

Traveller's cheques are another form of currency which can be bought in sterling or foreign currency and are safer for the customer to carry around than cash.

MEMORY JOGGER

What must you remember to check when exchanging foreign traveller's cheques?

You may already know that when you buy traveller's cheques from your bank or travel agents that you pay an extra one per cent at the time of purchase which insures the cheques against loss or theft.

At the time of purchase you must keep a note of the numbers so that you can report missing or stolen cheques immediately and they will be replaced.

When you collect them from the bank or travel agent you have your signature on each cheque but they can only be cashed when you sign them again and date them.

As there is a signature already on the traveller's cheque, it is easy to check the second signature against the first when they are cashed. However, it also makes it easy

Traveller's cheques

for a forger to copy the first signature. If in any doubt, ask the customer to sign again on the back of the traveller's cheque where there is nothing to copy from.

Service to the customer

As with any other service you provide, ensure you are efficient and helpful to the customer. In this instance there may be the added difficulty of a language barrier.

Try not to keep the customers waiting too long while you are making the calculations and, if necessary, contact your superior or senior receptionist if you are unsure of the procedure. He or she can then watch over you while you complete the transaction.

Calculations can be made by pen and paper, by using a calculator or by computer according to house custom.

Accepting traveller's cheques

When accepting traveller's cheques for either payment of an account or in exchange for sterling the procedure should be followed very carefully.
- Ask for a passport or some other proof of identity.
- Check that the amount to be exchanged is within house limits.
- Check the currency exchange rates, make the calculation, deduct the establishment's commission and then tell the customer how much money they will receive.
- Make sure that you see the customer sign the cheque. Do not let yourself become distracted so that you miss the actual signing. The customer may have written one earlier and then slide this into place when you are not looking.
- If in any doubt about the signature, or if you do not witness the signature, ask them to sign again on the back of the cheque where they have nothing to copy from.
- Make a note of the customer's room number and enter this on the back of each cheque so that it can be traced back if required.
- Refer to your warning lists to ensure that the cheques have not been reported as stolen.
- Give a receipt for the traveller's cheques stating amount of cash received.
- If in doubt check it out.

A traveller's cheque for U.S. $50

Essential knowledge

- Customers should be advised in advance of the exchange rate you are offering.
- When exchanging foreign currency all exchanges of traveller's cheques should be conducted in a quiet and, if possible, screened area of reception.
- Correct exchange rates should be used and accurate calculations should be made.

Calculation of the exchange rate

In large establishments where cashing foreign currency is a regular service the current exchange rates on offer are likely to be displayed. In a smaller establishment it is best to contact your bank in the first instance to obtain the current rate. Outside banking hours, look in the financial section of a newspaper and add a charge on to make sure that you do not lose on the exchange.

The actual calculation can be carried out on your front office system if you have the relevant program and this is a very simple operation. The exchange rates are updated as necessary.

Otherwise you have to resort to a calculator, pen and paper to make your calculation.

Do this

- Practise calculating various exchange rates obtained from the financial sections of newspapers.
- Role play the steps listed for accepting traveller's cheques so that you are absolutely certain what to do in which order.
- Learn to recognise the different types of cheque.

Unexpected happenings

A customer may approach reception with traveller's cheques that are not signed so that you will have no signature to compare with the second signature when they sign to exchange them.

Ask the customer to sign in the space allowed for the signature. (See the illustration on page 188.) Ask for proof of identification and also retrieve and examine the registration form. If all three signatures match you can accept the cheques in the normal way once the customer has signed and dated the cheque.

Also if the customer has no proof of identity you should be suspicious. A foreign customer, unless resident in Britain, would usually carry a passport. Foreigners living in Britain should have some proof of identity, such as a driving licence or something with which you can compare the signature before any exchange takes place.

Case study

You are working in the reception of your hotel one Sunday morning when one of your French guests approaches you to change a 1000 franc traveller's cheque. Because it is Sunday, the banks are closed, so you cannot check the exchange rate with them.
- *Where else can you look for the exchange rate?*
- *Check the source and calculate the value of 1000 French francs at the quoted exchange rate.*

What have you learned

1 List in detail the steps to be taken before exchanging currency.
2 What should be done if the signatures do not match?
3 As well as handing over the money what else should be given to the customer?
4 Why is it essential to conduct exchange of traveller's cheques and foreign currency in a secure area?
5 Give two reasons why customers should be given accurate information about exchange rates and commission.
6 List in detail the steps you would take when a customer has requested a currency exchange according to your house custom.

Answers to the question on currency on page 185

Australia	Dollars
Austria	Schillings
Belgium	Francs
Canada	Dollars
Cyprus	Pounds
Denmark	Kroner
Finland	Markka
France	Francs
Germany	Marks
Greece	Drachmae
Holland	Guilders
Ireland	Punts
Israel	Shekels
Italy	Lire
Malta	Pounds
New Zealand	Dollars
Norway	Kroner
Portugal	Escudos
South Africa	Rand
Spain	Pesetas
Sweden	Kronor
Switzerland	Francs
Turkey	Lire
United States	Dollars

Get ahead

1 When you have the opportunity to visit technological exhibitions look out for computerised systems which automatically calculate exchange rates and see them in operation.

2 Advance payments and deposits from overseas customers may be received by your establishment. Find out the average time that this currency, usually in the form of a cheque, takes to clear once banked. The currency has to be 'sold' on the open market and selling rates will vary from day to day.

Maintain data in a computer system

This chapter covers:
ELEMENT 1:   **Input data and text into a computer system**
ELEMENT 2:   **Locate and retrieve data from a computer system**
ELEMENT 3:   **Print documents using a computer system**

What you need to do

- Use suitable computer software.
- Correctly enter and retrieve.
- Obtain directions from an appropriate person when the source data is incomplete.
- Obtain directions from an appropriate person when the source data is unauthorised.
- Identify errors in inputting and coding and correct in accordance with organisational procedures.
- Generate reference codes as necessary.
- When it is not possible to work to specified deadlines, report reasons promptly and accurately.
- Achieve work within agreed deadlines.
- Locate, access and retrieve data within time limits using appropriate search methods.

- Print correct and complete documents.
- Ensure that the hard copy is clean, clearly printed and correctly aligned.
- Minimise paper wastage.
- Keep print area clean and tidy.
- Correctly collate documents and distribute as directed.
- Store source material in accordance with organisational procedures.
- Safeguard equipment and data against damage.
- Ensure confidentiality and security of data in accordance with organisational requirements.
- Disclose data only to authorised people.
- Work following safe working practices.

What you need to know

- What software and hardware are available, their uses, and how to operate them.
- How to correctly code data and the importance of using codes.
- Formatting procedures and how to format discs.
- How materials are stored and filed within your organisation.
- How to locate details in a computer system.
- How to safeguard equipment and data against damage and why this is important.

- The organisational procedures for security and confidentiality of data.
- How to back up data and why it is important.
- What are print characteristics and how to use them.
- How to use and operate printers.
- What is your organisation's house style, and when it is important to use it.
- What the relevant legal requirements are.

ELEMENT 1: Input data and text into a computer system

THE COMPUTER HARDWARE AND SOFTWARE

The actual computer is called the hardware which is made up of the central processing unit (CPU – the box and brain), the screen and the keyboard.

Computers can be purchased with loaded software, or programs can also be bought separately and installed onto the computer and these are generally specific to your organisational needs. For example, your establishment has a reception area which takes reservations for your service and so a suitable software package will have been purchased from one of the computer houses to deal with reservations or your system may have been custom designed.

Computer hardware – screen (VDU), central processing unit (CPU) and keyboard

Innovations and new programs evolve all the time and there are many suitable software systems available to deal with all types of reservation whether it be bedrooms, conference rooms, restaurant tables, appointment times, etc.

As well as taking reservations many systems will also operate billing systems incorporating front and back office, payroll, energy and yield management stock control, etc.

Innsite, Remanco, Welcome, are just a few of the companies that supply dedicated reservation systems.

Essential knowledge	● Whenever you use a computer to do work it is important that you take precautions to ensure that you always have safe copies of your material. If you do not have copies, and the system goes down or a file becomes corrupted, you risk losing everything. ● In order to protect your work you should back it up regularly, i.e. take a safe copy on a separate disk. In this way, should the worst happen, you will still be able to access and retrieve copies of what may be a very important or long document.

ENTERING TEXT

Before entering text it is necessary to prepare a disk to be used as a back-up in case the system should crash. If this should happen all the information could be lost and this can be many months' work.

MEMORY JOGGER

Why is it important to format and prepare back-up disks?

A disk should be *formatted*. This means that it is wiped clean and prepared for use. Most computers are different but it is well worth the few minutes it takes to prepare new disks for use. Type 'FORMAT' on the appropriate disk drive that you will place the disk in, this would be 'A:' if the floppy disk is in drive A, 'B:' if in B drive, etc.

It is a good idea to back up your work regularly. In your organisation it may be the policy to do this every page, half hour or for a reservation system twice a day. Failure to do this can result in loss of data. At the very least there should be a daily back up of work, with a set of disks for each day of the week.

In the normal course of events, to open a file or create a file you have to give the file a name and as long as you can remember the name of the document it is quite simple to call this back up and re-enter the document. The file name should also be entered on the printed document with your reference as another aid to trace it if it is later required for retrieval.

Do this

● In your organisation find out how often disks are backed up, and then ask if you can format a new box of disks to become familiar with this task.

A 'floppy' disk

If you are making reservations your system will probably automatically generate a reservation number each time a reservation is made and you can easily recall the reservation by this method, or perhaps by the customer's name, or date of arrival.

Reference codes are very useful when confirming reservations to customers and they can quote them back to you when making further reservations or amending their booking. This provides proof that the booking has been made.

Sometimes it is difficult to find a reservation if you do not have the full information so other methods have to be used to trace a booking. Most systems also have a guest history file and you can trace a customer's last date of reservation from this updated information.

In the worst scenario you may have to go through all the screens to find the reservation or use manual systems to trace a confirmation letter duplicate from files.

In all establishments there are peaks and troughs when there is too much work to be done and so inputting information has to be prioritised: the most urgent being inputted first. As with any system, it is only as good as the information it contains so if garbage has been put in, garbage will come out – you can't blame the computer if wrong information comes out!

Billing is a good example of this. If the wrong information has been placed on the wrong account it is either a wrong room number on the docket or the operative has made inputting errors – the computer cannot mix things up!

Everyone usually wants their bill at around about the same time so it is important that you have prepared the account by posting charges previously. It is a simple matter of printing out the account and presenting it to the customer.

The copy printed must be clear, easy to read and be without errors. You can produce printed copies in your house style by the use of a logo and other establishment embellishments. (More about printing in Element 3.)

CONFIDENTIALITY

Most computer systems have different levels of access to allow operatives access only to parts of the program they require for their work. Access to the system is usually by code or password to keep access to authorised personnel only. Management need access to all parts of the program for the financial aspects and to monitor the work and bookings and appointments.

The Data Protection Act 1984

Any information held on computer about an individual requires the establishment to be registered under the *Data Protection Act*. Failure to do so can result in a fine of up to £2000. Therefore it is against the law to hold information on file without registration and any information held must be correct and lawfully obtained.

SAFE WORKING PRACTICES

There are strict health and safety codes for operatives using VDUs and they should be provided with an annual eye test, an anti-glare screen, posture supporting chair, and a footrest.

Do this

- Using your word processing software, prepare a letter in answer to a request for a brochure. Save this on disk under reference ENQI.
- Find out who you should contact within your organisation if you find errors or incomplete data.

Case study

One of the VDU operators is complaining of eyestrain and constant headaches. He is a full-time worker and all his working day is spent inputting data.
- *Under health and safety legislation, what equipment and services should be provided for the VDU operator?*
- *Who is liable in the case of any industrial injuries?*

What have you learned

1 Describe hardware and software.
2 Find out the software that is available for use in your organisation, and what are its uses.
3 Why should a disk be formatted before use?
4 Which tasks should be prioritised when inputting text?
5 How can a computerised system be safeguarded against access by unauthorised personnel?
6 Why is it important to produce documents in 'house style'?
7 What should be provided for the VDU operator to work safely?

ELEMENT 2: Locate and retrieve data from a computer system

MEMORY JOGGER

Why are reference codes useful in retrieving information?

Inputting text is only part of using a computer system. Another major part is to be able to locate and retrieve text that has been saved on the hard disk or a working disk. If text has been saved on the working disk this enables data to be copied from one machine to another (this is called down-loading). Information saved on a back-up disk can be put back into the computer in case of system failure or work continued on another machine.

All entered text if saved has a file name and one way to retrieve text is to look through the directory of file names, put the cursor on the correct name and call-up to amend.

Another method of finding text is to look at the final printed document which will state the file reference and the document can be retrieved by this information also.

Reservation information is entered by code number and name. Reservations can be recalled by name, date, time, type of accommodation, area, and a search can be made by the computer for any of these which are called 'fields'. Reference number is usually the easiest to locate a missing reservation.

If you call up a name, e.g. Wilson, the computer will list on the screen all the Wilsons with relevant addresses so that you can select the correct one or make further searches within the list.

Essential knowledge

Whatever software your organisation uses you must be able to store and retrieve data quickly and accurately.
- To find files you need to remember the file name and look at the file index.
- Sometimes a file cannot be retrieved because it has become corrupt and you will have to use your back-up disk to retrieve this information.
- Documents can state the file name either in the reference or in additional comment on the 'footer' with the page number.

Do this

- Find your letter in answer to a brochure request and add an additional paragraph advising of a special offer of 10% discount if a booking is made by the end of the month.
- Search through your customer files for any customers called Saunders.

CONFIDENTIALITY

You must remember that you may not disklose information about customers as they may not wish their presence to be revealed to callers. You might see from your guests in residence list that Mr and Mrs Jenkins are staying, but you must not state this information to anyone enquiring.

You may have access to some financial information such as how much the takings were yesterday, but again this information is confidential and should not be disclosed to anyone else.

Do this

- Find out what information should be kept confidential in your organisation.

Drinks should never be taken near a computer

SAFEGUARDING AGAINST DAMAGE

Damage can be caused to computers maliciously or accidentally. A very common accident is liquid such as coffee or tea spilt on the keyboard or into the computer. Therefore no drinks should be taken near to a computer or the system may be damaged.

Malicious damage can be caused to computers by wiping all the data from the computer and this can be done within seconds and can take some hours to re-program. Therefore passwords are important and free access to systems should be unavailable.

Thunder and lightning are another threat to computer systems, as sudden surges of power can affect the programs and lose data. In this case there is little to be done except ensure that back-up files have been made in case of damage.

Many organisations pay an annual fee to computer software companies who installed and trained staff in the system. They can be called upon when there are difficulties in the program or systems.

Do this

- Find out what support systems your organisation has available in case of accidental or malicious damage.
- If when retrieving data you are unsure of the file name, where could you find this information?

Case study

A customer arrives waving a confirmation letter for tonight but you can find no trace of the reservation. Using your computerised system how can you find out the following information:
- *Who prepared the confirmation letter and where can it be found?*
- *What is the reservation number?*
- *The gentleman says he has stayed before, how can you find out when?*

What have you learned

1 How can you ensure that no accidental damage occurs to the computer?
2 What steps can you take to ensure that no malicious damage occurs to the computer?
3 What methods can be used to retrieve a reservation?
4 How can a file be accessed?
5 If you cannot remember the file name, where can you look?
6 Why might you wish to retrieve a document or a reservation?

ELEMENT 3:   Print documents using a computer system

Before printing documents it is essential that the copy you will produce is accurate and well presented.

The types of data that you are likely to print will be very varied and will consist of some of the following items:
- Personal replies to enquiry letters.
- Menus.
- Accounts.
- Reservation information.
- House lists.

- Mailshot letters – personalised.
- Registration forms and key cards.
- Fax messages.
- Reports.
- Graphs, bar charts and tables.
- Spreadsheets.
- Databases.
- Desk-top publishing.
- Forms.
- Name badges.
- Tabular documents.
- Appointment lists.
- Arrivals list.
- Financial information.

Essential knowledge	<ul><li>Data should be accurate in terms of spelling, names and information.</li><li>Computerised information cannot be held on customers without registration under the *Data Protection Act*.</li></ul>

You should check the data on screen carefully for errors by reading through the text to make sure it makes sense and then using the spell checking program to ensure that there are no spelling errors.

Once this has been done and the work saved, you can print a draft copy first on rough paper and when satisfied with this can print the best copy.

Previously printed sheets that contained errors can be retained and used again on the back for rough copies to minimise the use of paper.

Layout of a document is of particular importance and use should be made of any house logo, house stationery and house style of print.

Many organisations now have laser printers which produce excellent results with a good choice of fonts or print styles. Other types of printer are bubble jet, daisy wheel and dot matrix.

THINGS THAT CAN GO WRONG

You can get paper jams, the printer may fail to work because it has run out of ink, equipment can be faulty or could have been maliciously damaged, etc. Often these errors are easy to correct yourself, but sometimes you have to call in an engineer to carry out repairs.

Once the printing has been successfully completed and you are satisfied that there are no errors you can distribute the papers to the appropriate areas or post out the document after signature.

You may find that the printed document is not as the layout you viewed on the VDU and this is because you failed to set tabs or margins to ensure that your work was correctly aligned. This is especially important if your work contained financial lists or columns.

It is not an ideal situation for an organisation to rely on one piece of equipment to print out important and necessary information. Usually there will be another compatible printer in the establishment that can be 'borrowed' in case of emergency. Another solution is always to have at least two pieces of equipment in case of a breakdown so that normal service standards can be provided.

Do this

● Recall your document ENQI. Check it for accuracy, spell check it, save it, and print it out on your establishment's stationery.

STATIONERY

MEMORY JOGGER

Why is it important that paper is not wasted whilst printing?

Stationery can be continuous on computer paper or single sheets. The choice will depend on the purpose of the document to be printed. Arrival lists could be printed on continuous stationery, but a personalised word processed letter will be on headed paper and a matching envelope will also require printing, unless window envelopes or envelope labels are used.

The final document is most important as to the style and impression it can make and whether it is to be used as a selling tool or just to impart information within the organisation.

Stationery is a high cost to an organisation and every effort should be made to minimise wastage.

Do this

● Find examples of stationery used within your organisation and find out what they are used for.
● Print out an example of each and retain them for your file.

PRINT CHARACTERISTICS

As stated earlier, there are many different types of font and print style. The finished result is chosen for required impression and space available for the text.

Methods of work

You should work in a neat, tidy and organised manner. Keep the documents that you have printed in appropriate order ready for distribution.

It would be unsuitable to have drinks and food in the printing area as accidental spills could severely affect the equipment, and if your only printer goes down, this could jeopardise the whole operation.

You should work quickly and efficiently to agreed deadlines. If for some reason you are unable to produce this work, you should inform your superiors who may be able to help you achieve your goals.

Case study

Your reception billing system only has one printer to print out all the bills. Unfortunately, just when you have a queue of customers wishing to obtain their accounts, it refuses to print.
● *What can you do in this situation?*
● *How can you ensure that this will not happen again?*

<table>
<tr><td>

What have you learned?

</td><td>

1 Before printing, what should be checked?
2 How can paper wastage be minimised?
3 Why are different print fonts used?
4 What can go wrong when you are printing?
5 What suitable stationery should you use for different situations, e.g. internal and external communications.
6 Why is it important to safeguard against damage?

</td></tr>
</table>

<table>
<tr><td>

Get ahead

</td><td>

1 Read computer magazines to keep up to date with new developments in hardware and software.
2 Attend specialist computer exhibitions for hands-on experience of new systems and developments.
3 Study computer skills to gain recognised qualifications in the areas of word processing, spreadsheets and databases.

</td></tr>
</table>

Index

Page references in italics indicate illustrations